PREDATOR OF THE SEAS

By the same author

THE MIGHTY NIMROD
A Life of Frederick Courteney Selous

SHAKA'S CHILDREN
A History of the Zulu People

LIVINGSTONE'S TRIBE
A Journey from Zanzibar to the Cape

THE CALIBAN SHORE
The Fate of the Grosvenor Castaways

STORM AND CONQUEST
The Battle for the Indian Ocean, 1808–10

COMMANDER
The Life and Exploits of Britain's Greatest Frigate Captain

DEFIANCE
The Life and Choices of Lady Anne Barnard

SONS OF THE WAVES
The Common Seaman in the Heroic Age of Sail

PREDATOR OF THE SEAS

A History of the Slaveship That Fought for Emancipation

STEPHEN TAYLOR

YALE UNIVERSITY PRESS
NEW HAVEN AND LONDON

Published with assistance from the Annie Burr Lewis Fund.

For information about this and other Yale University Press publications, please contact:
U.S. Office: sales.press@yale.edu   yalebooks.com
Europe Office: sales@yaleup.co.uk   yalebooks.co.uk

Set Adobe Garamond Pro by IDSUK (DataConnection) Ltd
Printed in Great Britain by Clays Ltd, Elcograf S.p.A

Library of Congress Control Number: 2024940498

ISBN 978-0-300-26399-2

A catalogue record for this book is available from the British Library.

10 9 8 7 6 5 4 3 2 1

To the two faithful readers who have accompanied me on
every page over many years,
my friend Tom and my wife Caroline

CONTENTS

CONTENTS

ILLUSTRATIONS AND MAPS

PLATES

1. Baltimore near Whetstone Point, 1831. Heritage Image Partnership Ltd / Alamy.
2. John Robert Mather, after Nicholas Matthew Condy, *Shipping Slaves, West Coast of Africa*, 1860. © National Maritime Museum, Greenwich, London, Michael Graham-Stewart Slavery Collection. Acquired with the assistance of the Heritage Lottery Fund.
3. The capture of slaves by an African slaver in Africa, undated. Wellcome Collection.
4. Slaves aboard a slaveship being shackled before being put in the hold, by Joseph Swain, *c.* 1835.
5. Francis Meynell, watercolour of the lower deck of a slaveship, 1840. Hirarchivum Press / Alamy.
6. J.M.W. Turner, *The Slave Ship*, 1840. incamerastock / Alamy.
7. Edward Finden, after Augustus Earle, illustration of the slave market at Rio de Janeiro, 1824. Wellcome Collection.
8. P. Fumagalli, after J. Mawe, *Ilhéus, Bahia, Brazil*, *c.* 1821. Wellcome Collection.

9. Slaveship fleeing cruisers, 1844. Morphart Creation / Shutterstock.
10. Daniel Orme, *Nelson Coming on Deck at the Battle of the Nile, 1 August 1798*, c. 1800. © National Maritime Museum, Greenwich, London.
11. George Morland, *Smugglers*, 1793. Yale Center for British Art, Paul Mellon Collection.
12. A Kruboy rowing, undated. © Thaliastock / Mary Evans.
13. Nicholas Condy, *Capture of the Spanish Slave Brig Almirante by H.M.S. Black Joke in the Bight of Benin, Africa*, undated. Courtesy of Bonhams.
14. William John Huggins, *Black Joke Engaging the Spanish Slave Brig El Almirante*, 1830. Heritage Image Partnership Ltd / Alamy.
15. Auguste François Laby, *Freetown, Sierra Leone*, c. 1850. Yale Center for British Art, Paul Mellon Collection.
16. Thomas Walker, wooden wine cooler, 1830–1. © National Maritime Museum, Greenwich, London.
17. Samuel Crowther, 1888.

IN TEXT

p. 38. *King Gezo of Dahomey.* Universal Images Group North America LLC / Alamy.
p. 69. Thomas Goff Lupton engraving after Gildon Manton, *Hugh Clapperton*, 1829. © National Portrait Gallery, London.
p. 94. *Francisco Félix de Souza*, oil painting photographed by Centro de Estudo Africanos, before 1849.
p. 137. 'Departure of the Ex-Governor from Freetown, Sierra Leone', 1854. Penta Springs Limited / Alamy.
p. 179. Cornelius Varley, 'Ship Study', 1823. Yale Center for British Art, Paul Mellon Collection.

p. 220. Thomas Rowlandson, 'The Dying Sailor', undated. Yale Center
for British Art, Paul Mellon Collection.
p. 265. W. Clarkson Stanfield, 'Old Seamen', 1840. World History
Archive / Alamy.

MAPS

AUTHOR'S NOTE

History is ever susceptible to new ways of telling. In a maritime world once dominated by battle and biography, rich layers of the seafaring past have been opened up through the lives of ships, from those titans of war, the *Temeraire* and *Bellerophon*, to such agents of discovery as the *Beagle* and *Erebus*. This narrative takes what many readers – like the author – may find a more disturbing passage.

The transatlantic slave trade has generated a vast compendium of books, treatises and analyses. Given the significant – and at times dominant – role of Britain in that atrocity, the country's involvement remains the subject of tortured reflection and recrimination, and of heated debate on such matters as the need for reparations. In a parallel strand of the story, numerous volumes have been dedicated to the abolition movement in Britain and, more recently, the Royal Navy's campaign to suppress the trade.

The present book may be found to inhabit an awkward place in these bibliographies. In following the story of a single vessel, it is set in the two distinct and separate theatres that she occupied – Brazil and West Africa. The time frame too is narrow – covering less than a decade in the aftermath of the Napoleonic Wars, when European nations were coming to terms with peace, Britain was trumpeting its status as a world power and, across the Atlantic, new states were on the rise in the former Luso-Hispanic colonies which had broken away from their European rulers.

In approaching these two worlds I anticipated a narrative that would emerge in fairly stark terms: the malignancy of the trade in humans needs no emphasis, and in the new world order that was taking shape in the 1820s Britain was setting a reformist agenda for European states. Yet there were cautions too against casting this as an allegory of good versus evil, the Royal Navy against the slave trade. In the words of the philosopher Walter Benjamin: 'There is no document of civilisation which is not at the same time a document of barbarism.' The extent to which British seafarers and merchants had previously participated in trafficking, and that West Indies plantation owners continued to supply British consumers with the fruits of enslaved labour until the 1830s, set that in context. As it turned out, the case could be taken further: in the polemics surrounding imperialism, an argument has been made that in trying to stop other states profiting from slavery Britain was merely protecting its own economic interests.

Within the narrow time frame defined by the life of the brig that set sail as the slaver *Henriqueta* and was mourned as the acclaimed rescuer *Black Joke* is to be found ambiguity and complexity in various forms. The life of a single vessel that occupied both these worlds evolved into a metaphor for the paradoxes of humanity.

I have written previously about aspects of Britain's maritime past in the age of sail – mainly naval, with diversions into trade and social history. Researching this book opened up a quite different world. The bravado, the derring-do and victories of the war years were not to be seen. What is revealed instead by the campaign to end transatlantic slavery is the mishandling of a great endeavour. The Preventative Squadron was not lacking in able and dedicated officers and men, but it was neglected by the authorities at home and so deprived of resources as to leave it constantly outrun by a new enemy at sea. The Royal Navy itself, it may be argued, had been left demoralised and vastly reduced since 1815, with many ships laid up, officers sent ashore and almost the entire force of seamen discarded without pay; in the post-war years, sailors made up the largest contingent of London's beggars.

Of the history of slavery I had little knowledge. Research into that subject, the extent of British involvement and, in particular, details of the conditions in which men, women and children were transported – the latter in harrowing numbers – proved long and grim. Africans' engagement in enslavement came as another discovery. I have written about, and spent much of my life reflecting on, Africa's colonial past. Southern Africa was the world into which I was born and raised and which, well after I departed as a young man, bequeathed a longing that drew me back as a news correspondent and to travel across the continent from east to centre and south. West Africa's history opened a further door.

In seeking to distil these worlds I have been bound to pass over a great deal of history: the transatlantic slave trade lasted nearly 400 years, while ships and vessels of the Preventative Squadron spent more than half a century – 60 years in all – cruising off West Africa before it could be said that battle had been won.

The most comprehensive study of the squadron's campaign is Peter Grindal's *Opposing the Slavers*, a work to which I returned repeatedly for the overall picture and have cited throughout. Grindal was a long-serving navy officer and his landmark work was the product of experience, meticulous research and care. It is no disrespect to say that the vastness of his canvas obliged Grindal to pass over some of the individual stories, nuances and details cast up by a more narrow focus.

What emerged most strikingly from my research were the voices of those drawn in by the campaign, in Africa as well as at sea, women as well as men. The period – the start of what has been termed the Age of Reform – was one in which views and values were evolving both significantly and rapidly, and the accounts of witnesses, and often their actions, speak for the heartfelt instincts of common humanity. Of those who served, many died, and some were traumatised.

The resources for telling this story were highly variable. While naval records for the Preventative Squadron are comprehensive, most of the documents relating to Bahia's slave trade were destroyed in the 1890s and research done on my behalf at Salvador's state archive brought little to light that had not already been set down in previous studies; the *Henriqueta*'s life is thus darker than that of the *Black Joke* in more respects than one.

The most significant gap, however, lies in Africa. The archives in Sierra Leone relating to the men, women and children rescued from slavers and resettled in Africa have deteriorated yet been salvaged and digitised thanks to the efforts of academics. But no amount of doctoring or research can bring to light details of the millions of Africans carried into enslavement, or their personal stories from origin to destiny.

As to the central figure of this narrative – the *Black Joke* herself – she was, it should be said for the sake of clarity, never a ship. In the age of sail, that term was applied to a square-rigged structure of three or more masts. As a brig, she had just two masts and was otherwise described as a vessel.

In seeking a metaphor for this object launched as an agent of suffering but seen as a thing of exquisite beauty by seafarers, I was repeatedly drawn to a piece of music by a great composer, the master of German lieder. Amid the outpouring of masterpieces that defined the final months before his death in 1828 from syphilis aged 31, Franz Schubert penned perhaps the most haunting of all his songs. 'Der Doppelgänger' is a dead or dying man's vision of a tormented, ghostly double – of his younger self; in another definition, the word *doppelgänger* represents an evil twin.

As it happened, the *Henriqueta* had at that point just set forth on her mission of rescue as the *Black Joke*.

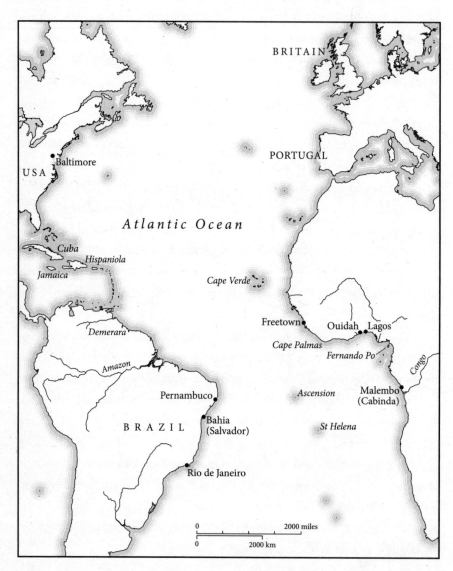

1. The Atlantic Ocean, showing key ports of the slave trade in the 1820s.

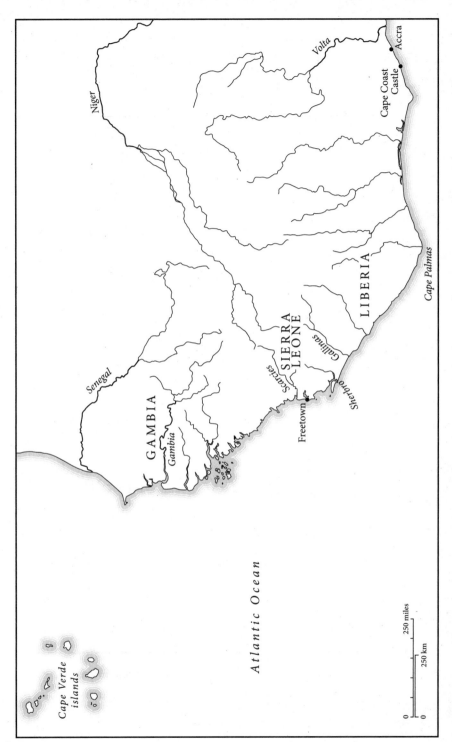

2. The corner of West Africa with the colonial settlement of Freetown.

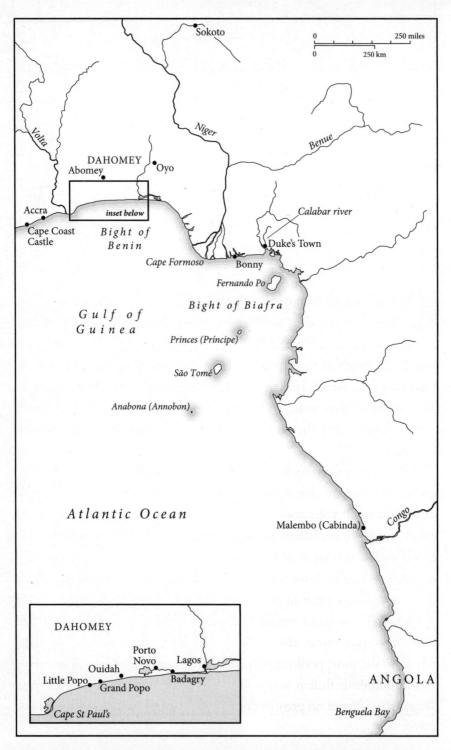

3. The Bights of West Africa, central source of slaving in the 1820s.

PROLOGUE

Ten years after Napoleon sailed into exile on St Helena, the frigate *Maidstone* stood at anchor off another tiny Atlantic landmass. Princes Island was an unlikely refuge, scarcely 10 miles by 4 and lying just 1° 37' north of the Equator within the Gulf of Guinea, but for the flagship of the Navy's latest campaign it provided a welcome respite. In September of that year, 1825, the temperatures of equatorial Africa were tolerable and the tornados had passed, along with the wettest weather.

From his quarterdeck in West Bay, Commodore Charles Bullen could look out on dense jungle, a land of green swept by the jagged outline of spent volcanoes. With its rich soil, abundant vegetation and sweet scent, Princes Island had resources essential to his squadron's well-being and in this week at rest Bullen indulged *Maidstone*'s hands. Off duty, men dangled lines from the forecastle for fish. Boats went ashore daily, returning with fruit and water, but seamen were no bathers so the palm beaches at hand would have had little allure. Besides, they had other matters in mind. This idyll was going to be brief. Soon they would return to the most perilous peacetime operation in the Navy's history.

Commodore Bullen was late to this fray, still finding his way in waters that offered no prospect of reviving past glories. Aged 45, he had been at sea since he was 10, rising to command through distinguished service – along with a degree of patronage – and with battle honours from Camperdown and Trafalgar to show for it. Years on half pay followed Napoleon's defeat before he was offered the *Maidstone*, flagship of the Preventative Squadron in West Africa, and command in a war like no other.

It seems unlikely that Bullen had embarked with any particular notions of service to humanity. Resilience, popularity with his fellows and experience were what suited him for the gruelling task: patrolling the Bights of West Africa was a dreaded duty, carrying the highest mortality rate of any navy station. It had, indeed, been the death of his predecessor, an old friend, Sir Robert Mends. Like others who served here, however, Bullen soon found himself affected by new visions of suffering. Although familiar with sea battle, the calamity wrought on bodies by cannon balls and flying shards of timber, he was overwhelmed by discovering the conditions in which captive Africans were being transported across the Atlantic. He wrote after boarding his first slave vessel:

> The filthy and horrid state I found her in beggars all description. Many females were in an advanced state of pregnancy & several had infants of four to twelve months of age. All were crowded together in one mass of living corruption.[1]

The torment of captive women and children is a recurrent theme in the observations of those who served in the Preventative Squadron.* A year since arriving in Sierra Leone, Bullen was getting to grips with other grim aspects of his command. The squadron, established six years earlier to enforce the Act of Abolition declaring the slave trade illegal, may have reassured reformers at home that Britain was doing its righteous duty. But

* Navy vessels had started cruising from Sierra Leone in pursuit of slavers soon after the 1807 Act of Abolition, but it was only in 1819 that the Preventative Squadron was permanently stationed there.

those on navy vessels ordered to halt the flow of bodies taken from Africa north of the Equator knew better: Whitehall's diplomatic efforts had failed to deter states determined to continue the trade; the Admiralty, still basking in the naval triumphs of the Napoleonic Wars, was detached. To put it charitably, the lords who composed the Navy's administrative board were oblivious to the scale of the challenge. More explicitly, they appeared disinterested. Bullen's squadron lacked the resources to confound, let alone thwart, the slave traders of Portugal, Brazil, Spain and France.

A week's respite at Princes Island (known today as Príncipe) was all the *Maidstone* could be spared and, having obtained water, wood and fruit from the Portuguese governor, Don José Ferreira – who, it was known, was a keen slaver himself and would be engaging in the trade again as soon as they had departed – she raised anchor on 13 September and sailed north for the Gulf of Guinea.

As sea conditions go, these were not especially hazardous waters. Ships' logs often refer to storms in the gulf as 'tornados', but these were violent squalls rather than the cyclonic hurricanes of the Indian Ocean and Caribbean – though they did descend so suddenly as to evade warning by barometers and were accompanied by thunder, torrential rain and lightning that could topple a mast. The Guinea Current, pulsing steadily eastward along the coast at up to 3 knots, was a more predictable factor, albeit one that frustrated and hindered mariners beating westward into south-westerly monsoon winds.[2]

The real perils came not from the sea, but the shore.

European seafaring states had by now been engaged for more than three centuries in trafficking humans from a stretch of coast running some 3,300 miles along the latitudes of West Africa. The 'White Man's Grave', they called it. For the naval personnel assigned to suppression operations, yellow fever and malaria were the main causes of mortality, but other conditions, from leprosy to yaws, rendered even their Sierra Leone base what one called 'a pestiferous charnel house'. As for the glory to be won in battle, there was none. In truth, the enemy had the upper hand. The insatiable appetite across the Atlantic for slave labour

– principally in Brazil and Cuba – had stimulated a surge in the number of vessels engaged in trafficking. Over the previous five years, it is estimated, some 226,500 captives on 200 vessels had eluded the Navy's patrols and been landed in those two states.[3]

The problem, as was often pointed out to the Admiralty, was insufficient and unsuitable ships. Bullen's squadron was larger than its predecessors thanks to political pressure, yet it still amounted to a single frigate, four smaller warships or sloops and two gun-brigs; and even some of these were notorious laggards. As one old politician of the day would reflect bitterly: 'If there was a particularly old slow-going tub in the Navy, she was sure to be sent to the coast of Africa.'[4]

No such sluggishness constrained the foe. Modern slavers, built for purpose and to order in America, were, as Bullen wrote, 'very fine, fast sailing' vessels.[5] For those being transported, conditions below remained hellish; but when it came to manoeuvrability and speed, the experimental two-masted brigs being turned out by Baltimore shipyards had no match in British designs that were steeped in tradition.

HMS *Maidstone* was a case in point. A 36-gun frigate made for war, she had storage enough to spend months at sea, was suited for blockade duty and had quite enough firepower to reduce equivalent French or Spanish ships. She had a reasonable turn of speed too, capable of 9 knots – in the right conditions. But as well as a tendency to plunge, she could slow to 3 knots with the sea on her bow; and in these waters that was no match for the pace and dexterity of a slaver brig.[6] Moreover, with three tall masts she could be sighted a great way off from those low-slung racers.

There was just one element Bullen had in his favour, one he could rely upon to get the most out of *Maidstone* and serve the cause they had been assigned: his crew. The officers were young, proud of a naval heritage that had come to define British power and desperate to make the most of what little opportunity came their way in this post-war era of a much reduced Royal Navy. The seamen, products of the same tradition, had a pride and resourcefulness all of their own – being, as one of their officers wrote, 'pugnacious kind of animals, fond of a little excitement'.[7]

And while they were all vulnerable to disease, another human resource had started to make up *Maidstone's* company: Kru – or Kroomen as they were termed by the Navy – were sturdy West African mariners who served alongside and aloft with Jack Tar and proved more resistant to the fevers that would carry off hundreds of their white shipmates.

A week after sailing from Princes Island, Bullen had resumed patrolling the ill-named coast of Bonny. It was wearisome work for the hands: tacking, or altering the frigate's course by bringing her head to the wind and round; and a frequent raising and shortening of sail, all in equatorial temperatures and humidity. Nothing had altered this routine for days when, early on 24 September, a brig was sighted coming up on the wind with the port of Bonny just 26 miles to the north-east. There could be little doubt: she was a slaver.

The company mustered by divisions, gunners to the 18-pounders, marines bearing muskets. But no warning shot was necessary, no resistance offered. The brig came to, a boat crossed from *Maidstone* and a boarding party went up the side.

A grim-faced lieutenant returned shortly to confirm what Bullen had by now concluded from similar previous encounters. The brig's captain had, in a frosty manner, produced papers showing that she was indeed carrying captive Africans – indeed, no fewer than 499 in number. However, she sailed under French colours.[8]

Well might Bullen have ground his teeth. The French ensign was being used as a flag of convenience by slavers of various states because France remained exempt from the treaties that defined Britain's campaign. Repeatedly frustrated, Bullen had proposed to the Admiralty that such vessels be seized and subjected to judicial scrutiny but this had been expressly forbidden. So another slaver with almost 500 humans aboard started across the Atlantic.

Two weeks later the *Maidstone* had taken up a position off Lagos. The island town set on a lagoon was emerging as a focal point for the trade, so the presence of six sail at anchor demanded investigation. Once again, boats set off under the orders of a lieutenant. Once again, he came back exasperated: the four Brazilian and two Spanish vessels were clearly on slaving voyages, carrying all the usual trading goods, but none had captives stowed below. However tempting it might be to seize these fiendish agents and thus neutralise them, it was forbidden by treaty. Only loaded slavers could be detained, and even then nothing was resolved until they had been sent on for adjudication by a court known as the Mixed Commission.

The following day, 7 October, began with humdrum routine. Eight bells were struck at 4am for all sail, men brought up their hammocks and by mid-morning they had fed off biscuit and suet. The *Maidstone* was in 6° 30′ N and 3° 44′ E, still some 5 miles south of Lagos, when, at around 10am, a lookout shouted down. A strange sail was in the south-west.

Men raced aloft and to their stations. The *Maidstone*'s log relates events over the next nine hours in stark terms: 'At 11, Employed as most necessary . . . tacked . . . Noon, light breezes and fine . . . 4, Moderate and cloudy . . . tacked . . . 6, Chase on weather beam . . . 8, Lost sight of chase.'[9]

The stranger had simply vanished, stealing over the horizon like a phantom.

An account, gathered weeks later by a British intelligence source, provides more detail of the incident. The 'strange sail' had been among the six vessels anchored at Lagos. A two-masted Brazilian brig, she had been in the process of loading a cargo of captives when *Maidstone* appeared. Hastily they were disembarked, the source reported, just in time 'to escape capture'.

> On the departure of the *Maidstone* the slaves were again embarked and they proceeded to sea. Soon afterwards the *Maidstone* appeared and gave chase – a calm or light winds enabled the brig . . . to escape. She is armed and had prepared her guns for resistance.[10]

Twenty-two days later, the *Henriqueta* – for that was the brig's name – landed 504 captives at Bahia in Brazil. Her owner, José de Cerqueira

Lima, was there to welcome his favourite vessel, celebrate the fortune she was making for him and chortle with her master at having reduced the mighty Royal Navy to bumbling fools.

Another resident of Bahia, William Pennell, watched and fumed. The British consul was a bitter foe of Bahia's slavers and had been making enquiries of his own about *Henriqueta*'s voyage. Some captives, he reported, had died on board, 'but with regard to the circumstances and number there has been concealment'.[11] On one point, however, he and Cerqueira Lima agreed. 'The British naval force,' Pennell went on, 'has been ineffectual as regards the illicit trade.'[12]

Commodore Bullen was no less exasperated. By the end of 1825, having flogged his squadron around the Gulf of Guinea, he had lost forty-eight officers, warrant officers and seamen to disease in largely futile pursuits of nimbler quarry. His own ship was feeling the strain as well as being constantly outrun. Her sole trophy was a Spanish schooner, the *Segunda Gallega*. For all Bullen's exertions, the 292 men, women and children found below and taken to join the rescued population of Sierra Leone were the only souls saved by the *Maidstone* that entire year.

Yet in the chase off Lagos the commodore seemingly had a moment of epiphany. Visions of that disappearing vessel – low-sided, raked at both ends and the sweetest sailer he had yet seen – returned to him in haunting form. On receiving consul Pennell's report, he discovered her to be the *Henriqueta*, and she may have been the inspiration for his idea.

Later that year, another American-built slaver brig was captured. As was standard practice, she was taken to Freetown, Sierra Leone, condemned and put up for auction. The buyer was Bullen. Bidders at these events were usually local traders, but the commodore had drawn wisdom from a fourteenth-century proverb. An old poacher makes the best gamekeeper, as they used to say. Or, simply, set a thief to catch a thief.

The fast-sailing slaver was renamed *Hope* and assigned to duty with the squadron. Bullen's innovation was met with thorough disapproval by the Admiralty, but it marked a turning point in the campaign.[13]

Part I
HENRIQUETA

CHAPTER 1

FROM BALTIMORE TO BAHIA
January–October 1824

Quite where her life began is not possible to say. Somewhere among the forests near America's eastern seaboard, perhaps those of Massachusetts or New Hampshire, is as close as can be stated. Her true nature, too, is unclear. The native inhabitants here included oak, pine, larch, maple and elm, of which oak would have been a natural choice, being the most durable; but she was never resilient enough to demonstrate that particular quality, so even her very essence must be left open.

Life. Use of that term may be questioned – being applied to a structure of dead timber and a small amount of iron, along with elements of canvas and hemp. Yet old mariners who had spent more years afloat than ashore and were inclined to invest their sea habitats with character, bad as well as good, were not so constrained. 'The charms of a ship,' wrote one hand, 'are to a seaman what the charms of a mistress are to a poet.'[1] And if one thing can be said about the brig that started her life as the *Henriqueta* it is that she was symptomatic of the human condition. She proved capable of instilling dread and hope, misery and devotion. Her story may be likened to a biblical parable.

Evidence lacking on *Henriqueta*'s origins extends to the identity of her maker; and because of the manner of her death, a further mystery surrounds just what it was that made her unique. An act of pure destruction would ensure she remained forever an enigma.

What can be said is that she emerged from one of the nine shipyards that lined Baltimore harbour in 1820 and were redefining America's scope as a maritime force. Britain had established itself as the world's naval superpower through fleets composed of ships of the line – great castles of oak bearing between seventy and a hundred guns. But since the War of Independence, the United States had been building a range of small, fast-sailing and manoeuvrable vessels that were also efficient sailing into the wind and highly adept at eluding British blockades. Speed, as one authority put it, was 'the great deity' of American seafaring;[2] and Baltimore shipbuilders like Thomas Kemp and William Price were turning out the fastest-sailing vessels to be found anywhere – two-masted schooners and brigs that served privateers and smugglers well but were especially prized by slave traders.

Among those with connections to Baltimore's shipbuilders was a powerful businessman living some 1,700 nautical miles to the south, in the Brazilian city of Bahia. José de Cerqueira Lima had been born in Portugal but, like many colonial entrepreneurs, preferred being in a distant quarter unconstrained by legal niceties. Cerqueira Lima had no time for the motherland's submissiveness to its British ally in signing a treaty in 1815 which defined as illegal the loading of African captives from any point north of the Equator. Like others who had supported Brazil's bitterly divisive declaration of independence in 1822, he sensed fresh opportunity. Bahia (now known as Salvador) had, after all, been founded as the capital of this Portuguese colony in 1549 and remained not only its most important port but the centre of a sugar trade booming on the back of enslaved Africans. For the economy to grow further – as production in Britain's West Indies colonies must eventually decline following the Act of Abolition – many more would be needed. Cerqueira Lima saw humans as a commodity he could supply.

Records of his dealings with Baltimore shipbuilders have not survived. The brigantine *Cerqueira*, bearer of his name, was perhaps the first to come from their yards. She was followed by the *Carlota*, a schooner named after his wife, a reputed beauty. Both vessels had made profitable voyages to the Slave Coast by 1824 when he acquired another – the perfect vehicle for his trade.

Mysteries apart, it is known that the *Henriqueta* evolved from a design called the Baltimore clipper. In simple terms, she was a two-masted brig of 256 tons, low-sided and raked at both ends, with dimensions of 90 feet 10 inches on the upper deck and 26 feet 7 inches in the beam. Even on launching it was unknown how fast she would prove.[3] It was only when she was set under sail that it became clear her shape and form captured seafaring magic.

With one vessel in his own name and another in his wife's, it is possible that Cerqueira Lima called his new brig after another member of his large and diverse family. Brazilian slavers saw nothing bizarre in investing their vessels with names drawn from holy scripture, such as *Bom Jesus*, *Nova Virgem* and *São Jago*, but Cerqueira Lima's taste was for the more personal; *Henriqueta* offered a dainty, sweetly feminine persona. With a prow and setting of masts that proclaimed her speed, she sailed into Bahia and what would be her home port for the first time in mid-1824.

The entry point for Portugal's settlement in the Americas was a panorama of stunning grandeur, a natural harbour extending more than 30 miles from north to south and a similar distance across. An English woman traveller of the day, entering the Bay of All Saints on a sea breeze, described Bahia as 'one of the finest sights my eyes ever beheld'.

> A city, magnificent in appearance from the sea, is placed along the ridge and on the declivity of a very high and steep hill: the richest vegetation breaks through the white houses at intervals . . . and reaches along to the picturesque church and convent of Sant Antonio da Barre . . . The very form of the bay, with its promontories and islands, altogether finishes this charming picture.[4]

Bahia's paradoxical essence only emerged after Maria Graham and other arrivals came ashore. The natural beauty of the bay, the city's holy splendours – the centuries-old Cathedral Basilica of All Saints, the cobbled square of Pelourinho – were set about on all sides by scenes of human degradation and enslavement. 'The whole lower town of Bahia is,' Mrs Graham wrote, 'without exception, the filthiest place I ever was in.' Enslaved men bore their burdens to and fro while vendors and workmen in ragged garments plied their trades on a single narrow street divided by a gutter funnelling household waste which fed pigs, dogs and poultry.

From here the privileged were borne by more slaves in *cadeiras* – a form of sedan chair – to the upper town, and another world, 'beautifully situated on a ridge between the sea and a freshwater lake', Mrs Graham reported with relief. Here dwelt the city's white gentry.[5]

From its founding almost three centuries earlier, Bahia had quickly evolved into a fulcrum for slave trading across Brazil, its harbour lying on a broadly similar latitude to regions of West Africa directly across the Atlantic. Rio de Janeiro, some 800 miles to the south, became more dominant early in the nineteenth century as the capital of Portugal's royal family in exile during the war raging in the Iberian Peninsula.[6] Then came peace in Europe, and with it turmoil in Brazil. The royal family was divided – Dom João VI returning to Portugal as king while his rebellious son Pedro remained at Rio, declaring 'Independence or Death' and proclaiming himself Emperor of Brazil.

In a brief *guerra da independência*, Bahia's white elite were torn between loyalty to Dom João and the lure of unfettered opportunity under Pedro. There was little question where those in favour of sustaining the slave trade stood. How could their country join Portugal in bowing to the domineering British over abolition when African labour was the only means of enriching Bahia? For months the city simmered violently, family against family.

By a quirk of fate, the struggle was in large part resolved by a renegade Royal Navy captain. After his dismissal over allegations of Stock Exchange fraud, Thomas Cochrane had acted as a mercenary naval commander, first for Chile in its war for independence from Spain, then accepting a similar role in Brazil's nascent navy. In 1823, a year before *Henriqueta's* arrival, Cochrane brought four ships to off Bahia where a Portuguese fleet of thirteen ships lay at anchor and, deploying his fearsome reputation in psychological and tactical manoeuvres, intimidated the army general commanding the city to evacuate the garrison. The Portuguese fleet sailed north for Maranhão, carrying thousands of troops, but was beaten to it by Cochrane who again outwitted the local authorities to take possession before it arrived. In just a few weeks, he had delivered northern Brazil into the hands of Emperor Pedro.[7]

Thus was the die cast. Brazil had won its freedom with a centre of power that now lay in the south at Rio. But distant Bahia retained its own form of independence. It was still bursting with profits, being ideally located for voyaging to West Africa and the heart of the slave trade – the Bight of Benin. More than 10,000 captives were being brought to Bahia in shackles every year for auctioning at the slave market: the more fortunate went to local buyers for labouring in the city; a worse fate awaited those destined for the interior – distant sugar plantations or mines. Cerqueira Lima and other leading traders were also shipping Africans here for transporting on to Rio or Pernambuco.[8] Brazil was on its way to becoming the world's largest slave market.

All the while, the indigenous population withered. The fact that Africans were found to be sturdier and more resilient – 'a finer, stronger race than any I have ever seen', wrote Mrs Graham – only increased the demand for their labour. Another English visitor, James Wetherell, observed Bahia to be 'a mixture of . . . every complexion and colour of hair, every kind of feature and stature, from the white to the deepest hue of the African'.[9] But whites made up less than a third of the state's 65,000 population. The great majority were blacks, either born in Brazil to previous generations of enslaved Africans or transported in their own lifetimes; a proportion of both these black groups were known as *libertos*, former slaves who had acquired the resources to buy their freedom.[10]

In this land of extremes, the wealthy lived on the spectacular Corredor da Vitória which ran along a ridge perched about 600 feet above the sea. They included twenty or so British merchants, fellows whom Mrs Graham thought 'not of the first order', their minds so 'engrossed by sugar and cottons' that they took not the slightest interest in cultural matters or the vivid natural life on their doorsteps. Like the Portuguese residents, these 'incurious money-makers' had household slaves and were themselves involved in the trade, selling cotton goods from the mills of Lancashire that could be bartered for humans across the Atlantic.[11] It was hardly surprising, Mrs Graham concluded, that such philistines had no interest in the opera house, a grand if faded monument of the colonial period with its discordant singers and grubby seating. Only a tolerable orchestra held it together.

This same sumptuous neighbourhood was home to José de Cerqueira Lima.

Like his prize new vessel, Bahia's rising tycoon remains something of a mystery. Of his Portuguese origins nothing can be said. As to age, he was nearing 40. Greed apart, what distinguished him was opportunism and cunning. During the turbulent transition to independence, Cerqueira Lima played a shrewdly equivocal hand though his own convictions were never in doubt. In the years before he became directly involved in state politics, he exercised influence through his capacity to supply Bahia with enslaved labour. After Portugal lost power, his status soared. As a statement of allegiance and intent, he called his next slaving brig *Independência*. Until recently a monopoly on shipping Africans had been in the hands of one Vicente de Paula Silva.[12] But in acquiring the latest Baltimore technology, Cerqueira Lima was set to become, in Mrs Graham's words, 'the greatest slave merchant here'.[13]

His residence was Bahia's most imposing, a baroque palace on the Corredor da Vitória dating from the birth of Portuguese colonial architecture and containing a collection of gold plate, furniture and fittings that rendered it suitable for hosting Emperor Pedro on visits from Rio. In more ordinary times, Cerqueira Lima held court surrounded by his large family, who included his white wife but also children by African women, and a retinue of slaves.[14]

He rubbed along well enough with his British neighbours. They were Protestant heretics in his eyes, naturally, and there was little social mingling, but they did have useful products and common business interests. In January 1824, however, he had suffered a severe blow with the capture off Lagos by the Royal Navy of his first vessel. Although the *Cerqueira* had no human cargo on board, she was plainly on a slaving voyage and the frustrations felt by the West Africa Squadron had led on this occasion to a breach of the 1815 treaty stipulating that only loaded slavers could be detained.[15] An outraged Cerqueira Lima vowed to fight Britain, in the courts and by any other means necessary.

When *Henriqueta* came into view a few months later she may have appeared a weapon of retaliation.

From their subjective points of view, José de Cerqueira Lima and Maria Graham had little to agree on. Yet a historical perspective threw up paradoxes that an English lady, horrified by what she saw of slavery, might have found discomforting.

Just as Portuguese mariners had been the first to circumnavigate the globe, so they were the first Europeans to engage in slaving by sea: West Africans were being trafficked to Portugal and Madeira as early as the mid-fifteenth century. But it was discovery of the New World that caused the ancient institution of slavery to evolve in new forms. Initially, Spain took the lead, so that by the 1530s the island of Hispaniola (present-day Haiti and the Dominican Republic) had more inhabitants of African than Spanish origin. The Portuguese followed in their wake, founding settlements in Brazil, 'the Land of the True Cross', and towards the end of the sixteenth century it was their trade that started to accelerate, especially to Bahia.[16]

English slave trading is said to have been initiated by John Hawkins, who sailed to the coast of Guinea in 1562 with the consent of Queen Elizabeth. Despite her somewhat fanciful desire that Africans should 'not be carried off without their consent', Hawkins proceeded in 'burning and spoiling their townes' before trading his victims in Hispaniola.[17] The French and Dutch too joined in the trade, but once British settlements were founded in the Caribbean islands and North America, Iberian power across the Atlantic was gradually usurped.

The Royal African Company, founded in 1672, united the royal family and English noblemen with wealthy merchants as investors in a trade based at Cape Coast Castle in modern Ghana. By the turn of the century the company had trafficked nearly 175,000 Africans across the world.[18] A royal charter proved no obstacle to interlopers; private traders set up in Bristol, which was to generate an estimated 2,000 slaving voyages before the Act of Abolition. Other English ports followed, notably Liverpool, which went on to become the largest slaving harbour in Europe and the starting point for almost twice as many voyages as Bristol.

In the decade from 1720, British vessels transported some 100,000 captives across the Atlantic. That figure rose in the 1730s to 170,000, more than were shipped by the Portuguese to Brazil. A new slaving enterprise appeared in the form of the South Sea Company and as Britain emerged as the paramount slaving nation, so did new markets: the majority of African men, women and children transported by British vessels were landed in Jamaica and Barbados, but Spanish ports in the Caribbean and the American states of Virginia and Carolina also served as markets.

Statistics in such instances become wearisome as well as dehumanising, as they can only be grotesquely rounded up. But they need to be spelled out as best we can: in the 1740s, British ships transported more than 200,000 captive Africans. When trading by the monopoly companies gave way in 1750 to a free-for-all, slaving surged further – to some 325,000 in the decade up to 1790.[19]

It was with due honesty that, when the tide started to turn, William Pitt the Younger, addressing Parliament in 1792, said: 'No nation in Europe has plunged so deeply into this guilt as Great Britain.' By the time the Act abolishing the slave trade in Britain and its colonies was passed fifteen years later, an estimated 3,260,000 captive Africans had been loaded onto British vessels, of whom perhaps 700,000 had died at sea.

For astute slavers such as José de Cerqueira Lima, speed was the prime virtue in a vessel, not simply as the means to escape a pursuer but so that the human beings festering below could be delivered as quickly as possible and thereby have the best chance of surviving a transatlantic voyage and turning a profit.

For that very reason a Baltimore clipper was a desirable possession. Yet the design had other qualities too, being suited to close work on an African coast dissected by creeks and rivers and lacking any sheltered harbours. There was a further aspect to these vessels, something chilling in the light of the atrocities that defined them. With sleek, sweeping lines, they were objects of exquisite elegance.

Slave traders themselves could be enchanted. As one wrote on first seeing Baltimore clippers at anchor:

> There was something bewitching to my mind in their racehorse beauty. These dashing slavers, with their arrowy hulls and raking masts, got complete possession of my fancy.[20]

Although a hard-nosed magnate, Cerqueira Lima may well have felt the same sensation on beholding his new brig. The man given command of her certainly did.

João Cardozo dos Santos was a protégé of Cerqueira Lima's – strikingly youthful, just 20 when he was presented with the *Henriqueta*.[21] As such, he could have been in no position to take charge of a voyage requiring the skills of a seasoned seafarer, knowledge of haggling for Africans and a steely-eyed indifference to their sufferings. All of these he would develop over years of association with his brig. What launched him, though, was a family connection. An older brother, Manoel

Cardozo dos Santos, was one of Cerqueira Lima's most trusted associates and master of the *Cerqueira*.[22] That was Cerqueira Lima's way of doing business, cultivating a body of loyal attendants who owed him allegiance and extended his circle of influence. For those he favoured, fortunes beckoned. Such were the profits from the human trade that within two years Manoel dos Santos would be able to buy his own vessel.[23]

His younger brother João was now set on a similar course, but on his first voyage would need guidance: Cerqueira Lima assigned him an adviser to handle negotiations in Africa and an experienced mariner to take *Henriqueta*'s helm, quite possibly the American master who had delivered her from Baltimore; new Brazilian vessels were known to have been sailed in this way, with the nominated master as a pupil at his side.

In September 1824, within weeks of her arrival, plans were in hand for *Henriqueta*'s departure. Now Cerqueira Lima had the irritating bureaucracy to deal with.

Slave trading, even in Brazil, was notionally limited by treaties initiated by Britain, specifically that with Portugal which prohibited loading captives north of the Equator. Trafficking had once been mainly from regions south of the line, such as Angola and Mozambique, which remained legal sources. Brazil's demand for bodies, however, had overtaken the capacity of those parts to deliver them, so traders had turned to the ports on the Gulf of Guinea once favoured by Britain.[24] This gave rise to a systematic deceit. The authorities in Bahia and Rio issued so-called passports, permitting vessels to import captives loaded south of the Equator. In reality, more and more cargoes had their origins north of it – especially those landed in Bahia.*

* For this reason, reliable data for the origins of captives brought to Brazil from the 1820s onward remains elusive. Figures for slaving voyages to Bahia and Rio supposedly from ports south of the Equator and cited on valuable databases such as slavevoyages.org need to be treated with caution. As will be seen, passports were routinely falsified to show captives had been loaded at Malembo, for example, when they had in fact come from the Bights. Most of the Brazilian vessels captured north of the Equator carried passports for ports to the south. The origins of the numerous vessels that escaped capture cannot, therefore, be properly quantified.

The British government was not ignorant of this violation. At almost the same time that Cerqueira Lima was applying for *Henriqueta's* passport, George Canning, the foreign secretary, wrote to his consul-general in Rio, Henry Chamberlain, pointing out that these permits allowed slave vessels to touch at Princes Island, which offered 'an excuse for being seen near the Slave Coast north of the Equator' – an opportunity they seized to 'procure their cargo in these ports'. Canning went on: 'I hope that the Brazilian authorities, when made aware of these evils which are produced by the form in which their passport is drawn up, will lose no time in altering it.'[25] As if to drive the point home, Canning enclosed the note written by Commodore Bullen off West Africa after his first shocking sight of conditions on a captured slaver: 'The filthy and horrid state I found her in beggars all description.'[26]

The fact was, however, that the chaotic state of affairs in Brazil following its secession from Portugal had reduced British diplomats to hapless onlookers. And so riven by conflict was the young nation that whatever pact might be reached with Rio would not serve in Bahia – now a law unto itself. As for events there, both London and Rio were largely in the dark because the consul, William Pennell, had been stricken with a stomach ailment that for a while appeared likely to carry him off.

Another aspect of trafficking to Bahia gave particular cause for concern. This was the corrupt local method of measuring ship displacement. Under a recent decree issued in Rio, no more than two humans were supposed to be loaded per 2 tons of a vessel.[27] In reality, records were being falsified in Bahia, so that one slaver of 162 tons had been measured to show an additional 83 tons, another of 108 tons a further 59 tons, and, even worse, one of a mere 84 tons another 57 tons.[28] The atrocious conditions of transportation were thus being rendered all the more torturing: a small vessel designed to carry no more than 168 Africans in some supposed state of relative security was being authorised to take on at least 282.

Henry Chamberlain, Britain's senior envoy in Rio, could only bleat feebly to the Brazilian government: 'It is difficult to understand how the measurement by the authorities at Bahia can have been correct.'[29] The recipient, José de Carvalho Mello, replied that he would, of course, take up this important matter with the president of Bahia, in full knowledge that nothing would be done.

All of which suited Cerqueira Lima's purposes admirably in obtaining a passport for *Henriqueta*'s maiden voyage. The tide was running his way in the battle against these British hypocrites. Following the capture of the *Cerqueira*, her master Manoel dos Santos had performed valuable service with an outraged protest to the authorities at Sierra Leone. His only reason for calling at Lagos, he declared, was 'because the winds [for Angola] were uncertain' and he needed 'to resupply myself with beans, oil and other provisions'.[30] As no captives had been found on her, the brigantine had to be handed back.

The *Cerqueira*'s return to Bahia, empty of cargo, on 24 May galvanised her owner. He resolved to launch an unprecedented legal claim against the British government 'for the losses, damages and prejudices arising out of [her] capture and detention', for the stupendous sum of £60,000 (equivalent today to £3.4 million).[31]

William Pennell's recovery and return to duty brought renewed scrutiny to events. Among those battling the inhuman trade, few did so with more quiet dedication than Britain's consul in the outlaw province. A corpulent, avuncular figure who preserved his diplomatic bearing even in the midst of violence, Pennell had seen enough in seven years' service at Bahia to turn him from dispassionate observer to dedicated abolitionist.

Born in Topsham, Devon, the son of a prosperous merchant, he appeared more respectable gentry than ardent crusader. Among his most devoted activities had been fathering twenty-two children by his wife Elizabeth, a clergyman's daughter, while running a shipping business between Ireland and Newfoundland. Profits enabled him to take up voluntary service at the age of 50 on behalf of the Crown, initially as consul at Bordeaux. Elizabeth, no doubt exhausted, did not accompany William when he accepted the same role at Bahia in 1817 – again without pay.

Despite persecution by gout, he remained an amiable soul.[32] Mrs Graham recorded his generosity as a host, welcoming her into a garden house on the Corredor da Vitória perched at the edge of the bay where 'flowers and fruits mingled their sweets even down to the water's edge'.[33] She was not his only guest. British visitors were invited to dinners and parties where two of his daughters acted as hostesses, fiddlers performed and quadrilles were danced. Pennell's hospitality was extended to Bahia's white residents, though Mrs Graham was not taken by their manners: even dressed in the best of French fashion the Portuguese ladies lacked politesse; the men stood about scowling; and both gambled prodigiously.

The source of the locals' dyspepsia in British company is readily discernible. During the independence crisis, Pennell had steered a cool path between secessionists and loyalists and, at especially precarious moments in Bahia, offered asylum to various endangered individuals. For these mercies he retained the gratitude of some residents.[34] But with the province's enduring demand for slave labour, and Pennell the visible representative of an obstructive power, he had a growing number of foes.

The paradoxes of British foreign policy were, naturally enough, deeply resented in Brazil. The same nation that had dominated transatlantic slavery – having transported at that point more African captives than any other European state – and that still reaped the profits from its survival in the Caribbean, was now trying to prevent other, younger states from obtaining the same benefits. Here, surely, was evidence of a sly economic strategy to preserve British dominance. It was not lost on Bahia's administrators that significant numbers within the British establishment still claimed ownership of hundreds of thousands of enslaved men, women and children.

Righteousness, it might have been added, was hard to discern across Brazil's northern border. Just a year earlier, the British colony of

Demerara-Essequibo (modern Guyana) had been the scene of an uprising by enslaved labourers against conditions which – as it emerged – were barbaric even by the standards of most Caribbean plantations, and lacked so much as the liberty of assigned rest days granted to labourers in Brazil.[35] Cerqueira Lima and his like may not have known details of the merciless suppression and executions that followed what had been a relatively restrained uprising; but they were kept informed on matters of common interest to local British merchants – the *Inglezes*, as they were known – who had been drawn here by Bahia's potential, who lived high on the bounty of an economy driven by enslavement, and among whom Cerqueira Lima had useful contacts.[36]

Publicly, at least, Pennell remained an integral part of this society. As consul he had a fine house and, along with his hostess daughters, a staff of black servants. This raises a question, for it is possible that they too were enslaved; Mrs Graham made no exceptions in observing: 'The English are all served by slaves.'[37] It is more feasible, however, that his retinue was drawn from Bahia's population of freed *libertos*. Of his devotion to the abolitionist cause there is no doubt. While continuing in his diplomatic duties, his primary role had turned to intelligence-gathering. Pennell was London's most reliable agent for information on illegal slaving voyages.

For the Grahams, who had come to Brazil assured of Britain's virtuous stand but no direct experience of slavery, Pennell suggested a visit to the nearby island of Itaparica. Mrs Graham, having been unable to pass the slave market 'without shame and indignation', was slightly taken aback to find at each sugar plantation a 'little community of slaves . . .':

And in their huts something like the blessings of freedom are enjoyed, in the family ties and charities they are not forbidden to enjoy. I went into several of the huts and found them cleaner and more comfortable than I expected; each contains four or five rooms, and each room appears to hold a family.[38]

These conditions were a world away, as we will see, from those endured in the interior; the enslaved of Itaparica were also fortunate, as they told the English visitors, in being distanced from their owners – while those in the city were subject to constant, often cruel, attention. 'They have a little church and are more contented than I thought a slave could be,' Mrs Graham wrote.[39]

Deeper comprehension came with the sight of a vessel discharging her human cargo in port. 'They are singing as they go ashore,' she observed. 'Poor wretches! Could they foresee the slave-market, and the separations of friends and relations that will take place there, and the march up the country, and the labour of the mines and the sugar-works, their singing would be a wailing cry.'

But it was a meeting with a British naval officer that revealed to her the full horror of the trade, epitomised by the voyage of transportation. Commander William Finlaison of the sloop *Morgiana* had brought to Brazil a slaver captured off West Africa as evidence of treaty violations that were becoming increasingly flagrant. He also related to Pennell's guests the atrocities being committed on such vessels to escape detection by the Navy. These were tales which, Mrs Graham wrote, 'made my blood run cold':

Of young negresses headed up in casks and thrown overboard when the ships are chased. Of others, stowed in boxes when a ship was searched, with a bare chance of surviving. Where the trade is admitted, no wonder the heart becomes callous to individual sufferings.[40]

Commander Finlaison, for his part, was still fuming at the Brazilian authorities' refusal to discountenance violations in which they were directly involved. Off Lagos, he had captured a schooner, the *Emilia*, grotesquely overloaded with 398 captives, many of them already 'fearfully diseased' and, much to his credit, taken 100 on *Morgiana* to save lives.[41] Having since escorted the *Emilia* to Rio as ordered, in anticipation that she would be condemned, he had encountered obstruction from the Mixed Commission – the arbitrating court sitting in Rio.

Still worse, as he saw it, was the rejection of his attempt to save five Africans who had been among *Emilia*'s crew. These men, themselves enslaved, had been taken in by his own company – only for the British judge on the commission to inform Finlaison that he was not authorised to liberate men deemed Brazilian property. Ordered to hand them over, he refused until the Rio authorities issued an ultimatum.

The curious aspect of this case, from the British perspective, was that the five black seamen – named as Jodi, Gorge, Lauriano, Balthasar and Domingo – evidently had no desire for a new life in the Royal Navy. One of them, Jodi, drowned while trying to swim ashore from *Morgiana*, while Gorge told a hearing he wanted to stay in Bahia. He and the other three were duly returned to their owners.[42]

The *Morgiana*'s brief stay in Bahia brought fresh evidence of hostility to the British. A few seamen allowed ashore to carouse in the lower town came under attack. One hand was fatally stabbed. The incident may have been due to a drunken quarrel but, Mrs Graham reported, fear spread in the British community that Commander Finlaison was 'so hated here on account of his activity against the slave trade that none of his people are safe'.[43]

By early October, Cerqueira Lima had his passport. The *Henriqueta* was licensed to import captives from Malembo, a port 5° 5′ south of the Equator, some 50 miles from the mouth of the Congo River. The number of captives permitted to be loaded was not stipulated but, by her tonnage measured as a brig, she could ship 600 African bodies under the old Portuguese regulations.

In this pantomime Cerqueira Lima and the provincial regulator were openly complicit. All of Bahia knew that the *Henriqueta* would be shortly sailing for the Bight of Benin, in all likelihood Ouidah, almost 7° north of the line.

Her crew had been assembled by methods unique to Brazilian shipping. Slaves served in various forms here – in households and on plantations, of course, but also as the porters, stall-holders and craftsmen thronging the streets around the harbour, the 'fruit-sellers, vendors of sausages, black-puddings, fried fish, oil and sugar cakes', observed by Mrs Graham, along with those busy 'plaiting hats or mats'.[44] These were men and women who would return to their owners at the end of the day to hand over their earnings – a proportion of which they would usually be allowed to retain. Slaves also acted as boatmen and loaders, however, ferrying goods to ships at anchor. Records show that nearly 90 per cent of Bahia's maritime labour force were black.[45]

For those who showed aptitude, the next step was going up the side – and then setting sail. Like every other aspect of Bahia's economy, from sugar production to street commerce, the maritime industry was dependent on black labour. It is a jarring but simple truth that virtually every vessel departing for Africa had among her seamen the likes of Jodi and Gorge who would be sailing back to their motherland, there to participate, however reluctantly, in the trafficking of those who might have been deemed kith and kin.[46]

This is not to suggest complicity, though it has been argued that the enslaved males of Bahia who acquired seafaring skills gained not only mobility but a degree of autonomy from those who claimed to be their owners. As one study has noted:

Bahia's slave trade, unique in the Atlantic, was based on the assemblage of small-scale investments, mostly in goods not currency, purchased on credit with the promise of small-scale returns. In lieu of complex financial instruments, investment in such voyages was organized around familial and patronage ties, which allowed maritime laborers as well as the slaves of Atlantic merchants to participate in long-distance commerce through their personal connections with wealthy elites.[47]

Cerqueira Lima claimed ownership of many Africans and his involvement in the slave trade made it inevitable that some would be forced to become crew on his vessels. As *Henriqueta*'s nominal master, João dos Santos, his new protégé from that family, may also have had a role in selecting her company after receiving petitions from interested families seeking a stake in this particular investment. While no crew record – or muster list, as it was known – survives from *Henriqueta*'s first slaving voyage, later events suggest that the pilot and two mates were Portuguese.

The manual work, the hauling, the setting and stowing of sails, was to be done by thirty-two seamen. Of them, it is likely that at least a dozen were of African origin – men in the ownership of Cerqueira Lima or his associates.[48] In this respect, *Henriqueta*'s company would have matched the standard shipboard diversity found in Bahia. The case of the five black hands found by Finlaison on *Emilia* was far from rare; a study of slaving vessels based in Bahia has established that between 30 and 40 per cent of crews were African-born.[49]

They were useful hands too. A British observer in Rio thought trading would be reduced if black men could be prevented from serving on slavers 'as they are generally the most useful and effective part of their crew'.[50]

Cerqueira Lima was in the habit of issuing strict written instructions to the masters of his vessels, rounding off with a characteristic farewell: 'Wishing you a good voyage and hoping that it may be as happy in its results as we can all desire.'[51]

On the morning of 30 October 1824 *Henriqueta*'s company went to their positions along her 90-foot upper deck and up the two heavily raked masts. It could be taxing labour in that humid season, with occasional torrential rain followed by sunlight and slow breaths of air, reaching a point that sails might be shaken down. Then vast spreads of canvas lifted slowly, limply, before bursting into life and, with her deck leaning sharply, she turned away from the shore, out of the bay and into the Atlantic.

CHAPTER 2

A HELL AFLOAT
October 1824–January 1825

A slaveship was the most vile form of confinement devised by man, and there are no grounds for suggesting that the *Henriqueta* was any kind of exception. At best, the loading of these vessels below decks was carried out with some thought as to how many human bodies might be stacked side by side and still survive from embarkation to landing. At worst, whether from brutality or stupidity, disease or starvation, it led to forms of suffering drawn from the realm of biblical prophecy. The term Hell Afloat was applied to naval ships in isolation under mad or tyrannical captains, but it ought properly to have been born from a slaver.

No first-hand account exists of *Henriqueta*'s maiden voyage to Africa in 1824. The record of a later passage survives, from which may be inferred the likely course taken, along with the way she responded to weather conditions.[1] To these may be added other known facts to compile a picture filling in the spaces around a number of particularly dark episodes.

The *Henriqueta* took to the Atlantic like a bird. Escaping the coast against the prevailing forces of the South-East Trades and the South Equatorial Current taxed all shipping for Africa, yet she managed 77 nautical miles on day two, 114 miles on day four and 141 miles on day five.[2] On a course east by north-east that hardly deviated, she ran steadily towards the Equator, still against variable winds while reeling off between 183 and 198 nautical miles a day. Square sails set fore and aft, her arrow-like form swept along at 14 knots; and sweet though that was, with a following wind she had more in her yet.[3]

Her speed was partly due to lightness of construction – a feature of these American vessels which Spanish traders in Cuba had been quick to discern and employ. By comparison, the Portuguese schooners and brigs trading out of Brazil had been dull sailers, and Cerqueira Lima may indeed have been the first of his countrymen to have taken a lesson from Havana.[4] Being made for speed had its drawbacks: the lightly built Baltimore vessel was a thing of delicate beauty; but she was not durable. An officer given command of *Henriqueta* in her next life, who would exult with the wind at his back as she whipped ahead and marvel at how 'she could forge ahead even in a calm', would also bear witness to her frailty.[5] Now, though, sails set square on the yards, spanker and jibs filling, she flowed sweetly until, with wind on the quarter, she could be racing.

João Cardozo dos Santos stood braced on a sloping deck as she cleaved the swell. Still *Henriqueta*'s master in name only, he took daily instruction in the craft of sailing from his appointed mariner. The Baltimore clipper, it was pointed out, had a tendency to plunge, driving under the waves, especially at speed in a squall. There was no need for haste, however, considering the lengthy process ahead; and, with no threat at this stage of interference from those British despots, Dos Santos's exploration of his vessel's qualities could proceed at ease. They had 2,100 nautical miles to run to Cape Palmas, the southernmost point of West Africa at 4° 36′ N and 7° 72′ W, bypassing the British base at Freetown in Sierra Leone. With good weather that would take just over two weeks.[6] There they would pick up the easterly Guinea Current and proceed more cautiously along the coast towards the Bights of Benin and Biafra – black heart of Bahia's slave trade. As *Henriqueta*'s records show, the outward voyage could be accomplished in twenty-two days.[7]

While their identities are unknown, her company on this high-investment enterprise would have been selected, experienced hands and – whether of Portuguese or African origin – hard-bitten fellows. Handling captives, observing their trauma during loading and the inevitable deaths on the return passage, all while enduring wretched conditions themselves, bred callousness, an indifference to suffering for which the end of a voyage was the only relief.

Still supplied with fresh provisions from Bahia, they had time to contemplate their present ease. It must have been hard for them to visualise how a space which now accommodated up to forty men in a degree of comfort – some preferred to sleep on deck rather than below, especially in tropical temperatures – was likely to be loaded on the return voyage with more than 500 Africans. *Henriqueta* would be carrying twelve times as many human beings as when outward bound.

Rainfall was often in the air. The torrential downpours that fell mid-year on passages through the doldrums had passed but rain could still come in copious measures – up to half an inch in a day. Further turbulence awaited in the Gulf of Guinea along the African coast, where the violent squalls termed 'tornados' burst out of the sky at rates of up to 50 knots, challenging the strength and agility of seamen in furling sail.[8]

Passing Cape Palmas at the start of the third week in November, *Henriqueta* ran east, holding to around 3° N. Directly to the north lay the thousands of miles of coast that had constituted slavers' trading grounds for almost three centuries. The principal source for vessels from Bahia, however, was a stretch of 600 miles east of the Volta River. It was at this point – crossing 0° longitude to the eastern hemisphere – that *Henriqueta* shaped a course east by north-east to enter the Bight of Benin.

The first land to be sighted was a flat, featureless coastline that emerged so gradually as to be almost indistinguishable from the horizon. Dos Santos had the *Henriqueta*'s topsails stowed and she came to off a beach-encircled lagoon. Ashore, a mile or so inland, stood the town of

Ouidah, once a bastion for European slave companies, now the fiefdom of one Francisco Félix de Souza. In launching his new venture, Cerqueira Lima was following a familiar and trusted regime. Business would be conducted through a fellow native of Bahia, a trader willing to exchange African captives for a product no other marketplace would accept.

Slavery had been widely practised by large, dominant societies across West Africa from ancient times. Trading by outsiders began in the seventh century, when Arab merchants started trafficking captives northwards across the Sahara.[9] But the appearance of white men from over the horizon – the Portuguese, followed by the Spaniards, English, French and Dutch – was a metamorphosis. Centres of trade shifted to the Atlantic coast, giving rise to new kingdoms. In around 1700, the town of Hueda – or Ouidah, as it became known – emerged under its rulers as the hub of slaving in West Africa.[10] Over the next decade, about 15,000 enslaved men, women and children passed through Ouidah every year.

The novel offerings which beguiled Ouidah's rulers also spurred their downfall. The inland kingdom of Dahomey, with a capital 60 miles to the north at Abomey, had evolved as a highly militarised society that also brandished feminine power through a cohort of tall armed women warriors known as the Mino. Ouidah was invaded in 1727 and, despite intermittent conflict, became absorbed into Dahomey. The European traders, established in forts of red clay located in separate quarters of the town, continued to receive captives through royal hands while coming under the control of an African authority figure: the Yovogan, or 'Chief of the Whites', ruled on behalf of the king in Abomey.[11]

Turbulence in Europe, arising from the Napoleonic Wars and an age of reform, was felt in Ouidah too. The French were the first to depart, followed by the British with the Act of Abolition, and the Portuguese. Thus was the way opened for the rise of Francisco Félix de Souza.

The figure of De Souza has assumed an enigmatic, even mystic, place in both folklore and historiography: the founding father of an Afro-Brazilian community on the Bight of Benin where he is still honoured despite having enslaved tens of thousands of Africans; a figure sinister or benevolent, depending on the narrator, but unfathomable too, hence the fascination he has exerted. Like many of those who appear in this narrative, his origins are obscure although one study of his life has concluded that he was born into a Bahia family – his father a Portuguese settler turned slave trader, his mother an indigenous Amazonian – and arrived in Africa for the first time in around 1788.* An older brother, Jacinto José de Souza, held a senior position at the Portuguese fort while it was still channelling captives to Brazil and encouraged the younger man to conduct private trade up and down the coast. Yet when he moved to the fort himself it was as a lowly clerk – until his brother's death, whereupon De Souza took charge.[12] Meanwhile, tensions within the kingdom had been on the rise.

A turning point came when De Souza visited King Adandozan in Abomey to seek payment of a debt. The monarch responded by imprisoning him. He escaped, to form an alliance with Adandozan's brother, Gezo, that led to the king's overthrow in 1818. De Souza's reward from Gezo was control of the kingdom's slave trade. It was long believed that he had absolute rule over the town and its environs, giving rise to the title Viceroy of Ouidah, but recent studies have established that political authority remained in the hands of the Yovogan.[13]

De Souza's domain was no less grand for that. He took possession of Ouidah, including the eighteenth-century French fort, extending the town with new streets and spreading prosperity. He built his own mansion, a substantial residence that stands to this day. While all of this was established on the back of slavery – which, it may be added, was rife well before his arrival – he was revered by a population estimated to

* De Souza is the subject of Bruce Chatwin's *The Viceroy of Ouidah*. The author, it is said, wanted to write a life of the slaver but, failing to find enough material, turned his research into a novel. The subject similarly fascinated the film-maker Werner Herzog, inspiring his film *Cobra Verde*. The only biography is in Portuguese: *Francisco Félix de Souza, ercador de scravos*, by Alberto da Costa e Silva; but Verger and Law have described De Souza's rise to wealth and power in their cited works.

have reached about 20,000 at the time of *Henriqueta*'s first voyage.[14] Tradition has it that he was instrumental in persuading Gezo to abolish human sacrifice. He also had a reputation for keeping families together as entities when buying captives (though that was plainly not sustainable in large-scale negotiations).[15] Honoured by Gezo with the title Chacha, he won further respect for a king-like virility: descendants claim that he fathered no fewer than 201 children.[16]

Cutting so theatrical a figure, the Chacha impressed strangers too. A naval officer described him as living 'in prodigious splendour' attended by petitioners and slaves.[17] Another described 'a sallow, corpulent, heavy-featured man' in his sixties, wearing 'a loose dressing robe with a small velvet cap, from which his long hair is flowing'.[18] On the occasions when he ventured out it was under a parasol carried by a slave with an armed guard and a company of musicians. As well as selling Africans in large numbers to the Brazilian and Cuban traders anchored offshore, De Souza owned several slaving vessels of his own, including at least one Baltimore clipper.[19] He was clearly known to Cerqueira Lima through mutual connections and, with their heritage and ostentatious lifestyles in common, may well have served as a role model for his younger Bahia compatriot.

Dos Santos went ashore with an example of his wares. Humans were once exchanged for cowry shells, which had evolved into the local currency. Other enticing goods followed – sugar and aguardente, or firewater, a potent cane brandy which went down well here and was often used to lubricate trade. Weapons too were bartered, being much valued by Gezo's militia. But the product that defined Bahia's trade with this region was tobacco. Not just any tobacco, but tobacco of a quality rejected as unacceptable by Portugal, for which market it had been cultivated. A third-rate crop was the most highly valued commodity for buying humans at Ouidah, and Dos Santos had come well supplied.[20]

What slowed proceedings – to the point that it rendered unpredictable the timetable for any slaving voyage – was a shortage of human captives: the surge in demand from Brazil and Cuba had strained even

Dahomey's capacity to provide them. Other factors too were at work, as De Souza engaged in personal trade with his own vessels. The upshot was that Ouidah's six barracoons – the thatched enclosures where men, women and children were imprisoned while their destiny was haggled over – were almost invariably empty when slavers anchored. It might take anything between two and five months before they would be filled again.

De Souza was noted for his hospitality, whether to supplicant Brazilian traders or British adversaries. Navy officers and travellers were among those who made their way through the sprawling town – clusters of large huts composed from red clay and thatch shaded among cotton trees – past the marketplace generally accepted to be the best on the coast: 'The finest I have seen in Africa,' wrote one British visitor:

> well supplied with every luxury and many useful goods . . . As there are no shops, all trade is here . . . The market is divided into propor-tions . . . meat, fish, corn, flour, vegetable, fruit and foreign goods have all separate [areas].[21]

Another of Ouidah's features was a temple enclosing a single large tree inhabited by reptiles. Earlier inhabitants had worshipped a sea-god, Hu, but rituals had become more diverse since the Dahomean invasion; Ouidah contained various 'public fetish temples', including one to serpents such as boa constrictors.[22]

Nearby stood Ouidah's most prominent structure. Quite apart from its size, Francisco de Souza's residence was noted for its sumptuous contents, notably a dinner table set with china, cut glass, silver plate and, it was said, gold spoons and forks.[23] Nothing of De Souza would be seen during the day, while traders in their straw hats were left to themselves with tea, coffee, claret and beer. Early in the evening, a robed figure appeared, taking his seat without a word before motioning those assembled to follow suit at a table which was by now 'covered in luxurious confusion'. De Souza, 'a man of strange, sullen and solitary habits', ate in silence while 'sedulously attended by Africans', and retired as soon as he was done. This entire production served as a display of his paramountcy.

As one visiting naval officer reported:

> He holds a most absolute control over [the traders]; it would be impossible for them to take a slave on board without his permission. In short, they are as much under his command as is the ship of war under the admiral. No captain knows the moment he may be called upon to prepare for sea. De Souza will suddenly order one of them to be ready by a certain day ... De Souza again sinks into his apparent lethargy and the captains are left to feast, gamble and speculate upon the next of their number to be sent off.[24]

But for all De Souza's apparent supremacy, he was only the final link in a chain that, ultimately, lay in African hands. While eager traders were kept waiting at his table, De Souza himself was largely dependent upon the monarch who reigned inland at Abomey.

So, for the time being, the *Henriqueta*'s master joined those given lodgings beside De Souza's residence; in the time João dos Santos was here, weeks would turn into months.

Since seizing the throne six years earlier, King Gezo had extended his military hold over neighbouring states to the point that Dahomey exerted unrivalled regional power. Raiding forces ranged to the west, east and north, taking captive up to 15,000 men, women and children annually from the Mahi people to the north and from the Yoruba country to the north-east; even Hausa speakers in the more distant north were known to have been carried off. While the great majority – an estimated 12,000 – would be transported across the Atlantic from Ouidah, the remainder of these captives would be enslaved locally.[25]

British travellers had been reluctant to explore West Africa's interior. The doughty Mungo Park was the first to do so, in 1795, observing similar patterns of war being waged for human prisoners in the Mandinka country, more than 500 miles to the north-west. However, it was not until the post-abolition era that Britons ventured to Dahomey's hinterland. Among them was John Duncan.

Duncan was a rare species – like Park a Scot but with little education and of low rank when he left service in the Life Guards for African travel. As in the case of many seized by Britain's new-found abolitionist fervour, he arrived quick to inveigh against what he termed the barbarism and savagery of local customs – known to include human sacrifice, the display of decaying bodies after execution and the use of skulls for decorating buildings and as drinking vessels.

Duncan's path to the interior from Ouidah was smoothed by none other than Francisco de Souza, who, he noted, although 'a professed slave-dealer . . . a circumstance likely to produce an unfavourable opinion of him', appeared to have a healthy respect for the English, and who, having obtained permission for him to visit King Gezo at Abomey, provided him with supplies and bearers.[26]

The former Life Guard set out to impress. An exceptionally tall man – he stood well over 6 feet – Duncan wore his uniform jacket when brought before Gezo and was taken aback to find, instead of the ferocious despot he had anticipated, 'a tall athletic man . . . with pleasing expression, good features . . . and graceful manner'. Once their acquaintance had deepened, he went further. Gezo's 'noble mind seems to have been formed to govern', he wrote.[27]

As a military type, Duncan was also stirred by a parade by thousands of warriors shortly before they set off on a slave-raiding expedition. The men he thought not particularly disciplined and orderly. But the Mino, the king's elite troop of Amazons, made a deep impression: a regiment of 600 women, smothered in red dust, their heads shaved apart from a cockade-like tuft, presented arms with their muskets in a great hurrah before racing about the parade ground. Armed additionally with short swords and clubs, 'these women certainly make a very imposing appearance, and are very athletic', Duncan recalled.[28]

King Gezo of Dahomey.

In the course of his journey, which lasted more than a year and took him 400 miles into the interior, Duncan shed more prejudices and formed an abiding respect for Gezo's people. The Dahomeans, he declared, were 'a fine, intelligent race . . . much more industrious than the natives of [Ouidah] or other parts of the coast'.[29]

But perhaps the most challenging insight he offered to readers of the travel account published on his return to Britain concerned slavery within the kingdom.

> Domestic slavery to the native is, I have frequently observed, nothing more in the interior than easy servitude; the slave in the Mahi country is the same as one of the family. They eat together, work together, and are in every way associated together as one family. Their labour is easy and they are much better provided for than they could for themselves.[30]

Duncan remained nonetheless alive to the horrors of the Middle Passage, and on his return to Abomey had thoughtful conversations with the king about abolition. While drinking toasts from human skulls, Duncan explained that Englishmen had become 'disgusted with the conduct of their forefathers in making a property of the poor black man'. Gezo responded that this might be humane:

> . . . but that it would be difficult to abolish slave-holding in his country, as the children of all slaves were the property of the owner of the parent, and were treated as one of his own family; and that if a king were to interfere and abolish this law it would cause a revolution as it would affect all his head men and half heads, besides rendering these domestic slaves homeless and destitute.[31]

It was also the case, Duncan believed, that the contentment of Gezo's people was largely because 'slaves are only extorted from neighbouring kingdoms' and that when 'this source of revenue is exhausted, in all probability recourse will be had to contributions [from] his own subjects'.[32] These paradoxes, and memories of what appeared to him a relatively benign form of slavery, stayed with Duncan on his return to Ouidah – there to witness fellow humans of the kind among whom he had wandered for a year awaiting their embarkation into bondaged exile.

He was equally torn, not to say confused, in parting from De Souza, the slave-king who had provided the assistance essential to his journey and demonstrated all the 'undoubted and inflexible integrity' described by another bemused British visitor.[33] How could such a man, Duncan wondered, 'be coupled with traffic so abominable as that of buying and selling human beings; for he bears the character of the most generous and humane man on the coast of Africa'.[34]

The answer to such a conundrum of human nature is beyond reach now. It may be pertinent, however, to note the power of Catholicism in Bahia, where De Souza was born and, in his youth, worshipped at the altar of the Cathedral Basilica of All Saints. Portugal was unique in having decreed that all Africans taken into slavery be received into the Church: those traded in Angola were baptised before embarkation; at Ouidah there were no clergy to perform the sacraments, but captives bound for Bahia would be baptised on landing.[35] While De Souza, in the words of one guest, had become 'altogether African', a Catholic heritage could run deep. It is not impossible that faith had convinced him that transporting enslaved Africans to his native land was somehow delivering them into the arms of God.

After months waiting at De Souza's table, the traders received their bounty. How the barracoons had been filled is unclear, for while King Gezo's forces supplied the great majority of captives, profits were now also being pursued by freebooters – independent African merchants with their own methods of procurement.[36] On this occasion, however, it appears that more than a thousand prisoners had been marched down from Abomey in a multitude. Buyers were stirred from their drunken lassitude to frantic bartering.

João dos Santos had been under instruction throughout these past months. Having started his apprenticeship as a seafarer, he was introduced to negotiating for humans. It could have been no coincidence that two more of his mentor's vessels, the *Carlota* and *Conceição Estrela*, were anchored off Ouidah at the same time; Cerqueira Lima had a fortune riding on these transactions and an appointed broker may have overseen bartering with De Souza on behalf of the three masters.

In all, five Brazilian slave vessels were at anchor in the early days of 1825 as dealings wound towards a conclusion. From *Henriqueta*'s hold tobacco was unloaded along with textiles – possibly manufactured in Lancashire and shipped once before, from Liverpool to the British merchants of Bahia – and brought ashore in canoes. These small craft were an essential element of trade to and from Ouidah, as shipping had to remain well offshore in what were shallow waters; and, because folk here remained wary of the sea, the canoes were handled by men known as Accras, a seafaring tribe from the Gold Coast about 200 miles to the west.[37] Their next task would be to paddle hundreds of other Africans out to the anchored vessels.

Inside the barracoons the air was tolerable – temperatures being mild and humidity moderate at this time of year. But weather apart, they were filled with panic.

The mystery for Africans of why they should be so wanted by pale-skinned people that they should be captured and taken down to the sea, there to disappear forever, had by now endured for centuries. Thirty years earlier, Mungo Park was repeatedly asked on his travels if his people were cannibals. He noted: 'A deeply-rooted idea that the whites purchase Negroes for the purpose of devouring them . . . naturally makes the slaves contemplate a journey towards the Coast with great terror.'[38] From the moment of their capture, it would seem, the chained men and women, with their children, had realised they were not to remain among those destined for local servitude. For days they had been marched in columns from Abomey, and once the sea itself came into sight, a dazzling blue space beyond the sands of the lagoon, they knew it was to consume them. The final unknown was just what suffering it would inflict.

The form in which it next came, once negotiations between vendor and buyer had been resolved, was branding.[39] First the captive was made to kneel. Then, as a mark of his or her buyer, a burning iron was applied to a part of the body – usually the shoulder or breast 'anointed with a little palm oil' – inflicting a distinctive pattern that left a scar.[40] Lists kept at Sierra Leone of men and women removed from captured Brazilian vessels cite specific marks, such as 'cuts on the forehead' and 'cuts on the cheek'. In the case of women, these include 'cut under the right breast', 'large cut on the right breast' and 'cuts all over the body'.[41]

The only captive to leave an account of being embarked at Ouidah passed lightly over the excruciating pain inflicted by red-hot metal: 'A man went round with a hot iron and branded us, the same as they would [a] barrel.'[42] Mahommah Baquaqua, a Muslim from the interior, went on to wolf down a meal of 'rice and other good things', unaware that 'it was to be my last feast in Africa'. Next, he was chained to others – 'tied with ropes round about our necks, and drawn down to the sea shore'.[43] Only then did he feel the dread that had gripped so many before.

> I had never seen a ship before, and my idea was that it was some object of worship of the white man. I imagined we were all to be slaughtered and were being led there for that purpose.[44]

Baquaqua was aged about 20 at the time and, like the great majority of captives, had been picked for his youth; Portuguese and Brazilian traders like Cerqueira Lima were known to favour adolescent males in particular.[45] They, however, were in short supply: a register of those found on *Henriqueta* three years later listed 85 boys up to the age of 16, compared with 261 men in their mid- to late twenties, along with a poignantly high number of women and girls.[46]

The difficulties of embarkation further prolonged their terror. All vessels at Ouidah had to anchor a mile offshore, so prisoners came down to the lagoon, the sand soft under their naked feet, to canoes drawn up on a sun-drenched beach that in different circumstances might have appeared an arcadia. Here the Accras, or canoemen, loaded up to thirty bodies at a time for a passage out through surf that surged under and over, from bow to stern, and carried its own perils.

Vessels at anchor attracted sharks. A sailor recalled the sight of one of these predators circling, 'with his black fin two feet above the water, his broad snout and small eyes, and the altogether villainous look of the fellow'.[47] Sharks swarmed the entire Gulf of Guinea but were especially visible off Ouidah, where captives had to be paddled out through the surf and a body overboard could trigger a feeding frenzy. During Baquaqua's embarkation, a canoe with thirty occupants capsized with the loss of all but one of them.[48]

The presence on board *Henriqueta* of other Africans, former tribesmen of similar tongue and heritage, may have brought some initial reassurance. Such, indeed, was a practical reason for Cerqueira Lima to take on slaves and freed blacks as crew. Vessels bound for Brazil had until quite recently borne a reputation for less inhumane treatment than those of other slaving nations. A Danish abolitionist, Hans Monrad, who lived on the Guinea Coast for six years until 1809, wrote that captives on Portuguese vessels were 'most mildly' treated compared with those in Dutch and French hands. Each seaman was allocated fifteen people to his personal care.[49] They were allowed on deck, 'and to a degree, mingle with the crew'. Monrad went on:

I often saw the sailors make as much of the small Negro children as if they had been their own.[50]

Such intimacy had ceased since the Navy's surveillance of West Africa began. The priority now was to maximise loading, to confine the human cargo below, where they would be out of sight, and to hasten back to Bahia with all speed.

The conditions that awaited those coming aboard *Henriqueta* in the first week of 1825 can be partly defined in terms of space. Her quarters – if those of a floating dungeon can be so termed – ran a length of 90 feet (yet narrowing fore and aft) and a breadth of 26 feet. While she was at anchor the carpenter had installed platforms on either side of the lower deck, adding what amounted to another layer in the space for confinement. A passage down the centre made movement just about possible but headroom between the levels was limited to about 3 feet.[51] Women and children tended to be contained separately. Wherever they were, all captive bodies reclined hard up against one another so movement by one was felt along the rest. Facilities for bodily functions were limited, so piss, shit and vomit either gathered or passed into the hold, where others might also be confined. A clergyman who came aboard a captured Brazilian slaver noted:

> [What] struck us most forcibly was how it was possible for such a number of human beings to exist, packed up and wedged as tight as they could cram in low cells three feet high ... The heat of these horrid places was so great, and the odour so offensive, that it was quite impossible to enter them, even had there been room.[52]

The *Henriqueta* was fully loaded, along with Cerqueira Lima's two other slavers, the *Carlota* and *Conceição Estrela*, when the terrible fate of their captives took an even more harrowing turn.

It could not have escaped the attention of João Cardozo dos Santos and his aides that for some time several Spanish vessels had also been at anchor off Ouidah. As all of them were there for the same purpose, their masters may even have joined the Brazilians at De Souza's table. So Dos Santos could have recognised danger: it was well known that pirates sailing under Spanish colours were active along the Bights and as far south as Angola – plundering captives from vessels already loaded. Heavily armed with between fourteen and twenty guns, and crews of up to eighty men, the marauders posed an intimidating threat to slavers far better equipped to resist than the *Henriqueta*.

They may have sensed menace. Her master and crew could still only watch when the pirates came surging up *Henriqueta*'s side.

CHAPTER 3

'THE MOANS, THE WEEPING, THE CRIES'
January–July 1825

The attackers were Spanish pirates notorious for their violence in extracting plunder of any sort. They evidently encountered little resistance boarding *Henriqueta* as there were no casualties. João dos Santos and his crew were reduced to observers as hatchways were opened and the men, women and children recently embarked and now cringing below were summoned out. Slowly, and as mystified as they were terror-struck, they emerged into the light again.

This much is known of the attack at Ouidah that day in January.[1] In every other respect the records are silent. As to the fate of *Henriqueta*'s first human cargo, all that can be added is that the 572 captives were directly re-embarked on pirate vessels to sail for Cuba in the hands of predators even more callous than those from whom they had been seized.

An explanation of sorts was offered by a naval officer, Hugh Clapperton, who arrived at Ouidah a few months later at the start of an expedition into the interior. Like other visiting Britons, Clapperton was taken aback to find Francisco Félix de Souza 'not all evil', and paid tribute to his trustworthiness as well as his vigour, 'having upwards of fifty wives and nearly as many children'.[2] But he concluded that the slaver baron had offended Spanish traders by 'not fulfilling his contracts with them' and that they had consequently 'plundered his vessels of upward of twelve hundred slaves'.[3] It is just as likely, however, that the raiders were simply one of the bands of voracious marauders active along the African coast: it was not only De Souza's vessels that had been attacked; four Brazilians were stripped of their captives that day, two of them owned by Cerqueira Lima – the *Henriqueta* and *Carlota*.

Dos Santos, having submitted to the marauders, would have been apprehensive. Youth and family connections had secured him sponsorship, but his future with an irascible patron may now have hung in the balance. With the *Carlota*'s master, he had gone back to De Souza and another consignment of human beings was obtained with relative speed. An element of trust was also necessary as their trading goods had already been exchanged. De Souza was left banking on the fidelity of a fellow Bahian.

So it was that when land came in sight again on 13 March, *Henriqueta* contained hundreds more men, women and children in the darkness below, festering survivors of a passage from Africa that had taken twenty-eight days.[4] For the crew who had set sail with her 134 days previously, some features along the coast may have appeared familiar as they ran south-west, but it was only when the grand structures of Bahia came up on the headland, and the Cabo de Santo Antônio opened into the Bay of All Saints, that they could say they had safely returned. João dos Santos – still only 20 – concluded his turbulent initiation with no illusions as to the ruthlessness required for commanding a slaveship.

Anxious to account for himself, Dos Santos would have been relieved on coming ashore to find that Cerqueira Lima had already received tidings of the pirates' raid from another returning vessel.[5] Bahia's slaving tycoon, never a man of easy temper, had gone straight to the provincial president, Francisco Vianna, demanding action. It is a measure of Cerqueira Lima's influence that Vianna addressed his appeal to Emperor Pedro in Rio, while still basing it on a deceit: *Henriqueta* and the other Brazilians, he stated, had been 'violently attacked' by Spanish pirates in Ouidah, resulting in 'grave financial losses to their owners'. Of captives there was no mention, merely that one vessel had been plundered of 572 'ounces'. This apparent reference to gold was, as one study has pointed out, a coded euphemism for the *Henriqueta*'s first human cargo.[6] Vianna went on to declare the raid 'offensive to human rights' and to advise the emperor: 'Free and independent nations do not tolerate injuries which insult them . . . leaving such proceedings unpunished.'[7] There, however, matters rested.

After more than four months away, the number of captives finally landed by the *Henriqueta* on her maiden voyage was 504.[8] The *Carlota* followed in her wake some weeks later with 352 more men, women and children.[9]

There to note these events was a watchful William Pennell. Of the details he knew nothing, but the consul was certain of what amounted to flagrant treaty violations: while official papers showed that both vessels had embarked captives at the Angolan port of Malembo, it was common knowledge that they had come from Ouidah. Pennell could prove nothing, and there was no possibility of relieving these 856 enslaved souls from their fate. But in this campaign against Cerqueira Lima, he had another strategy in mind.

What had passed on *Henriqueta*'s homeward voyage is a matter of speculation.[10] In the view of contemporary observers, however, this was the point when captives' trauma reached its peak. An account by two German travellers expressed a belief that it was the passage, rather than their subsequent enslavement, 'that tortures their souls, the separation from family and inhuman treatment during the crossing – horrors from which large numbers of these unfortunate victims die'.[11]

With her captives secured, *Henriqueta* had sailed from Ouidah in the first week of February, a timely point to escape the monsoon squalls about to descend.[12] Then, with a priority to avoid the British ships prowling the Gulf of Guinea, Dos Santos set a southerly course to carry her south of 0° latitude. At this point – where he could inform any interfering navy captain that his cargo had been legally boarded south of the Equator – the *Henriqueta*'s master was able to breathe more easily.

For the captives below, the ordeal was just beginning. There is no way of knowing their number at the time of sailing, but it probably exceeded the 504 who were landed. No fewer than 572 had, after all, been loaded in the first instance. Gambling with how many could be stowed below and endure such a passage was standard practice among slaver masters.

The *Henriqueta*'s owner had staked everything on her speed. While voyages to Bahia from Angola had in recent years averaged twenty-eight days, from the Bights they could take forty days, and any added time at sea extracted a human toll.[13] Cerqueira Lima had been assured by her Baltimore suppliers that his new brig would significantly cut voyage times. So she did. But attempting to maximise profits also led to atrocious and deadly overloading.

Having been stacked in rows across two levels with about 3 feet of headroom and left in the dark to purge fluid through sweat and urine, their next sensation was the bewildering nausea of seasickness. Vomit mingled with those other excretions, to which were soon added faeces as, although large buckets were placed in each section, access was limited. A doctor familiar with the lower deck of a slaver wrote:

> It often happens that those who are placed at a distance from the buckets, in endeavouring to get to them, tumble over their companions, in consequence of their being shackled . . . In this distressed situation, unable to proceed, and prevented from getting to the tubs, they desist from the attempt; and, as the necessities of nature are not to be repelled, ease themselves as they lie.[14]

The shackling of male captives, already stripped naked, was standard practice. Women were not chained and might be given the modesty of a light covering.[15] Once a vessel was well under way, and the danger of interception by British ships had passed, a sensible master allowed them out on the upper deck in groups to take in fresh air and follow the sailors' example in defecating over the side. Whether Dos Santos felt sufficiently confident to permit this on his first voyage must be left an open question, as such brief sensations of liberty could trigger resistance by captives.

Catholic ritual had a place in Brazilian slaving at sea as well as ashore. Time was when most vessels carried a priest, who would minister to captives as well as crew. Hans Monrad, the abolitionist who thought the Portuguese the least brutal of slaver nations, ascribed this in part to their faith. 'These padres,' he wrote, 'keep a sharp lookout on the captains and when they have returned home can report them and have them punished if they have treated the slaves inhumanely.'[16]

Cerqueira Lima did not keep a priest on the *Henriqueta*, trusting rather to the care provided by his African seamen, themselves former slaves, who, Monrad believed, were the most valuable resource when it came to reassuring captives at moments of panic and, therefore, to the preservation of order on board.[17]

Within days of crossing the Equator, the *Henriqueta* picked up the South Equatorial Current. Running south-west, she was on course for Bahia; but at some stage in an Atlantic voyage, turbulence was likely to arise and renew terror in the darkness of the lower deck; and low-slung brigs of her kind shipped seawater in large volumes that swept below, drenching stacked bodies. A Portuguese master recorded the reaction to a storm: 'The din from the slaves, chained to one another, becomes horrible . . . the moans, the weeping, the cries . . . Many slaves break their legs and arms, others die of suffocation.'[18] In addition to fractures, the shackles inflicted wounds on men jolted by movement, which, combined with high temperatures and humidity, led to infections that could prove fatal. As often at sea, however, the main causes of death were dysentery, or the 'bloody flux', and scurvy. With food as meagre as it was basic coming from *Henriqueta*'s steaming cauldrons – yams or beans – it became a race to reach home waters before the symptoms often observed on a lower deck became manifest:

[It] was so covered with the blood and mucus which had proceeded from [the slaves] in consequence of the flux that it resembled a slaughterhouse. It is not in the power of the human imagination to picture a situation more dreadful or disgusting.[19]

Shortage of fresh water was another hazard, leading to death by dehydration. As some West African societies believed sickness was caused by malevolent spirits, the spread of disease confirmed to captives that they were in the hands of white devils and wizards. That belief could only have deepened when the bodies of the dead were cast into the sea where sharks followed in the vessel's wake. As suffering accumulated, so did another cause of death: despair led to men and women jumping overboard.[20]

A paradoxical reaction was often noted among the survivors of a passage: having been stripped of their identities and shared cultures, they developed new kinship groups based on shared pain, experience and understanding; different language groups found means of communicating. The common bond formed among seafarers was, it seems, replicated among these captives. In Brazil, they adopted the term used for shipmates. They were *malungo*.[21]

No deaths at sea were reported on *Henriqueta*'s first voyage. That was probably no more true a picture than that she had returned from Malembo, though her speed did produce fewer losses than the average 7 per cent death rate recorded on Bahia slavers.[22] What could not be concealed were deaths on arrival. The city's Santa Casa da Misericórdia hospital noted that *Henriqueta* came in with two dead on board and that three more captives died soon after being landed.[23]

Survivors often came ashore singing. Music as an expression of hope as well as pain was one of the recurrent sounds from slaving vessels and was noted by, among others, Maria Graham on her visit to Bahia. 'This very moment,' she wrote, gazing from her cabin window, 'there is a slave ship discharging her cargo, and the slaves are singing. They have left the ship and they see they will be on the dry land.' And quoting from Alexander Pope's *Essay on Man*, citing lambs skipping on the way to slaughter, she went on: 'That "blindness to the future kindly given," allows them a few hours of sad enjoyment.'[24] Mrs Graham had some knowledge of what awaited: 'the labour of the mines, and the sugar-works'. She could, though, barely have comprehended the full reality.

Enslaved Africans made up the great majority of the state of Bahia's population. But without constant renewals, their number would have steadily diminished: the birth rate was low, with roughly eight men to every two women, and infant mortality high.[25] The same was to be said of the death rate in the *senzalas*, the quarters of plantations and mines inland where epidemics of cholera and smallpox added to the toll of intensive labour – all at a time when Bahia's economy was sustained by Europe's insatiable appetite for sugar and Africa's discovery of tobacco. The interior's vast space of fertile, virgin land only awaited cultivation.

Cerqueira Lima had been keenly anticipating the *Henriqueta's* return. The balcony of his whitewashed mansion overlooked the Bay of All Saints, so it is possible that he saw her sail into view on 13 March, followed a few weeks later by the *Carlota*, the schooner named after his wife. Despite recent setbacks, he was set to recover and prosper anew: of the 1,571 captives landed at Bahia in the first six months of 1825, 1,035 were recorded as the property of Cerqueira Lima.[26]

Of Senhora Cerqueira Lima there is no account, apart from her reputed beauty as a young woman. She had borne her husband six children, however, and Bahia's ladies did not age well if Mrs Graham is to be believed. 'They marry very early and soon lose their bloom,' she observed in her diary. 'The figure becomes almost indecently slovenly . . . and this is the more disgusting as they are very thinly clad.' Moreover, although women dressed fashionably to display their wealth at dinners and balls, when visited at home:

> . . . they wear neither stays nor bodice. Hair black, ill combed, and dishevelled, or knotted unbecomingly, and the whole person having an unwashed appearance.[27]

Cerqueira Lima and his family inhabited their grand palace on the Corredor da Vitória, but Mrs Graham was not impressed by the households of the wealthy either, finding them 'for the most part disgustingly dirty'. The lower level was occupied by slaves and horses; located on the floor above were dusty, cobwebbed sitting rooms with 'a sofa at each end, and to the right and left a long file of chairs which look as if they never could be moved out of place'.[28]

Cultural differences were more thoughtfully described by Robert Walsh, a chaplain at Rio who travelled widely in the interior. Walsh's searing descriptions of the brutality to which he was a witness, on the one hand, did not blind him to a common decency he perceived on the other. Of white Brazilians he wrote:

> They are naturally a people of a humane and good-natured disposition, and much indisposed to cruelty or severity of any kind. Indeed, the manner in which many of them treat their slaves is a proof of this, as it is really gentle and considerate.[29]

Walsh did not shy either from making uncomfortable comparisons with Britain's slaving colonies. In Brazil, he pointed out, former slaves could be admitted to holy orders and 'officiate in churches indiscriminately with whites'. In Barbados, such status was unthinkable, and one minister, a Reverend Hoste, who had the temerity to administer sacraments to black worshippers, caused outrage among his white flock.[30] In Demerara-Essequibo, scene of the recent uprising, plantation owners had long prevented their workers attending Sunday worship or having a rest day at all.

Another British traveller drew similarly unfavourable parallels. Henry Koster wrote that slaves in Brazil had 'many advantages over their brethren in British Colonies', including the festivities of the Catholic calendar, which gave a male slave 'days of rest or time to work for his own profit. Thirty-five of these and Sundays besides allow him employment as he pleases.'[31] Bahia, moreover, had a significant population of *libertos*, former slaves who had been able to buy their freedom.

The fate of the *Henriqueta*'s 504 surviving men, women and children was as random as the events that had brought them to the lower town of Bahia. Among the street stalls and arcades, goldsmiths and haberdashers, stood the slave market where the new arrivals were paraded, examined, prodded and purchased. Walsh observed among the men a defiant spirit, 'a certain ferocity of aspect that indicated strong and fierce passions, like men who were darkly brooding over some deep-felt wrongs and meditating revenge':

When one was ordered, he came forward with a sullen indifference, threw his arms over his head, stamped with his feet, shouted to show the soundness of his lungs, ran up and down the room and was treated like a horse; when done, he was whipped to his stall.[32]

Most distressing of all, Walsh found, was seeing a group of children – girls of 'sweet and engaging countenances' – being brought forward for display. In what came close to challenging contemporary prejudices, he went on: 'You could not for a moment hesitate to acknowledge that they are endued with a like feeling and a common nature with your own daughters.'[33]

For these children, as with the men and women, everything was dependent on who would claim them as possessions.

The slaves of Bahia's city residents were seen as relatively fortunate. While their earnings as hawkers, porters, craftsmen and boatmen went to the owner, many of them were allowed to retain a portion and through years of profitable service were potentially able to earn their freedom. The *libertos* represented the mobility of Bahia society, an easy mingling of whites, blacks and mulattos on streets and in markets. Among them were Ana Josefa de Rego and her husband Rafael Cordeiro, born into separate ethnic groups in Africa, captured and transported from the Bight of Benin into slavery of an unstated form, but who had – as her will testified – earned enough to buy their freedom and marry. Ana's legacy, while deemed insignificant in terms of property and possessions, included four slaves, António, Rita, Angélica and Esperança.[34] Hers is not a rare story. Statistics for the period are unverified but, according to one study, in 1835 the city's black population (whether of African or Brazilian birth) numbered some 47,000, of whom 19,500 were *libertos*.[35]

The enslaved majority of about 27,500 included at this point domestics in the Cerqueira Lima household. His wife, Carlota, had a headman, a cook, a chambermaid, a laundress, a seamstress and sedan-chair carriers.[36]

Common sense, if not decency, indicated that treatment should not be overtly inhumane. Yet monsters lurked as well. Having noted the 'gentle and considerate' treatment of slaves by many Brazilians, Robert Walsh went on to cite cruelty as causing 'the daily practice' of suicide in Rio. On one occasion, after hearing constant 'dismal cries and moans' from the house of a saddler who had two enslaved boys, he entered to find 'a tawny, cadaverous-looking man' with a leather knout 'in the act of exercising on one of the naked children'.[37]

Conditions on the plantations where the great majority of slaves ended up were generally far worse than those in the city. Most of Bahia's cultivation took place on the Recôncavo, the fertile belt that ran almost 200 miles around the Bay of All Saints and into the interior. Between 1790 and 1820, the state of Bahia doubled its number of sugar mills while the enslaved population rose to almost 150,000.[38] Larger plantations were worked by about 200 men.[39] Tobacco was cultivated on smaller plots by groups of between ten and twenty. Owners were advised in a manual of the day that the way to force slaves to work was to instil 'fear, and only fear, but employed with system and art, because excessive fear will be counterproductive'.[40]

On top of disease, men died of exhaustion. One study has noted that 'the annual importation of considerable numbers of slaves was necessary simply in order to maintain the *existing* population'.[41] Among the earliest observers to make that very point was William Pennell. In a despatch to George Canning, the foreign secretary, he noted that few children were being born in the *senzalas* of plantations or mines, due to the imbalance of males to females.

> The annual mortality on many sugar plantations is so great that unless their numbers were [renewed] from abroad the whole slave population would become extinct in about 20 years. The proprietors act on the calculation that it is cheaper to buy grown male negros than to rear negro children.[42]

What those prices amounted to in Brazil's wildly fluctuating currency at the time tells us little in terms of modern values. By Pennell's estimate, however, a voyage was earning Cerqueira Lima 'upwards of £30 a head' for each captive brought ashore (equivalent to about £1,700 in purchasing power today).[43] Quite simply, the transport and auctioning of humans was turning him into the wealthiest tycoon in Bahia.

What men like Robert Walsh saw as the paradoxes all around, between acts of kindness and brutality, go to the heart of oppression from time immemorial – a tendency to cruelty among humans of all kinds when constraints are lacking.[44] That – and what he believed to be 'the baneful and enervating effects of having all labour performed, and wants supplied, by slaves' – may offer insights into the likes of Cerqueira Lima.[45]

As a sociable being, William Pennell was an envoy more naturally suited to affable circulating than campaigning. In his early years as consul he had ministered to various needs of the British community, hosting regular garden parties and conducting weddings in the absence of an Anglican clergyman until he was ordered by Canning to desist. Even now it would have been easy enough to retire to the splendour of his mansion on the Corredor, shrugging off his helplessness while continuing to act as Whitehall's informant on the spot. But the abuses to which he was a witness, and the complicity of British merchants, were increasingly discomfiting. Pennell could not prove that the

Africans brought to Bahia were being loaded illegally, but he could show they were being loaded excessively.

The *Henriqueta* had landed 504 African survivors. Pennell was convinced she had taken on a significantly higher number, yet even so she was overladen. In an attempt at reform initiated from Rio, a *portaria*, or imperial decree, issued in the emperor's name on 12 August 1824, had specified that the number carried on a 256-ton brig such as the *Henriqueta* should be no more than 490. Pennell had, moreover, obtained from the official in charge of loading – the *intendente da marinha*, or marine steward – a statement that even 490 humans 'appears to me excessive for so small a vessel'.[46] For a solitary official to have taken a stand against Bahia's most powerful plutocrat required courage.

Citing these authorities, Pennell wrote on 16 September to the new provincial president, the Marquês de Queluz, pointing out – in diplomatic terms – this and other recent violations of the *portaria*.

Cerqueira Lima had meanwhile demonstrated he would have nothing to do with a regulation that reduced to 490 a cargo of 600 *escravos* permitted under the old system of admeasurement. He started with an appeal to Rio lamenting 'the very considerable damages [he] has to suffer' from the *portaria*. It could not be observed, he went on, 'as it is contrary to both law and treaty'.[47] In lobbying behind the scenes in Bahia, he was more direct: whatever the views of Rio (and therefore the emperor) he would continue to load *escravos* in the same numbers per ton as set down by a Portuguese charter dating from 24 November 1813.

This dispute, over degrees of inhumanity, would grind on. The *intendente* retreated, Pennell noted, 'apprehensive of the enmities which [his] disclosures excite in this city'.[48] Gross overloading continued. In essence, an order from Bahia's president had prevailed over the emperor's decree. Years later, Pennell reflected: 'The Intendente ... made a bona fide attempt at Reform in the case of the brig Henriqueta and was overruled by superior authority.'[49] It was not only the official who had made enemies. Pennell was careful to eschew naming Cerqueira Lima in his despatches. There can be little doubt, however, who he had in mind writing to the president about 'the odium . . . my conduct may excite'.[50]

His foe and neighbour had the wind in his sails. Cerqueira Lima was always quick to point out how the self-righteous British continued to reap the rewards from centuries of slaving by their own nation. That year furnished him with opportunity to mock them too.

In January of 1824, an English merchant brig, the *Accession* of Whitby, had come in at Bahia with thirty-nine Africans rescued at sea. As the master Robert Roddam explained, he had been bound from Rio to Hamburg when a wreck was sighted some 540 miles east of the Brazilian coast – a brig, her masts toppled, abandoned by the crew and with black bodies floating nearby.[51] Coming on the ruined vessel, however, Roddam 'found there were living creatures inside'. He took thirty-nine survivors on the *Accession* and, breaking off from his voyage, brought them to the nearest port. Despite their desperate state, all but two survived to be landed at Bahia.

What followed amounted to a bleak charade. At first the Bahia authorities wanted the castaways sold into slavery. With Pennell briefly absent on leave, his deputy objected and it was accepted that they should be shipped to Rio, on the understanding that they would be treated as emancipated men – provided all costs were borne by the British exchequer. The contract for transporting them went to Cerqueira Lima. The vessel he assigned was the *Cerqueira*, recently returned by the Navy and the subject of his ongoing claim for £60,000 in damages. Papers signed by her master, Manoel dos Santos, declared: 'I shall receive 8 mil-reis for the passage of each Black.'[52] The money was less significant than the satisfaction of extracting it from the enemy.

The castaways had barely been landed at Rio before two local traders came forward to claim them as property. José Silva and José Brandão stated that their brig, the *Lisboa*, had been lost at sea and these Africans must have been among those on board. Henry Chamberlain, the consul general, protested: they had been 'found in a state of freedom by a

British ship' and must be considered free men. The emperor himself, it appeared, was 'inclined towards justice and humanity'. As ever in such matters, however, it was the traders' interests that prevailed.

Under what was termed a compromise, the thirty-nine Africans were sold at auction to buyers who undertook that those termed their 'apprentices' would be 'instructed in religion' and in 'some trade or work' before being hired out to labour. After fourteen years, during which all their earnings would be paid to the owners, they would be freed to pursue their own trades. Provided, of course, they survived that long.

In casting a positive light on this outcome in his report to Foreign Secretary Canning, Chamberlain might be thought to have been unduly blithe:

> The Negroes have been rescued from Death and from Slavery. They are fitting for a state of freedom; and when the term of their servitude arrives, they will receive a small sum to enable them to begin the world on their own account.[53]

Whatever the opinions of British envoys, there was no ignoring the continuing and extensive engagement of their own countrymen in enslavement.

When the Act for the Abolition of the Slave Trade was passed by Parliament in 1807, some 700,000 men, women and children were in bondage in Britain's West Indies colonies. Almost twenty years on, their emancipation remained a distant goal. The primary campaigning body, the Anti-Slavery Society, had only been founded in 1823 and its champion, Thomas Fowell Buxton, was constantly being shouted down. That the most powerful men in the land remained loyal to 'the West India Interest' is well attested.[54] Taking the case further, it has been argued that Canning himself came under their influence, and that 'his opposition to emancipation was deep-seated'.[55] Certainly, in diverting early steps to 'ameliorate and then free' the enslaved through a parliamentary vote, the foreign secretary showed his position to be ambiguous.

A transition from outlawing the purchase of African captives to liberating those already trafficked was bound to be complex. In the meantime, those with investments in the West Indies were naturally enthusiastic to see sugar production by competitors constrained – especially those in Brazil: cut the supply of labour and crops would decline. In that respect, it might be claimed that agents such as Pennell (and, moreover, the Royal Navy's Preventative Squadron) were serving the national interest rather than a righteous cause.

Pennell would have seen no paradox. He had come to Bahia, in effect, as a volunteer and – like the vast majority of his countrymen – without ever witnessing slavery at first hand. As ever in the human story, distance from suffering and death helped to account for the apathy of most Britons, including the men in power. Those confronted with such visions either became desensitised or were roused to activity. Pennell had been taken on the latter course.

Earlier in 1825 he had reported to Canning his concern about British vessels sailing from Bahia for Africa, 'laden with articles usually shipped for the purpose of purchasing slaves'.[56] Asked to name specific vessels, he cited a brig, the *George & James* of London, owned by one Mathew Forster.* In another instance, Pennell wrote, a Captain Smith of the brig *Lupa* had been offered a charter for a port in Africa north of the Equator, 'to transport from one place to another a number of free Blacks'. On being questioned, he went on, Smith had 'admitted his belief that the ultimate object of the charterer was an illegal traffic in slaves'.[57]

---

* FO 84/42/280, Pennell to Canning, 5 Nov. 1825. The *George & James* was intercepted off Ouidah on 17 October by the frigate *Atholl*, taken to Sierra Leone and condemned. That same year an Act came into force declaring that British subjects convicted of slaving would be deemed guilty of piracy and be subject to the death penalty. The *George & James*'s master, William Ramsay, died before he could be brought to trial. It was stated that her real owner was 'Chacha' de Souza.

An additional source of concern was the number of British seamen being recruited here for service on slavers.

Britain's maritime power was supreme. Her Navy went unchallenged across the oceans, her merchant ships roamed the world in pursuit of trade, and her quest for knowledge – from mapping remote corners of the globe to seeking out further opportunities for imperial expansion – had opened new forms of voyaging. Her ships, bound for the Pacific or Indian oceans, often had cause to anchor at Brazilian ports where skilled sailors were in high demand and might be seduced by offers of bounty.

Mrs Graham had observed the system at work on the *Doris*, the 36-gun frigate which had brought her to Bahia. 'Several of our people have yielded to the temptations of some worthless persons in the town who induce sailors to desert', she noted in her diary.[58]

Among such 'worthless persons' was Cerqueira Lima. British ships might be found in every port, but their crews were often poorly rewarded; the Navy had paid off more than 120,000 seamen after the peace with France in 1815 and shipowners were quick to exploit impoverished hands in desperate need of a berth. Even on navy vessels pay rates remained low.[59] All of which may explain the success of Brazilian slavers in luring British seamen from their ships.

The *Carlota* was being prepared for her next voyage when William Pennell learned that she had taken on seven English hands. Their identities and how they came to be in Bahia at the time were left unstated in his report. But having confronted the men, and warned them not to proceed, he wrote to Bahia's president, the Marquês de Queluz, asking him to consider intervention. This was pushing the boundaries of diplomacy, as Pennell himself had to admit: *Carlota* was to sail under Spanish colours, and he had no proof in asserting that she was 'bound for the Coast of Africa for illegal objects'. He could only conclude by expressing 'an anxiety that the humane objectives contemplated by our respective governments should not be contravened'.[60]

Pennell received praise from the consul general in Rio for his 'exceedingly meritorious watchfulness', but there was no official response and the British hands continued to serve in Brazilian vessels. For many Jack Tars, the prescribed punishment of up to two years in gaol was a risk worth the rewards on offer.[61] Others would follow in their wake – notably, as will be seen, from one of the most famous vessels in maritime history.

Another of Cerqueira Lima's vessels may also have taken on British seamen that year. On 15 July, just four months after returning from Ouidah, the *Henriqueta* sailed for Africa again.

CHAPTER 4

GIFTS FOR THE KING
August–October 1825

The *Henriqueta* passed down the Bight of Benin once again in August, carefully but with more assurance. Their second crossing to Africa had given João dos Santos a clear sense of the brig and her ways. She was now his. He knew her responsiveness to a shift in the breeze, to another layer of canvas, and especially – as they ran down the coast – her deftness of manoeuvre. This was not a shore suited to any form of trade: long stretches of sandy beaches were broken by numerous rivers, but none opened into a natural harbour, so *Henriqueta*'s flexibility working close in was a gift.

She did not anchor at Ouidah this time, instead running another 100 miles down the Bight, past two other slaving stations, Porto Novo and Badagry. The pirate raid at Ouidah had decided Cerqueira Lima to take his trade to another port: Lagos – or Onim as it was also known – lay on a small island at the mouth of a vast lagoon running more than 30 miles along the coast. Yet as it came in sight, Dos Santos knew that here, too, he must be on high alert.

Spanish pirates posed a threat to Bahia's slavers, but it was of an occasional, transient kind. The same could not be said of British ships and since Lagos's emergence as a new hub of the trade, the Navy had directed its campaign here, to Cerqueira Lima's cost. It is feasible that the *Henriqueta* had first been sent to Ouidah rather than Lagos for that reason. This was where his battle with Britain, his ongoing claim against the government for damages, had begun.

The saga of the brigantine *Cerqueira* started, as has been seen, when Dos Santos's brother Manoel claimed that while on a 'legitimate voyage to buy slaves at Malembo', bad weather had forced him to put in at Lagos for provisions – only to be subjected to persecution.[1] Initially, according to his testimony, the British tactics had been harassment rather than violence: three times, while the *Cerqueira* was at anchor, officers of two navy vessels had come aboard and, on finding no captives, departed. But one, commander of the sloop *Bann*, would not let matters rest.

Versions of what followed are starkly different. On a few facts, however, there is agreement: on 30 January 1824, men from the *Bann* came up in boats, boarded *Cerqueira*, overwhelmed her crew and seized control; although she and two other Brazilian vessels still had no Africans held below, they were taken down the coast to Sierra Leone. There the British authorities, acknowledging that the Navy had exceeded its authority, agreed their release and return to Bahia.

Cerqueira Lima did not let matters rest there. Manoel dos Santos, acting on his proprietor's instructions, set down a righteous 'Protest against the British Nation' in which, swearing to his honesty 'on the Holy Bible', he declared the *Cerqueira* had only called at Lagos 'on account of the inconstancy of the wind' (a standard alibi of Brazilian masters detained in the Bights). The reason for her prolonged stay – she had remained at anchor for more than six weeks – was the difficulty of obtaining provisions and the Navy's harassment.

Warming to his theme, Dos Santos described how he had been ashore, still seeking supplies, when the British attacked his vessel. They then came into Lagos, confronting King Osinlokun and demanding that he 'deliver up the slaves' they alleged Dos Santos and other masters had bought. On being told by the king 'there were no slaves' and that his visitors 'were not there to buy slaves', the British turned violent and spiked the guns kept by Osinlokun to defend his port. At this point, Dos Santos went on, 'the blacks rose . . . [to defend] their guns'.

> In this disturbance . . . the Englishmen embarked upon their launch
> and opened a fire of artillery and musquetry, killing and wounding
> a great many blacks, and retreated.[2]

Manoel dos Santos rounded off his denunciation of British tyranny by stating that 'the cost of all and every prejudice caused in the course of my voyage' was £60,000. This was the amount, equivalent to £3.4 million, claimed in damages by Cerqueira Lima.

The report by *Bann*'s commander, Lieutenant George Courtenay, posted – as may be expected – a rather different version of events. He had indeed, he wrote, boarded the *Cerqueira* and two other Brazilians, while they were preparing to embark 700 captives. Two of his officers had then landed a party ashore to seize the vessels' masters and load the Africans – to take them to Sierra Leone and freedom. The violence, he went on, began when the king ordered the British to be detained and they retreated – pursued by the Brazilians at the head of hundreds of Africans firing muskets and arrows. Courtenay gave no estimate of their antagonists' casualties as fire was returned from the *Bann*'s pinnace and yawl. The naval party, he reported, had two men killed and six wounded.[3]

Whatever the truth of the matter, Courtenay had admitted capturing three vessels before any Africans had been embarked, for which there was no defence.

These events were still fresh in mind when *Henriqueta* came in sight of Lagos. And João dos Santos had a description from his brother of the vessel that posed their most serious threat.

Dos Santos was following in his brother's wake in other respects. Despite the efforts of the Royal Navy, it appeared that the future of the trade lay here, as Lagos was now able to offer captives in greater numbers than any other port in West Africa. On his first venture, Dos Santos needed to set his dealings with the king on a harmonious course. He came laden with gifts for the king, or *oba*, Osinlokun.

Forms of domestic slavery were rooted in West African societies.[4] Millions of Africans were forced into servitude as, for centuries, powerful men incorporated the vulnerable into their communities – wards, migrants, outcasts and the destitute.[5] A man's standing was measured by the number of individuals whose labour and allegiance he commanded. Rulers in precolonial Africa were defined not by possession of land, but of people.[6] This was true of Dahomey. It was also the case in the states directly to the east – Benin, Oyo and Allada, places of diverse affiliation but bound by a common language, Yoruba.

That slaving first by Arabs then by Europeans destabilised these societies is clear. Greed, driven by the alluring wares offered in exchange for humans, had deeply infected Dahomey. The same combination wrought even wider conflict in the eastern regions. The *obas* of Benin, rulers of the most powerful kingdom in the sixteenth century, had forbidden the sale of their people to white traders. Gradually, however, their authority was undermined by the neighbouring powers of Oyo and Allada, both of which sold captives for export and grew in strength on the proceeds.[7] Benin's decline made way for the kingdom of Oyo but brought no stability.

From the 1760s, Lagos started to emerge as a significant slaving port – its traffic driven by the deepening conflict among the Yoruba-speaking inhabitants of the interior. Another source of captives was the Hausa population of Muslims to the north, which added an element of religious strife to the venomous brew as humans plundered and traded within Oyo were sold on at coastal markets. Bahia's slavers profited most. It is estimated that above 80 per cent of the 251,000 captives shipped from the Bight of Benin between 1800 and 1825 were on vessels bound for Brazil, the vast majority to Bahia.[8] By now Oyo had been engaged in three decades of intermittent civil war and the kingdom was approaching collapse.[9]

The kings and their favourites also grew rich on the backs of African captives. The town on an island had evolved into a fortress-like realm of its own, ruled by men in thrall to the wares, glittering and empowering, proffered from Bahia. The *oba* Osinlokun had come to power by overthrowing his younger brother Adele in 1821, but both indulged their royal entitlements. Of Adele, an English traveller related:

> Everything he took a fancy to was put into his hands at his own request; but as it would be grossly impolite to return it after it had been soiled by his fingers, with the utmost nonchalance the chief delivered it over to the care of his recumbent pages . . . A large portion of almost every article . . . speedily pass[ed] through his hands into those of his juvenile minions.[10]

Osinlokun, it was said, had been schooled in the arts of trade as a boy and, having come to power by force, made weapons a priority. The previous year he ordered two artillery batteries from Brazil along with swords and muskets.[11] But like his brother – who was to be seen 'gorgeously arrayed in a scarlet cloak covered with gold lace and white kerseymere trowsers' – Osinlokun had an eye for luxury. Among his other imports from Bahia was a richly decorated chest containing coral beads and damask cloth embroidered with gold.[12]

Dos Santos came well supplied with sweeteners. A Brazilian source noted that Osinlokun demanded 'contributions from the captains . . . [to] authorise them to negotiate' and the *Henriqueta* had a companion vessel.[13] Before her departure, consul Pennell reported that Cerqueira Lima had chartered an American schooner, the *Lafayette*, 'to be subservient in her illicit operations'.[14] As well as bearing gifts for the *oba*, the *Lafayette* may have called at Ouidah to settle the outstanding debt with Francisco de Souza.

Once the royal tax had been delivered, bartering could commence. Virtually all the prominent traders at Lagos were tribal associates of the *oba* – family members and chiefs or, in some cases, wives and even slaves granted access to wealth as a reward for past services.[15] They made their purchases at the markets that flourished along the 30-mile stretch of the lagoon's northern shore. The fact that the Ogun and Osun rivers rose in the heart of the Oyo kingdom and flowed out here was a further stimulus to trade; captives, having been marched or brought by river down from the interior, were easily transported across to Lagos in canoes and traded on for other merchandise from Bahia – usually tobacco, cloth and alcohol.

One man to have made just such a journey, and who survived to pass on his story of capture and renewal, is a stand-out figure in the history of African slavery.

He was born Ajayi to a Yoruba-speaking family at Osogun, a rural settlement some 70 miles north of Lagos where his father scraped a bare living from the land. Theirs was a region marked from Ajayi's earliest years by conflict: he described Osogun as being surrounded by a wooden barrier about 4 miles in circumference with a force of warrior defenders. Yet he could still recall mornings 'fair and delightful . . . enjoying the comforts of father and mother, the affection of brothers and sisters'.

Ajayi was aged about 13 when, on just such a morning in 1821, word spread of a force advancing on the settlement. His father left their simple mud-thatch home to join the defenders but soon returned 'to give us the signal to flee'. It was the last the family saw of him. Their mother collected Ajayi, a sister and an infant and joined a mass flight.

Here the most sorrowful scene was to be witnessed – women, some with three, four or six children clinging to their arms, with the infants on their backs and with such baggage as they could carry on their heads, running as fast as they could.[16]

Ajayi's description of the raid by Muslim slavers on Osogun paints a picture of individual plundering rather than any organised enterprise. Few families escaped, yet they were broken up, 'violently divided between three or four enemies, who each led his [captives] away'. Ajayi's family were taken together and 'led in the manner of goats tied under the drove of one man', but once they had been marched to 'the town of the chief', they too became fractured: first Ajayi and his sister were separated from their mother – 'we dared not vent our grief in loud cries but by heavy sobs' – then his sister was taken away.

They had been caught up in the final stage of Oyo's civil war. As the kingdom disintegrated, Muslims once forced into servitude by Yoruba speakers had found their freedom and, joined by other Muslims from the north known as Fulani, created centres of power that now contributed significantly to Lagos's trade in captives. It was from one such 'town of the chief' that Ajayi was chained together with other boys and men and marched south.

Ajayi's experiences chime with the only contemporary account by a British traveller to the region. Hugh Clapperton, the naval officer who met De Souza at Ouidah at the start of an expedition to Africa's far interior in 1825, passed through a land ravaged by war. 'One town will plunder another whenever an opportunity offers,' he observed.[17]

On reaching Katunga, the capital of Oyo some 200 miles inland, Clapperton was taken to the king. Once a mighty regional power and beneficiary of the slave trade, Oyo's monarchy was in peril and the king – who said neither he nor his father before him had ever seen a white man – was relieved by the appearance of a visitor bearing firearms at a time when the kingdom faced rebellious Hausa slaves who had joined the Fulani and 'put to death the old and sold the young'.

> He was glad that white men had come . . . and now he trusted his country would be put right, his enemies brought to submission and he would be enabled to build up his father's house which war had destroyed. This he spoke in such a feeling and energetic manner, and repeated it so many times, I could not help sympathising with him.[18]

Clapperton was in no position to alter regional history and he did not linger, being bound for the Muslim states to the north. But he had warmed to these Yoruba speakers, 'a mild and kind people, kind to their wives and children and to one another', and a government that, 'though absolute, is conducted with the greatest mildness'.[19] He was struck, too,

Although a naval officer, Hugh Clapperton was among the earliest British travellers to West Africa's far interior.

by noble landscapes and the potential here for prosperity: 'Our road lay through beautiful rocky valleys, cultivated in many places with cotton, corn, yams, and bananas; and well-watered with many fine streams.'[20] Yet all the while, he noted, 'a war is now carrying on only a few hours from us – not a national but a slaving war'.[21]

Clapperton's journal sets Ajayi's story in context. And his note on a pattern to the trade – that it was not only those taken in war who were being sold into slavery but 'refractory and intractable domestic slaves' – helps to explain the boy's fate.[22]

For months Ajayi had been traded from hand to hand. Among his owners was a Muslim woman who put him to domestic work while allowing him to befriend her son 'with a degree of freedom'. Then, hearing that he might be sold to white men, Ajayi collapsed in dread. 'Several nights I attempted to strangle myself with my band but had not courage enough to close the noose tight.' The woman, 'perceiving the great alteration in me', sold him on to a buyer who, in turn, took him to a market on Lagos lagoon and exchanged him for tobacco.

The appearance of water, the notion of being set upon that element, always precipitated panic – of a journey seemingly to the underworld. 'Nothing now terrified me more,' Ajayi recalled. Still months passed in what appears to have been a barracoon with other boys and men held together by:

> a chain of about six fathoms in length thrust through with an iron fetter on the neck of every individual. In this situation the boys suffered the most: the men sometimes getting angry, would draw the chain most violently . . . Very often at night, when two or three individuals quarrelled or fought, the whole drove suffered.[23]

Ajayi had become almost resigned – 'having no more hope of ever going to my country again, I patiently took whatever came' – until the spectres that haunted local folklore appeared: '[With] great fear and trembling, I received for the first time the touch of a white man who examined me – [to see] whether I was sound or not.'

As Ajayi found himself among those picked out, word passed that another enemy lay out on the water. Dread deepened, for it followed 'that there must be wars on the sea as well as the land – a thing never heard of before'. So it was that after being loaded into canoes in the dark of night, taken onto the sea and up the side of a wooden island, Ajayi joined 186 other captives in the dark below. It began to move.

On this occasion, the sensations of life aboard a slaver were mercifully brief.

The next morning [we] found ourselves in the hands of new conquerors whom we at first very much dreaded, they being armed with long swords. Called up from the hold, we were astonished to find ourselves in the midst of ships.

What followed was as day to night. Ajayi and others, starving, desperate for food, started to search their prison vessel, and as they were not threatened, 'we began to entertain a very good opinion of our new conquerors'. In a few days, having been taken on another ship, 'we were quite at home . . . being selected by the sailors for their boys, and furnished with dress'.

Ajayi was among the 187 captives on a Portuguese polacca, the *Esperança Felix* bound for Bahia, when she was intercepted off Lagos in 1822 by the Royal Navy sloop *Myrmidon*. Over the following weeks, months and years, he entered a new world and discovered a new form of freedom. Not all of those taken off the *Esperança Felix* would be so blessed: 102 were aboard another captured vessel, the *Icanam*, carrying them to Sierra Leone when she ran into a tornado.[24] In all, almost 400 rescued captives were lost, an event which places the *Icanam* among the forgotten disasters from the age of sail.[25] While the twenty seamen who went down with them had often seen the sea's rage, these tortured souls discovered in their last hours new realms of terror.

But for a Yoruba boy – 'a veteran of slavery' he called himself – life had turned. Ajayi had begun his transformation to the man remembered by history as Samuel Crowther.

Royal Navy ships had begun patrolling the Gulf of Guinea in 1808, the year after Parliament declared the trade in humans illegal, but with the nation still at war, resourcing of this attempt at enforcement was limited and by 1815 fewer than 120 suspected slaving vessels had been captured and taken to Sierra Leone.[26] Peace introduced an era in which diplomatic initiatives were set in train to achieve the same objective, yet with even more meagre returns: the number of Africans trafficked annually to Cuba and Brazil surged from an estimated 39,000 in 1815 to 60,000 in 1819.[27] That year saw the first permanent naval squadron stationed at Sierra Leone but thanks to the Admiralty's blank refusal to assign either enough or the right kind of cruisers, the Preventative Squadron's voyage was one of frustration and frequent failure. The year of Ajayi's rescue, 1822, marked a rare high point with the interception and capture of twenty-eight mainly Portuguese and Spanish slavers. The following year that number dropped to just three, and in 1824, the year of *Henriqueta*'s first voyage, it stood at eleven.[28]

HMS *Bann*, the 20-gun sloop identified by Cerqueira Lima as the scourge of fair enterprise, had been significantly more successful than her companions, having captured eleven slavers. The fact that four, including the *Cerqueira*, had no captives on board may have been testimony to excessive if laudable zeal, yet she had still saved almost 1,500 Africans from slavery.[29] Among them was a young woman on the *Juliana da Praca* intercepted off Porto Novo, six months after the rescue of Ajayi. Their meeting and shared destiny – including what Ajayi recalled as 'our blessing of three children' – would prove another of *Bann*'s legacies.[30]

As João dos Santos came ashore from the *Henriqueta*, he was heartened to hear that this particular menace had not been sighted for months – an indication that after three years off Africa she may have departed, worn out, for home.[31] Having duly presented himself and his gifts to the *oba*, Dos Santos set trade in motion; but not through the usual network of Osinlokun's tribal associates. Scenting the fortunes to be made at Lagos, individual Brazilians had started forming alliances with the *oba* to set up their own barracoons. Among the first was Manoel Joaquim d'Almeida.

D'Almeida was a native of Pernambuco, the northernmost of Brazil's ports, some 500 miles up the coast from Bahia; but it was at the latter that he started slaving. Aged just 23 when given his first vessel (youth was plainly a factor in the selection of men to command them), he had made at least a dozen voyages from Bahia since 1814.[32] Twenty years on, d'Almeida had taken up residence at Lagos with an African wife and family and established a factory of his own. Here, it has been shown, he 'represented the interests of several Bahia merchants, including Cerqueira Lima'.[33]

Acquiring the hundreds of humans needed to fill a brig's hold was a prolonged process. According to one study, between four and six months was seen as normal, between two and four months as rapid.[34] On that basis, it must be concluded that d'Almeida was a chillingly effective negotiator. The *Henriqueta* had sailed from Bahia on 15 July and would return on 3 November. Based on her known voyage times to and from the Bight – twenty-eight days outward bound and twenty-eight homeward – that indicates she was at Lagos just over two months.

While d'Almeida's agents were crossing to the coastal markets, buying up groups of prisoners taken in war, the skies poured rain. With humidity high and the south-west monsoon blowing offshore, the season was not auspicious for the health of those about to be packaged below. One aspect was favourable. The yam crop was in. Provisions should be adequate.[35]

All the while João dos Santos had a telescope to the horizon. Of the *Bann* there was still no sign. Other navy ships also remained significant by their absence when his human cargo started to come down to the lagoon's edge early in October. Now was the time for utmost caution: the British must have learnt from the *Cerqueira* episode that seizing vessels without captives entailed risk, but from the moment they embarked, the *Henriqueta* would be vulnerable.

Loading began on 6 October. The sea was calm. Thunderstorms, the skies lit up by explosions of lightning, had passed. Canoes were bringing out glistening bodies, a dozen at a time, when, some time before noon, masts were sighted to the south. She looked far too large for a slaver. She was, in fact, a 42-gun navy frigate.

Because those captives already embarked were all male, they could be roused from below with some speed. The *Henriqueta*'s hands did not shy from wielding lengths of rope, driving the men back along the main deck and down into the canoes that had ferried them out just hours before. Another factor was that the frigate HMS *Maidstone* was a cumbersome sailer with a draught too low for close inshore work. She approached gingerly before anchoring in deeper waters some distance off and despatching a boat.

By the time a lieutenant from the *Maidstone* came up *Henriqueta*'s side, Dos Santos could gesture coolly for him to go below and inspect her. All the captives had been returned ashore. That there was specific evidence of human trafficking could not be disputed: numerous water casks, large quantities of provisions and, above all, the tiers of deck with just a few feet of headroom typical of a slaver. Yet, as both parties knew, these telltale signs no longer constituted sufficient grounds for detention. The officer may have glowered at Dos Santos as he left, but that was as far as it went.

The *Henriqueta* was not the only slaver off Lagos that day. Accounts reached the British consul William Pennell that altogether four Brazilian and two Spanish vessels had been boarded.[36] But it was Cerqueira Lima's brig that had run closest to the wind. 'She had part of her cargo of slaves on board,' Pennell reported, 'and had just enough time to land them and thereby escape capture.'[37]

What followed was a series of manoeuvres in which each of the two participants appeared to have an acute anticipation of the other's actions.

The *Maidstone* raised anchor and set sail south, hauling up soon after she crossed the horizon and commencing to tack to and fro. Commodore Charles Bullen, frustrated in his attempt to catch a slaver red-handed, was lurking just out of sight to await her departure.

On the *Henriqueta*, reloading captives began as soon as *Maidstone* disappeared. It continued until nightfall and resumed as dawn came up on a clear day. Around noon, with more than 500 men, women and children crammed between the twin slave-decks below, Dos Santos gave orders to make ready.

The risk was obvious. The navy ship was likely to be lying in wait, 4 or 5 miles offshore. The wind was light, with none of the urgency needed to sweep the brig out, starting a race south into the Atlantic and across the Equator. Could she but catch a breath of wind with the frigate to leeward, Dos Santos knew *Henriqueta* had the race won. The critical space was those first miles they would have to cover on quitting the shore to avoid interception. Here he had one vital advantage.

She made all sail in the early afternoon with a light breeze that carried her out slowly on a south-westerly course. Scarcely had Lagos passed from sight than a distinctive sturdy shape came up to the southeast. On *Maidstone*, a lookout shouted down that one of the slavers was on the move. The moment is noted in the log: 'At 3.30 Obs'd strange sail standing offshore.'[38]

Dos Santos ordered his men straight to the sweep ports. Long oars called sweeps gave a Baltimore clipper additional flexibility when working close to shore. They also added to her momentum when the wind fell slack. While *Maidstone* tacked again to come about and cut her off, *Henriqueta* hastened on.[39]

The frigate's log reports what followed in brusque terms: 'At 6 Stranger on weather beam. Moderate and cloudy. At 8 Lost sight of chase.'[40] That brief record does not even hint at a collective surge of anger and frustration as the *Henriqueta* outraced her pursuer. Yet there was also wonder at that light-weather flyer, with her heavily raked masts, sharp lines and shallow draught. Old naval hands, from officers to topmen, may have seethed that such vessels were evading their best efforts, all while being put to bear misery and death. What is not in doubt is that they envied those sweet-sailing qualities.

It was a turning point for Commodore Bullen. In their first year of duty on the coast, his flagship *Maidstone* had succeeded in intercepting just one slaver, a Brazilian brig *Aviso*, and he had now lost his most valuable resource: the *Bann* had indeed sailed home in May. But he had been given a vision of the way forward. Whether the Admiralty would approve was another matter; their lordships, it was often noted, had no liking for change or innovation.

It seems unlikely that Bullen ever learnt of one small but significant blessing his actions that year had conferred. Among the 431 captives taken off the *Aviso* and landed alive at Sierra Leone was a boy named Laiguandai. He too, like Ajayi, had been swept up at the age of about 13 in the wars ravaging the Yoruba region and had passed through various hands before being sold to traders on the coast. Like Ajayi too – or Samuel Crowther as he came to know his friend in Freetown – he married, fathered children and lived in Africa for the rest of his life, as Peter Wilson.[41]

'THERE HAS BEEN CONCEALMENT'
October–November 1825

She may have left one navy pursuer trailing in her wake, but the *Henriqueta* was not yet out of reach. For all her master knew, other ships of the British squadron could be cruising nearby and she had almost 450 miles to run before that risk was behind them. Only after she had crossed the Equator might Dos Santos declare legitimacy, as a slaver homeward bound from her licensed port of Malembo. The once-standard practice of claiming a vessel had been driven north by 'contrary winds' no longer held water.[1] Still under a faint breeze, the *Henriqueta* was set to run straight south for the line.

Of one thing at least Dos Santos now had certainty. In a chase, she could make a mockery of any British ship in pursuit. When it came to prevention and speed, the notion of naval superiority vanished in *Henriqueta's* wake along the Gulf of Guinea. Now he must utilise her pace in a rapid return to Bahia and so secure the best possible survival rate, among both her captives and her crew.

Next to speed, the key elements here were diet and health. Care for the one served the other. This was not down to any consideration of humanity. Margins of profit were the primary factor. The most successful slavers, among whom Cerqueira Lima was prominent, ordered masters to ensure their vessels were properly prepared for transoceanic voyages. In this respect, they had almost four centuries of tradition and knowledge to draw upon.

Portuguese mariners had been crossing the globe before any others, and far longer than the English. First to the New World after the Vikings was, of course, Christopher Columbus, an Italian in the service of Spain. But in wider seaborne exploration, Portugal led the way: once Bartolomeu Dias had used the powerful south-westerly winds to cross the Atlantic before rounding the Cape of Good Hope to the Indian Ocean, others followed: Vasco da Gama took it further, passing up the east coast of Africa to the East Indies in 1498; Ferdinand Magellan, the first circumnavigator of the world, was Portuguese; and, crucially for the present narrative, Pedro Cabral landed on the soil he claimed for Portugal as Brazil in 1500. Along with questing zeal came hardiness and indifference to suffering. These were seafarers who had been trans-porting Africans across the Atlantic for 250 years.[2]

The *Henriqueta* had a company of thirty-eight, of whom Dos Santos, his navigator, and two mates had all been born in Portugal, either Lisbon or Oporto. Of her thirty-two seamen – those who went aloft or were otherwise employed in handling her vast quantities of rope and canvas – twenty were also Portuguese-born and from cities with ties to the sea, Braga and Lamego.[3] A few would have had the additional skills needed on any ship, as carpenter and cooper. Pride in their tradition naturally coloured assessments of British seafaring abilities and nothing they had seen altered a belief that theirs were superior. Seamen were a tribal folk and the *Henriqueta*'s escape from Lagos was likely to have strengthened a bond between them. It certainly reinforced a conviction that in these waters, this arena, they had the upper hand.

More complex sensations may be imagined among her twelve African seamen, the majority of whom were Yoruba-born. Seven, described in the *Henriqueta*'s books as *escravos do proprietro*, were there-fore deemed the property of Cerqueira Lima, with given names such as Sabino and Bento. Five had originally been shipped from Lagos, including Ramar and António. Jorge was from Angola while Criolo was

Bahian-born, descended from an earlier generation of slaves.[4] It was no coincidence that most of them shared ethnic origins with those they would be helping to transport. They had been selected for that very reason.

Clearly, they had no choice in these roles. They were filling a need. Bahia appeared incapable of raising its own mariners. Having all significant labour performed by the enslaved had produced, it bears repeating, ennui and indolence among the white colonial population, hence a dependence on Africans as well as Portuguese for crew.[5] Between 30 and 40 per cent of Bahia's slaver crews were black. When it came to local shipping, that proportion rose to almost 50 per cent, of whom a significant majority had their origins within the Bight of Benin.[6]

Not all, however, could be described as strictly enslaved. Most were paid. In the case of the *Henriqueta*, all those on the muster were listed as receiving the same wage as their white fellows, and for good reason. As well as strength in handling ropes and agility in the tops, Africans brought to these vessels an essential ingredient as cultural go-betweens. Here were Yoruba speakers who could go ashore and act as translators between a vessel's masters and local traders. They were able to interact with the panic-stricken captives coming on board, assuring them that they were not about to be eaten alive – that, indeed, the life awaiting them was easier than the one they were leaving: just look at me, they might have said. African seamen, moreover, had a particular authority in dealing with ailments and disturbances below. In the words of one Portuguese master: 'These freed blacks can be very useful denouncing conspiracies and patrolling the slaves.'[7]

Whether Bento and Sabino, Jorge and Ramar received from Cerqueira Lima the full pay they were due remains an open question. As in the case of Bahia's enslaved street vendors, the *proprietro* might well have retained a portion for himself. But in time they would be *libertos*, and while at sea they were the equals of their white shipmates. Many fell into a category known as *ladino*, or culturally assimilated, speaking Portuguese as well as their own tongues. From the cramped spaces they shared to the dangers they faced, these were men dependent upon one another. All were enveloped by the same ghastly sights, smells and conditions. The kinship forged between men at sea endured in some form, even if purely as a means of survival.*

Religion may also have played a part. Having been introduced to Catholicism by the custom of baptising them, many slaves in Brazil gave the appearance of accepting the faith practised at sea and ashore. Robert Walsh, in his wanderings around the country, noted that they would greet him on the road with extended hands and the salutation 'Jesu Christo', for which the response was 'por sempre' (for ever) and which he likened to the tradition of his native Ireland. Commitment was another matter. 'Many still adhere to their pagan traditions,' he went on, 'though by far the greater number are anxious to seem rid of them . . . because it confers on them a certain consideration.'[8] Among the benefits were the Church's insistence that slaves had a right to the sacraments which overrode a master's demands, in effect freeing them for worship on Sundays and saints' days.[9] They had their own church in Bahia, the Nossa Senhora do Rosário dos Pretos, and Catholic ritual was observed even on slaving vessels when conditions permitted.

African culture and spiritual beliefs ran still deeper. What Walsh referred to as pagan traditions – magic rituals and witchcraft – had retained a place in these communities and, despite the opposition of slave-owners, were evolving into cults that absorbed aspects of Christian practice and even came to influence parts of white society.[10] The most visible was a faith known as Candomblé, a blend of Yoruba belief and Catholicism in which African deities and Christian saints were visible, and which endures in modern Brazil.

---

* Cerqueira Lima placed a high value on his African hands – quite literally, declaring them 'expert in the practice of the sea' and worth at least 500 milreis each, the equivalent of about £140 at the time. This statement was, however, coloured by the fact that it formed part of his claims against the British government for damages over the capture of another of his vessels, the *Independência* (Hicks, p. 125).

It might be expected that the return of black seamen to Africa, to the sight of their native land and tribal kin, would have stimulated large-scale desertions. No records have survived for an adequate analysis of this taxing subject, yet a British merchant who spent ten years in Brazil, having noted 'a great deficiency of sailors' among the white population, added with some bemusement, 'A great number employed on slave ships are black slaves, native to Africa and go oftentimes to their homelands but do not abandon their ships.'[11] The account of one slave-turned-sailor offers some insight into why men faced with this dilemma responded as they did.

He was known as Gorge, sometimes George, both being transliterations of the name given to him in enslavement. Nothing about his early life is known, other than that he believed his birthplace to have been Ouidah where he was taken captive, and that he had then been transported and sold at Bahia in 1805 aged about 15.

Gorge stated his owner to be Joaquim Carneiro de Campos, who, given the time frame and the similarity in name, appears to have been a politician who later became the Marquês de Caravelas, a prominent member of the Portuguese imperial administration in Brazil. Whatever his identity, the individual who paid for Gorge clearly saw this youth – broad, quite short in stature at 5 feet 4 inches, his cheeks scarred by branding – as healthy and strong.[12] Before turning 20, Gorge was introduced to seafaring, initially along the coast between Pernambuco and Rio, for which he showed aptitude. As he gained in skill, so did the rate De Campos could charge for hiring him out to ships' masters.

Gorge first appeared as a slaver hand in 1816 when the brig *Temerário* came to off Ouidah. This was his birthplace and a decade had passed since his departure into enslavement. The *Temerário* had been at anchor long enough to start taking on captives and he had seemingly made no attempt to escape to his native shore when a British vessel came in sight on 5 March.

HENRIQUETA

Gorge's role in events as they unfolded is a matter of speculation. He may have been among the *Temerário*'s hands who had just started to embark captives, reassuring Yoruba speakers that all would be well as they were directed below. Or he may have been on one of the boats which were rowing out more of these terrified individuals when a Portuguese mate gave the order to turn around and get them ashore again, *rapidamente*. Gorge may even have joined those who manned the *Temerário*'s eighteen guns – she was formidably armed – and opened fire as the British sloop approached.

Resistance was not prolonged. Men from HMS *Bann* (for it was she) came up the side, took possession and set the *Temerário* down the coast to Freetown, carrying the seventeen captives who had been found below, along with Gorge and the rest of her company.[13]

Seamen on slavers taken by the Navy were not subject to legal punishment (though they might well be knocked about) even in most cases where they had offered armed resistance, and would usually await the chance of a passage to a friendly port or home. Gorge was given the option of staying, with paid work at Freetown for Macaulay and Babington, which controlled trade in colonial Sierra Leone. But when a vessel bound for Brazil appeared, Gorge was among the *Temerário*'s crew to go on board. Back in Bahia, he was reclaimed as property by De Campos.[14]

Five years later, Gorge was captured again, this time on the schooner *Emilia* as she sailed from Lagos with 398 captives – a scale of overloading barbaric even by the standards prevailing in 1821. It was this case, to which Mrs Graham referred after the *Emilia* was taken to Rio by HMS *Morgiana* for adjudication, that led to a stand-off over enslaved seamen. Captain Finlaison of the *Morgiana* had recruited five of *Emilia*'s black hands, including Gorge, in what he saw as an act of liberation – while, naturally, strengthening his own depleted company – until being forced by the Rio authorities to deliver up men deemed Brazilian property.

Gorge gave testimony to the hearing by the Mixed Commission. Speaking under oath, he told a panel composed equally of British and

Portuguese judges that the 398 captives had indeed been loaded at Lagos, thus refuting an officer's claims that it was at Malembo.[15] Questioned by the British judge, Henry Hayne, he acknowledged that he had been captured previously on a slaver. His time at Freetown, he went on, had been spent as 'a prisoner', adding that although offered 'emancipation' and British citizenship, his allegiance was to the King of Portugal. Asked about his station, he said he was 'a mariner'.

Judge Hayne, in his report to the Foreign Office, concluded with obvious frustration:

> It would be a great object to prohibit slaves being employed in the navigation of slave vessels as they are generally the most useful and effective part of their crew.[16]

It has been argued that the case illustrates how the form of freedom offered to Gorge was not necessarily the best of all options available to individual slaves. In going to sea, he had acquired status, along with a degree of autonomy unthinkable for most enslaved blacks; as one study has pointed out: 'He was a seaman in the eyes of white seamen. And he was a seaman in his own eyes.'[17] It could be countered that, finding himself back in Brazil, Gorge had little option but to declare loyalty to those who had enslaved him. Yet he had passed up at least two opportunities to return to his native Africa. To that may be added evidence from papers found on *Emilia* showing that Gorge and two other black mariners owned goods on board – barrels of tobacco and aguardente – which were the standard merchandise of trade. They had profited sufficiently from their pay to invest in the purchase of fellow Africans.[18]

Gorge returned to the service of his 'owner' Joaquim de Campos. It may be concluded that when faced with uncertainty, he opted for the life he understood.[19]

The central figure in *Henriqueta*'s voyages remains an enigma. Still only 22, João dos Santos had acquired the sailing and trading abilities needed to enrich his patron and which would ultimately secure for him the prize coveted by all slaver masters – a vessel of his own. He went on to make a personal fortune. These few facts apart, Dos Santos's life and his methods in handling the many thousands of Africans he transported across the Atlantic over the years – all while sharing existence with them in a wooden shell little more than thirty paces in length – are subjects of pure conjecture. Some ships' logbooks can bring to mind life on board and the regime enforced by a commander, including his disciplinary style; the only surviving log of a voyage by the *Henriqueta* is a deadpan record of navigation in which even weather conditions are not mentioned.[20]

For a first-hand account of a slaver master's disposition we may turn to an Englishman schooled in the experience, John Newton, who before becoming a devout abolitionist made at least four slaving voyages, three in command.

> A savageness of spirit, not easily conceived, infuses itself (though, as I have observed, there are exceptions) into those who exercise power on board an African slave-ship, from the captain downwards. It is the spirit of the trade, which, like a pestilential air, is so generally infectious, that but few escape it.[21]

Hard-heartedness was combined with callousness when the torment of the brutalised souls below led to uprising. Episodes of resistance were growing in frequency, especially by captives being shipped from the Bight of Benin, and Dos Santos is known to have suppressed at least one uprising himself. At the same time, he worked with black seamen, relied on them, and to that extent at least must have gained some sense of a common humanity.

A possible explanation previously mentioned for these paradoxes – one which applies to Portuguese conduct over their history of enslavement – is the Catholic faith: the Church of Rome held that pagans taken from their heathen customs to a Christian land had been saved; baptising them on embarkation reassured the devout that even those who died suffocating within a darkness stinking of shit were in the hands of God. No such fancy could be conjured up on the *Henriqueta*, however, as she sailed without a priest; baptisms could be performed only after landing.

Dos Santos's main source of comfort was his pay. A single voyage earned him 2,400 milreis, or about £670 (equivalent in present purchasing power to £38,500), four times more than anyone else on board.[22] Next in line were the *piloto*, or navigator, a specialist from Lisbon who received 600 milreis, and the senior mate, also Portuguese, on 300 milreis, about £170 and £85 respectively. The *Henriqueta's* hands, whether of Portuguese or African origin, were paid 20 milreis, or £5, for a voyage lasting between four and five months.[23] (These rates were not vastly different from those on British ships: navy pay at the time was 33s 6d a month for Able hands and 25s 6d for those rated Ordinary; rates for merchant seamen were variable but usually higher.)

Among the *Henriqueta's* other high earners was an intriguing figure known as Sangrador Naraizo. Described as a Nagoa tribesman from the hinterland of Lagos, he too was enslaved, another *escravo do proprietro*.[24] His value to Cerqueira Lima, and to the captives, was as a healer and soother. Unlike the British slave ships of the past, *Henriqueta* had no doctor on board. The name Sangrador, translated as 'bleeder', signified a category of African crewmen found on most Brazilian slavers. They bore responsibility for the well-being, spiritual as well as physical, of the human cargo, identifying diseases and providing both traditional and European treatments. One *sangrador* described his craft as 'bleeding, scarifying, applying cups and leeches', while Cerqueira Lima praised one of his own medicine men for having a 'great expertise in his art', which suggests the use of magic rituals as well.[25] It was dangerous work, among the festering bodies of the lower deck, and its importance made *sangradores* the most affluent and mobile of Bahia's black mariners.

Sangrador Naraizo's duties extended to involvement in assessing the captives being held in barracoons, and possibly during negotiations.

Once a deal had been reached, he supervised branding individuals with the buyer's mark, first lubricating the skin with palm oil to ensure the iron did not cling and cause infection. His range of aptitudes and importance to the voyage's success were reflected in his pay. Sangrador Naraizo stood fourth in the *Henriqueta's* paybook at 200 milreis, or about £55 (equivalent to £3,150) – ten times the rate of her sailors.

As a seafaring company, all could celebrate escaping capture by the British. On 10 October, three days after leaving the frigate *Maidstone* floundering in the Bight, *Henriqueta* slipped across the Equator. At that point the last danger of naval interception passed and she started west by south.

The crew braced themselves anew for the confinement of the homeward voyage. Having reached Africa with thirty-eight men aboard, *Henriqueta* was now carrying almost 550 men, women and children. Dos Santos's quarters were shared with the pilot and mate. While the hands preferred the space and air of the upper deck to confinement amid the hundreds of other bodies, at least some of the African sailors were needed below to calm and keep an eye on the captives. Activity aloft came as a release, and with moderate seasonal temperatures, men like Sabino and his white counterpart Joaquin kept cool as well as exercising in the breeze passing through the tops. They had some 3,600 nautical miles (more than 4,100 miles) to run home and hopes were high that she could carry them there in four weeks. At this point, Dos Santos's thoughts turned to food and water.

Provisions were stretched on any fully loaded slaver. Only limited quantities of the yam, corn and beans available at Lagos could be stored now that the lower deck was stacked with humans. Water was potentially more of a concern. An early *alvará*, or regulation, stipulating that each captive should receive 2.5 litres a day, had long since been abandoned. They were likely to get half a litre or less.[26] Both food and water, essential to the survival of all on board, distilled the nature of power between crew and the enslaved. Should the *Henriqueta* be delayed by slack or contrary winds, there was no question which of the two groups would have priority.

On the lower deck, water had been discovered in a new essence. Few captives had previous knowledge of the sea, having been drawn from the interior, so the contrast between the life-preserving element of daily consideration in any African village and the immeasurable form that now surrounded them, one that stirred in them dizziness and a vomiting sickness, gave rise to renewed dread. After some days in this nether-world, with the words of comfort from countrymen who had survived here, the sickness passed, retching ceased.

But this new element persisted. With her low-slung beam, the *Henriqueta* took on sea even in light turbulence. It washed across bodies, drenching what little clothing they wore, and ran into the hold storing provisions. The taste of salt was everywhere, in the air, on the skin, in the food. It appeared to be bound up in this new existence from which there was no escape.

During *Henriqueta's* absence, Britain's envoys had started lobbying the Brazilian government for the objective that had eluded her Navy. On 18 July, Sir Charles Stuart landed in Rio with a diplomatic package intended to hasten progress towards an abolition treaty. The Portuguese government, in Britain's debt since the Napoleonic Wars, had submitted to pressure from George Canning at the Foreign Office finally to recog-nise Brazil as an independent state, and Stuart had Lisbon's authority to sign a document to that effect. In return, he was to table proposals for a commercial agreement – one based on the principle that Brazil would declare the slave trade illegal within four years.[27]

On 25 July, ten days after the *Henriqueta* sailed from Bahia, Stuart was spelling out Britain's position at a meeting with the Emperor Pedro. The envoy reported His Majesty as 'being anxious to put an end to the slave trade'. Whatever the emperor's opinion, however, he was in an awkward position – ruler of a young state intensely hostile to the poli-cies being dictated by a superpower. Negotiations proved tortuous and fraught; and whatever declarations might be made from Rio, Bahia would have none of it.

Diplomatic sensitivities were raised meanwhile by the scandalous case of a runaway slave. The man, known only as António, had fled the northern province of Maranhão on a Brazilian vessel before being discovered and landed at Rio. In what smacked of a ploy to embarrass the British, the local authorities chartered John Chambers, master of the *Minerva* brig from Scarborough, to take António back to Maranhão and deliver him to the consul, Robert Hesketh, for return to his owner.[28]

On the *Minerva*'s arrival, an outraged Hesketh reported that to add to the 'glaring impropriety' of a British vessel being involved, António had been taken off the brig and publicly flogged. He wrote to Henry Chamberlain, consul-general in Rio:

> I had no power to keep the slave from his owner here; but I hope you will obtain some order for his manumission and if that cannot be effected you may perhaps obtain some general orders that give freedom to all slaves who arrive by British vessels.[29]

No such orders were forthcoming, but Canning was moved to intervene. On 8 August, amid continuing negotiations, Chamberlain informed diplomats around Brazil of the foreign secretary's instruction: masters of all British vessels must be warned 'not to take on board slaves as passengers, unless in cases of absolute distress at sea'.[30]

Among the recipients was William Pennell, whose own growing frustration is evident in his despatches from Bahia. The northern capital's intention to establish itself as a virtual state within a state had just been emphasised by the dispute over admeasurement: the emperor's decree to limit the overloading of slavers had, in effect, been overruled by Bahia's president under pressure from Cerqueira Lima.

Pennell, although unable to prove that returning vessels had loaded their captives north of the line, persevered over admeasurement. In September, 303 captives were landed at Bahia from a smack, the *Caridade*, which under the decree was limited to a maximum of 220. Just one death was reported by the master. Pennell did some sleuthing and, in a report to his superiors in London and Rio, cited 'an intelligent and impartial witness' as saying he had found others in their death throes, and the real toll was significantly higher.[31] His request to the president that the case be investigated was deflected, and although Pennell wanted to pursue it, Chamberlain urged caution because of the treaty negotiations. 'I do not see any advantage likely to follow from fresh representations,' he wrote.[32]

Just weeks after *Caridade*'s arrival, another vessel put in from Africa – the *Lafayette*, which, as Pennell knew, had been chartered by Cerqueira Lima to assist in the *Henriqueta*'s voyage. Again he went in pursuit of information, questioning the master and establishing that he had 'left the *Henriqueta* at Onim [Lagos] expecting to receive a cargo of slaves'.[33]

Sure enough, twelve days later, on 3 November, the *Henriqueta* anchored back in Bahia. Just 112 days had passed since her departure, so more than three weeks had been shaved off her first voyage. The homeward passage had taken twenty-eight days, compared with an average of forty-seven days for slavers at the turn of the century.[34] As on her first voyage, she landed 504 living humans. While it is inconceivable that progress might be cited in any aspect of the trade, the speed of Baltimore clippers could certainly reduce the mortality rate at sea. The inevitable consequence was that masters would increase the numbers they loaded.

Now Pennell, piecing together intelligence from various sources, compiled the full and remarkably accurate account of events off Lagos which constituted his next despatch to Canning. As usual – he emphasised – the *Henriqueta*'s captives were reported as being taken 'from Malembo' when the *Lafayette*'s master had stated her to have been at Lagos. Pennell was able, moreover, to identify the navy ship as HMS *Maidstone*, to relate how captives had been hastily taken ashore on her appearance before being reloaded and how 'light winds enabled the *Henriqueta* to avail herself of her sweeps and to escape'.

As for the toll on the homeward passage: 'It is reported several deaths have taken place amongst the slaves but with regard to circumstances and number there has been equivocation and concealment.'[35] Further details from the *Maidstone*'s captain, he suggested, might still 'prove that the slaves could <u>not</u> have been shipped at Malembo or any point South of the Line'. He went on to sound a warning for future engagements with *Henriqueta* – 'she is armed and had prepared her guns for resistance' – before concluding with a damning summary of the campaign. By a conservative estimate, he declared, five-sixths of the captives being brought to Bahia were from prohibited regions, a fact that 'sufficiently shews how ineffectual the British Naval force has hitherto been'.[36]

Pennell was a phenomenon of another age: a father of twenty-two children, a diplomat who had moved from sophisticated Bordeaux to remote Bahia to serve his country, and did so out of his own pocket, a man of Devon aged 60 living in a corner of the world that lacked culture, refinement or any of the social pleasures with which he had once been familiar. In what amounted to a form of isolation – Bahia was more than 1,000 miles from Rio and five times as far from England – Pennell performed his duties diligently while surrounded not only by hostile locals but also by British merchants who drew their own benefits from the slave trade. His dealings with Moir & Co., for example, traders in sugar from Bahia, are unlikely to have been warm.

Frostier still were those with another neighbour whose enmity was now fully exposed. 'No one here,' Pennell reported to Canning, 'is more notoriously known to be engaged in the illicit slave trade than the owner of the *Henriqueta*, yet there is no Brazilian merchant who enjoys more consideration and <u>influence</u> with <u>all</u> classes of society.' The upshot, he went on, was that 'a popular odium is easily excited against those who endeavour to suppress it'.[37]

Cerqueira Lima's already vast wealth soared that year. Among his vessels, the *Henriqueta* alone had earned him an estimated £30 for each of the 1,008 living Africans she had landed, the modern equivalent of more than £1.7 million.[38] Bahia's slaving mogul was able, moreover, to boast of a triumph over the despotic British, having won his case for the illegal capture of his brig, the *Cerqueira*.[39] The vessel had already been returned to him. The damages he received were unstated, but while the sum did not attain the colossal £60,000 initially claimed, the British government, in Pennell's words, had 'made compensation so amply' as to cover the cost of the voyage and, 'I am credibly informed, increased the capital and added to the enterprise of the Speculator'.[40]

Cerqueira Lima's status had never been higher, yet his thirst for wealth was undiminished. Amid continuing negotiations with Britain, his immediate concern was that Brazil might sign a treaty to abolish the trade within four years. In the pursuit of profit, no time was to be wasted. On 29 November, just three weeks after her return from Africa, the *Henriqueta* sailed again.

CHAPTER 6

BONDED BY SUFFERING
November 1825–October 1826

Much of what passed on *Henriqueta*'s third voyage is a mystery. It is known she sailed from Bahia in November 1825 with the usual false passport for Malembo and returned 101 days later, with significantly fewer captives than on either of her previous passages. Rumours and speculation ensued. Where those Africans had come from and exactly what had occurred on board was not established. But the evidence that survives points to the darkest episode of her life.

There is no doubt that the Bight of Benin remained *Henriqueta*'s hunting ground, so it can be concluded that she would have passed Cape St Paul's to anchor along the coast by the time of the Nativity festivities: the Portuguese celebrated Jesus's birth on 24 December, so Dos Santos and some of the crew may have gone ashore to mark the occasion with a *fogueira*, a traditional Christmas bonfire, before bartering began. That could have been at one of the Bight's other sources, Porto Novo or Badagry, both of which were part of the trading chain that ran along the coast. A far greater likelihood, however, is that she was bound again for either Ouidah or Lagos.

Why Cerqueira Lima favoured these Bight ports over other regions of West Africa was attributed by William Pennell to the supposed sturdiness of its population – people, he reported, 'accustomed to hard work in their homeland'.[1] There were other factors as well. At Ouidah, trade was still in the hands of the old Bahian, Francisco 'Chacha' de Souza, agent for King Gezo of Dahomey. As for Lagos, it was now providing captives in numbers no other port in West Africa could match. By the 1830s, it would be accounting for almost twice as many shipments as Ouidah.[2] And all this was obtained due to the region's insatiable appetite for Bahia's third-grade tobacco, a commodity unsellable elsewhere.[3]

De Souza's reputation for integrity, however jarring it may sound, ensured he was never short of eager buyers, while his apparent decency continued to baffle those Britons who met him in the course of their efforts to put him out of business. Along with the travellers Hugh Clapperton and John Duncan, both of whom confessed to perplexity at finding 'Chacha' nothing like the monster they had anticipated, came Lieutenant Henry Huntley.

Huntley was a junior officer whose service in the Preventative Squadron would lead to an intimate connection with the *Henriqueta*. Over years of calling at Ouidah, he also became fascinated by the ruling figure seldom seen except when he appeared in a long robe and loose trousers to hold court at a dining table attended by slaver captains. 'His large dark eyes have hardly lost any of their early lustre; at a glance he recognizes everyone at the table, and notices all that is passing,' Huntley wrote.[4] He struggled to explain De Souza's hospitality towards naval officers such as himself – 'although [we] would be naturally obnoxious to him' – while reflecting on 'the remains of some noble traits of character' which suited De Souza 'for a life of less infamy than that which he has embraced'.[5]

De Souza was not alone in these paradoxes. His mentor, King Gezo, as has been seen, wielded absolute power from Dahomey's capital at Abomey, preserving order and authority over his people by extracting captives in raids on neighbouring states. John Duncan, who petitioned him unsuccessfully for an end to the traffic, had high respect for Gezo, a man 'formed to govern' who inspired the love of his subjects and had

Francisco 'Chacha' de Souza controlled the sale of captives from Dahomey.

abolished the tradition of human sacrifice. Yet in a conversation over the nature of authority, in which Duncan spelled out what he saw as the atrocity of enslavement – forcing others 'from their homes and kindred, separating them forever from all relatives, and dooming them to incessant labour' – the king:

asked me whether, when parents voluntarily sold their children, they would then feel any regret. I replied that if the parents did not, they were unnatural, and I was sure the children would; and to illustrate this, I pointed out a she-goat with two kids, and asked him if one were taken away, whether the young would not show symptoms of regret as well as the mother. At this he laughed heartily, but remarked that the he-goat, the father of the kids, would feel quite indifferent. I could not help smiling in return.[6]

Ouidah, however, was no longer receiving captives in the numbers that once made it the dominant port on the Bight of Benin, so De Souza had opened a trading station at Badagry, a port to the east where he installed his eldest son, Isidoro.[7] No such dwindling affected the traffic from Lagos. The constant state of war – factional, tribal and religious – across the tattered remnants of the Oyo kingdom continued to create large, steady flows of captives from the interior.[8]

It may be reasonably concluded that Cerqueira Lima had identified this as his preferred point of trade, and that, to take on her third load of captives, the *Henriqueta* put in at Lagos at the end of December.

Just days before she came to anchor, a British envoy began a mission into the war-torn interior of Oyo where those men, women and children were being rounded up. On 7 December, Hugh Clapperton started north from Badagry intending to combine diplomacy with exploration and to record his experiences. His journal, pored over and analysed since for insights into the region's largely undocumented history, stands as a compelling record of the societies and conflicts driving the trade at Lagos.[9]

Clapperton had visited Africa before, on an expedition to trace the course of the river Niger, when, travelling south across the Sahara from Tunis, he reached the caliphate of Sokoto. This Islamic state had emerged from the wars known as the Fulani jihads which, as has been seen, had engulfed Oyo and other West African regimes. In pursuit of orthodox doctrine, Sokoto's ruler had outlawed the sale of Muslim slaves to Christians, and Clapperton, having struck up what he reported as a cordial rapport with Sultan Bello, departed with the draft of a letter to King George IV in which the sultan undertook 'to prohibit the exportation of slaves by our merchants to Ataghira, Dahumi and Asanti', in exchange for arms and ammunition.[10] On arriving home Clapperton reported: 'Through our intercourse with Bello there is a fair opportunity of cramping, if not totally abolishing the nefarious [Atlantic] trade.'[11]

His travels in Muslim lands had left him in no doubt at this point where the greater evil stood.

> Domestic slavery is so interwoven with [Sokoto's] laws, their religion & state of Society that it never will, nor can, be dispensed with; but we are not to estimate the condition of such Slaves with that of those who are transported to the European Colonies; they are, in Africa, considered as Members of the Family in which they live, and, from their manners and appearance are a happy People.[12]

He was duly appointed by the Colonial Office to return and negotiate further with Bello on halting the passage of slaves through Sokoto, while continuing his search for the Niger. This time, though, he was to travel north from the Bight of Benin.

The perils of journeying into the heart of a fever-infested slaveland running from tropics to desert were obvious. Clapperton had been fortunate to survive his first African odyssey, and within weeks of leaving Badagry three of his companions were dead. As it transpired, the constant warfare carrying on along the route to Sokoto posed further dangers, requiring diversions that would extend their march to more than 1,000 miles.

Clapperton's observations as the first white traveller to the kingdom of Oyo have already been noted. He reflected how 'a people hitherto considered barbarians' were in reality 'civil and industrious' and possessed of 'more than common honesty'.[13] On seeing men 'preparing themselves to go on slaving expeditions', he countered that 'humanity is the same in every land'.[14] But just two days after departing the capital he was confronted by the conflict destroying Oyo – villages in ruins, inhabitants fleeing the marauding Fulani from the north and their fellow Muslims, Hausa slaves who had risen in rebellion. In their wake came raiders from other parts, seizing captives, livestock and crops. All of this added in his eyes to the importance of his mission to the caliphate.

Three months of hard travel brought him to a town called Kiama, a diverse cultural stewpot where the 30,000 inhabitants included 'Mahometans' as well as Yoruba-speaking 'pagans and fetishists'. Although 300 miles from the coast, he also observed that Brazilian tobacco, crucial for the trade, was sold here.[15] At nearby Wawa, captives were to be seen 'on a journey to some slave mar[ke]t . . . when on their march they are fastened night and day by the neck with leather thongs or a chain and in general carry loads'.[16]

Clapperton was no puritan. On his previous journey a companion had falsely and maliciously accused him of 'extreme impropriety' with a male Arab servant.[17] His sexuality was more conventional and the journal is peppered with references to the availability of enslaved young women. He also had a ribald side. At Wawa, he reported being pursued by a wealthy woman in want of a British husband. The widow Zuma had hundreds of her own slaves, hair dyed with indigo, hands with henna, and wore necklaces of gold and coral. Rotund, with 'tremendous breasts', she was 'a perfect Turkish beauty, just like a walking water-butt'.[18]

The farther Clapperton ventured, the more evident Islamic authority became. On reaching Bussa, a city on the Niger, he was brought before the sultan who, as well as expressing great interest in England, believed he had come to buy captives.

I told him there was nothing we so much abhorred in England as slavery; that the king of England did everything to prevent other nations buying slaves; that the slave trade was the ruin of Africa; that Youribba [Oyo] presented ruined towns and deserted villages; that it was very bad to buy and sell men like bullocks and sheep.[19]

An academic argument has been made that the trade from Islamic states to the Bight was by now limited, due to the prohibition on the sale of Muslims to Christians and the retention of large, enslaved labour populations.[20] The latter was certainly the case. At Kano, where Clapperton asked his Arab hosts about the make-up of the local population, he was informed there were thirty slaves to every free man.[21]

But trafficking from these regions clearly continued to feed the trade at Lagos. The anarchic state of conflict noted by Clapperton as he advanced was a driving force. So was the fact that, although the Sokoto caliphate had forbidden trading in Muslims, it still reaped the benefits of taxing those bearing captives through its territory. Clapperton observed: 'Young male slaves are carried down and disposed of in the Bight of Benin and Bello extracts an annual tribute from Traders to carry these unfortunate beings to the coast.'[22] Another factor driving the flow of human caravans was fresh sectarian strife between Sokoto and a neighbouring caliphate. Since Clapperton's previous visit, tensions had arisen between Sultan Bello and Sheikh Mohamed al-Kanemi, ruler of Borno, and at the city of Zaria tidings came that the two had gone to war. Fugitives were flooding in from the north.

On the approach to Sokoto, Clapperton's party was caught up in a ragged but intense battle, four hours of jihadist conflict accompanied by cries of 'Allahu Akbar' that ended with Bello's forces in retreat. Clapperton felt sufficiently armed to defend himself and continued onward, but his identity as a Christian had started to attract hostility.

While rivalry and differences over Islamic orthodoxy lay at the root of the war, another source of tension was suspicion between the two rulers over relations with white infidels. During Clapperton's earlier visit to Sokoto, as he was to discover, Bello had received a warning from al-Kanemi that the white man was a spy and that he 'should be put to death as the English would seize the country as they had done with India, which they had wrested from the Mahometans'.[23]

Almost a year after landing in Africa, Clapperton was ushered back into Bello's presence. He had returned, he said, 'as a messenger with presents from the king of England, for the purpose of putting an end to the slave trade'. Although the sultan received him politely enough, preoccupation with the war and a new wariness kept the white visitor at a distance – along with restrictions on his travel.

Weeks passed. Clapperton was ailing and his frustration rising. Worse was to come. Bello, who had been presented with swords, muskets and pistols from King George, received word that similar weapons were being taken by another member of Clapperton's party to his foe, al-Kanemi. This was true: the British diplomatic initiative to curb slaving had been extended to another powerful caliphate; but in Bello's eyes this, understandably, constituted an act of hostility.

In vain Clapperton protested: 'I am only one man. I cannot fight a nation.' He fell into a state of depression and, while awaiting Bello's permission to depart, the dysentery to which he had long been prone returned. In April 1827 he died, nursed to the last by his young servant, Richard Lander, who brought his journal back home, saw to its publication, then returned to Africa, following in Clapperton's footsteps.*

The mission to secure a Muslim–Christian pact on restricting the slave trade had failed. But Clapperton's observations on the conflicts between 'negroes and Arabs' that continued to supply captives to the Bight of Benin remain pertinent. Bello's followers once told him that, notwithstanding war between the caliphates, they encountered the

---

* Clapperton belonged to an indomitable succession of Scottish wanderers, men of humble origins who left their northern homeland for Africa, where they found purpose and common humanity. Having travelled in the wake of Mungo Park, he was followed by John Duncan and David Livingstone. All of them died in Africa. Clapperton's servant, Richard Lander, a Cornishman, having been similarly drawn, returned on further expeditions, first to trace the source of the Niger River, and subsequently to establish a trading mission. While travelling up the river, his canoe came under fire from native Africans. Lander was wounded and, although surviving to reach the coast, he too died there, aged 29.

greatest resistance from Yoruba speakers because 'they could not be made to believe in [the sultan's] doctrine'.

> They were confirmed Kaffers who, on the invasion, put all the Mahometans to death ... quite denying the plea that God had given to the faithful their lands and houses, and their wives and children to be slaves.[24]

What has been termed the Fulani jihad left an enduring Islamic influence in the regions that evolved into Nigeria, Niger and Burkina Faso. It also wrought devastation that shifted centres of power across West Africa. Those caught up in it included not only Yoruba and other ethnic groups – the Mina, Fon and Igbo – but Hausa Muslims. And the trauma it created led to forms of violent resistance that victims carried with them – on to slave vessels and across the Atlantic to Bahia.[25]

On 11 March the *Henriqueta* came to off Bahia after 102 days away, the shortest of her three passages. The number of enslaved Africans she landed set another marker. From both of her previous voyages, 504 survivors had come ashore. This time the number was 441.

William Pennell, his suspicions roused, turned sleuth once more. Within days he sent a despatch to London noting the large discrepancy in these numbers: 'On enquiring into the cause, I learnt that the slaves had risen on the passage and that many were killed.'[26] João dos Santos, as the *Henriqueta*'s master, was recorded admitting that eighteen had died in the violence.[27] Pennell was sceptical. 'Other reports make the number greater,' he reported. Who the consul turned to for the intelligence he mustered against Cerqueira Lima was not stated, but it was probably the *intendente da marinha*, or marine steward, who had taken his side on contentious matters before.

'Rebellions' on slavers were not uncommon. On British vessels, it has been estimated, resistance occurred on one in every eight to ten passages, although these were usually while captives were being embarked or before they set sail.[28] No similar picture can be compiled for voyages to Bahia, due to the destruction of records; and a cloud of secrecy cloaked this particular episode. But the evidence points to events on *Henriqueta's* third voyage as being hellish, even by usual standards. She never otherwise landed fewer than 504 survivors and once came in with as many as 544. Between 60 and 100 captives may therefore have died – if not in acts of sheer violent suppression, then through a combination of disease and bloodshed.

Stormy conditions could trigger trouble, seas swirling across decks, pouring through hatches onto those huddling in terror and effluent. Desperate hunger, too, starvation arising from delays caused by contrary winds. Even a small degree of liberty, allowing men up on deck, bringing reminders of freedom – light and air, along with the sight of weapons in their captors' hands. All these could set off a revolt.

But the fundamental spur came from brutal incarceration. The lower deck of a slaver could be likened to an oubliette – an underground dungeon of medieval times, accessible only from a single trapdoor above, into which victims were cast as an extreme form of punishment or torture to extract confession, and which inflicted psychological suffering.

Insurgencies ashore in Bahia may provide indicators. Men from the Yoruba region were familiar with warfare. Many, indeed, had been soldiers bearing spears and swords.[29] An early instance of rebellion in Bahia came in 1789 when a supervisor was killed and some 300 slaves fled into dense forest. Escape became common and runaways established their own communities across Brazil.[30]

The most significant revolutionary movements by the enslaved, however, were a series of rebellions in Bahia province between 1808 and 1835, mainly by Hausa Muslims yet with significant Yoruba participation. It started with an upheaval in the city, which was suppressed. An attack by a force of runaways on a town in the Recôncavo region in 1809 was also put down, with mass butchery. In the next five years, bloody uprisings were staged by plantation slaves and enslaved fishermen. Another was snuffed out in 1816. A decade later, in the year of the *Henriqueta* revolt, a runaway militia, armed with bows and arrows, pitchforks and hatchets, descended on the plantation district of Cabula, leading to a battle with state troops.[31] The peak of resistance was still to come.

Men habituated to violence turned to it instinctively at times of suffering, and whatever oppression captives had known in their homeland, nothing matched the trauma of mass confinement in the darkened sewer of *Henriqueta*'s bowels. Such shared pain, as has been seen, forged an attachment between victims that made them *malungo*, or shipmates.

Robert Walsh, who was aboard the frigate *North Star* when she captured a Bahia-bound slaver, the *Veloz*, wrote of coming on board to find captives between decks under hatchways but so confined that

> they sat between each other's legs and [were] stowed so close together that there was no possibility of lying down, or at all changing their position by night or day.[32]

Some 55 humans of the 562 embarked on the *Veloz* had already died and been cast overboard. In an especially atrocious case of overloading, the master saw total restriction of movement as a means to prevent revolt – as became clear when a naval officer ordered the captives to be allowed up for fresh air and water, and the master objected that he and his crew would be murdered. The officer insisted anyway. Walsh wrote:

> It is impossible to conceive the effect of this eruption – 517 fellow-creatures of all ages and sexes . . . all in a state of total nudity, scrambling out together to taste the luxury of a little fresh air and water. They came swarming up, like bees from the aperture of a hive, till the whole deck was crowded to suffocation . . . so that it was impossible to imagine where they could all have come from, or how they could have been stowed away.[33]

After two years in Brazil, Walsh believed it was only a matter of time before enslaved Africans, 'the most vigorous and athletic [people] it is possible to contemplate', rose up and overthrew 'the flabby [white] Brazilians who look the very personification of indolence and inactivity'.[34] He also noted that, although drawn from diverse groups, slaves shared 'a bond which connects them as firmly as if they belonged to the same race – that is a community of misery in the ships in which they are transported'.[35]

The outrage witnessed by Walsh occurred three years after the *Henriqueta* revolt. Of that episode, it can only be concluded that João dos Santos had deployed the usual sedatives – the reassurances of his Yoruba-speaking seamen, along with heavy doses of aguardente for male captives – without effect. A spirit of resistance tended to be contagious. It could be driven, moreover, by a belief in the transmigration of the soul; Africans embarked in the Bights were widely held to believe 'that as soon as death shall release them from the hands of their oppressors they shall be wafted back to their native plains'.[36]

Naked men, as described by Walsh, 'swarming up, like bees' to arm themselves with whatever objects came to hand – shackles, oddments of timber, pieces of rope – posed a fearsome vision. Just how many fell under the crew's guns and blows on *Henriqueta*, to be tossed overboard, must be left to Pennell's conclusion: 'A number greater than eighteen.' It may have been significantly greater.

There were other consequences. The numbers of captives embarked on the *Henriqueta*'s subsequent voyages rose sharply. Cerqueira Lima always had an eye for profit, but it is feasible to suggest that Dos Santos, having experienced one revolt, adopted the strategy seen on the *Veloz* – overloading to constrain movement and, thereby, potential rebellions.

The silence that was drawn over the incident had a diplomatic aspect. For more than a year, Brazil had been under pressure from Britain to abolish the trade, and giving any attention to the *Henriqueta* uprising would have been an embarrassment at a time when negotiations were delicately poised – particularly as Emperor Pedro had just arrived in Bahia from Rio. Whispers about the death toll went no further. Pennell reported to London that no legal investigation was to be held.[37]

The emperor had been at pains to assure his British interlocutors that he was sympathetic to abolition – as he was always bound to do, given that his country's independence had only been accepted by Portugal thanks to pressure from Britain. A sticking point in previous discussions had been a time frame. Now, visiting Bahia to hear from leaders in the most recalcitrant of his provinces, he was reminded forcefully of local opinion. Cerqueira Lima would have been to the fore among those described in a despatch as the 'certain merchants' who insisted to Dom Pedro they had nothing to do with the 'fraudulent practices' that British agents alleged were part of 'the illicit commerce in slaves'. Another leading trader, emboldened by Cerqueira Lima's victory, opened a legal claim against 'the British Nation' for damages from slave deaths on his brig, the *Segunda Rosália*, after her capture.*

On his return to Rio, the emperor changed tack, revoking his earlier agreement that Brazilian slavers would be prohibited from calling at São Tomé and Príncipe (or Princes) – the two equatorial islands in the Bight's vicinity used as sanctuaries from the Navy.[38]

That summer, Canning at the Foreign Office assigned a new envoy to Rio, again bearing the sweetener of a commercial trade pact to lever Dom Pedro's government into acceptance. Even as Robert Gordon was about to depart, the chargé d'affaires at Rio, Henry Chamberlain, warned that whatever Brazilian ministers declared publicly, privately they would 'encourage the continuation and extension of the trade'.[39]

Gordon came ashore at Rio on 13 October, offering a pact based on a two-year transition to total abolition. The Brazilians responded that

---

* The *Segunda Rosália* was seized by HMS *Atholl* with 258 captives loaded at Lagos. Placed under an inexperienced prize crew to sail for Sierra Leone, she became becalmed, ran short of provisions and lost seventy-two of those on board, mainly from starvation, before making port sixty-five days later. As a disaster attributable to incompetence, it was an embarrassment to the Navy. The legal claim failed.

six years would be necessary. Gordon's steeliness affronted the emperor, who called him an 'ill-mannered and obstinate Scot', but it proved effective. On 23 November, Dom Pedro signed a treaty declaring that three years from the point of ratification, it would be illegal for Brazilian subjects 'to be concerned in the carrying on of the African slave trade'. Violations would be treated as crimes of piracy.[40]

For the time being, captives could still be bought and transported from African ports south of the Equator. But the flaws of previous treaties with Portugal and Spain, which had confused navy officers as to whether they could legitimately seize unladen slavers – as when *Henriqueta* had been boarded by men from *Maidstone* – had been remedied. As one campaigner wrote:

> Under the defects, the slave dealer could bring his vessel fully equipped with slave-decks, water-casks and provisions; could land the merchandise required in his barter for slaves; could collect at his leisure his cargo of Negroes on the shore; could send out empty vessels to decoy any cruiser in the offing . . . so all the vigilance and zeal of the Preventative Squadron was effectually baffled by the cunning of the slave traders.[41]

In future, navy officers would not be constrained by such tactics. The squadron's commodore ordered that slaver vessels found north of the Equator could be taken, whether they were loaded or empty.[42]

Gordon was under no illusions as to Brazilians' view of the treaty, which had been ceded, he wrote to Canning, 'in opposition to the views and wishes of the whole Empire'. Britain, according to popular opinion, had imposed itself on a weaker power not out of humanity but to ruin Brazil's agricultural economy while British plantations in the Caribbean were still being worked by enslaved Africans.

Pennell went further, predicting the pact's failure. It would, he said, be treated by the authorities as 'a dictation of a superior authority from which it is lawful to escape, rather than as a compact which they are bound to enforce'.[43]

And yet, and yet – or so the consul appears to have mused. Visiting estates around Bahia had inspired in him hope as well as despair. On the one hand, he found an appalling disparity in the numbers of male to female slaves, in some cases seven to one – an acute social deformity arising from a vile system. On the other, here was a potential idyll – rich land capable of producing abundance in the right hands. His observations gave rise to a vision for the future spelled out in a personal letter to Canning of rare passion. What if, Pennell wrote, these same labourers, 'the finest race of men which Africa produces,' were encouraged to come to Bahia as free men and women – as immigrants?

The administration, he pointed out, had tried to lure white workers and settlers to Bahia, with little success because the climate and labour 'destroy the European constitution'. Africans, on the other hand, were able to perform heavy tasks – not only on plantations, but as the city's sedan-chair carriers, who, in being allowed to retain some of their daily earnings, showed what could be achieved 'by the stimulus of free labour'.

> Let the African know that on coming to this country he comes to a better climate where his free labour will procure for him an ample recompense with protection for his person and property and all the other advantages which a more civilized state of society holds out, and a disposition would be created in him to emigrate . . . I do not know any place more likely to benefit by freed labour than this province.[44]

Canning did not reply and may well have wondered as to his consul's soundness of mind: such matters were not in their hands and, moreover, discussion of free labour raised uncomfortable parallels with Britain's colonies in the West Indies. Yet just as Pennell had presumed to spell out his views to London, he had been pressing the same cause in his official and social rounds of Bahia.

The city's richest merchants – headed by Cerqueira Lima – were outraged by the abolition treaty and incredulous that anyone should dare to threaten their wealth and power. In his wrath, Cerqueira Lima pointed out his benevolence as a citizen, the public works he had bestowed upon the city; the São João theatre, for one, would not have been built without him. How were temples of culture to be funded in future if the state outlawed the means by which they were created? Ministers offered quiet reassurances that no such prospect was in sight. But the evidence shows that traders were unnerved. Cerqueira Lima and his ilk had already begun a race to fill their coffers while they could.

At the end of September, Pennell reported that twenty-five slavers had sailed from Bahia in the previous nine months.[45] This was a significant increase on recent years, and there was no doubt in his mind that all of them would be breaching the treaty already in existence: every master had availed himself of a licence to touch at São Tomé or Príncipe under the emperor's decree – a clear sign that they were sailing for the Bight.[46] Among them were three vessels owned by Cerqueira Lima, the *Henriqueta*, the *Carlota* and the *Bahia*. Pennell had a further scrap of intelligence for London. Cerqueira Lima had added to his fleet with the purchase of an English brig – the *Fanny* of Halifax.[47]

The *Henriqueta* departed on her fourth voyage on 24 June 1826. In subsequent weeks, Dos Santos resorted to a new stratagem for frustrating naval opponents. Vessels flying the US flag were exempt from inspection by the Royal Navy, and the *Henriqueta* was among seven Bahia slavers identified that year as having sailed under American colours.[48]

She returned to Bahia on 11 October with 524 surviving captives. Her largest cargo so far signalled what was to come.

CHAPTER 7

'THE MOST SANGUINE AVARICE'
October 1826–September 1827

Maria Graham retained vivid memories of Bahia long after her departure. Some were gratifying. As one of those intrepid British women
of her time who travelled widely and wrote perceptively, she recalled the
handsome upper town and its grand public buildings, and the warmth of
her host, William Pennell, who arranged a playful picnic in the country
'with a variety of adventures and accidents'. Above all, there was the natural
magnificence – noble views with 'the splendours of Brazilian animal and
vegetable life . . . the gaudy plumage of the birds, the brilliant hues of the
insects, the fragrance of the shrubs'. Then she would reflect that this was
also 'the principal slave port in Brazil', where although 'nature herself wears
an air of newness . . . the Europeans and their African slaves are too much
intruders ever to be in harmony with the scene'.[1]

Mrs Graham never mentioned José de Cerqueira Lima by name,
referring only to 'the greatest slave merchant here' – one who fell into
that group of white Brazilian males with 'a mean look' and a fondness
for the gaming table. 'None appear to have any education beyond
counting-house forms, and their whole time is, I believe, spent between
trade and gambling.'[2]

Whatever his gaming fortunes, Cerqueira Lima's riches had reached
a new high by the beginning of 1827. He owned eighteen vessels,

including his latest purchase, the English brig *Fanny*, and early that year at least four of them were either under way or about to sail for Africa. Along with his biggest earner, the *Henriqueta*, they were the *Independência*, the *Carlota* and the *Bahia*.

Even at the time, the traders' emphasis on purchasing young male captives who were unlikely to find wives and create families puzzled not just opponents of the trade, but also some supporters. Brazilian politicians, while debating the recent treaty with Britain, were united that year in declaring that because of 'the number of deaths among slaves being equal to, or greater than, the number of births', the country would still need a constant supply of African labour.[3] Despite the treaty's ratification in May, it was evident that when it finally came into force, in 1830, transporting African captives would continue illicitly, with government connivance.

In the opposition camp, William Pennell was baffled too. But the treaty had given him a clear programme and he had the bit between his teeth. Early in the new year, he toured a fishing settlement composed largely of *libertos*, freed Africans, and contrasted it with what he had seen on sugar plantations. Instead of those haplessly distorted societies with seven male slaves to every woman, the village of Santa Anna had a rounded population of 900 *libertos*, mainly families, all engaged in agriculture as well as fishing with their fellow inhabitants, some 50 whites and 50 slaves.

I visited several of their cabins and learnt the history of the inhabitants from their own mouths and I held afterwards conversations with the parish priest and some of the white inhabitants . . . I have derived a conviction that free labour is <u>eminently</u> favourable, not only to the increase of numbers but to the improvement of moral habits.

Within 25 years the population of Santa Anna has more than doubled . . . The negroes are mostly married and the priest reports most favourably of them. [He] assures me they are very attentive to the indigent . . . From the number of healthy children at the cabin doors, it is evident to the most cursory observer that the population of Santa Anna is in a very progressive state of augmentation.[4]

Pennell concluded his frontline despatch with high optimism: a school had just been opened by one of the white inhabitants; and, despite recent violence involving slaves at another fishing village, the whites at Santa Anna had 'the greatest confidence' in the 'peaceable disposition of the free negroes'.*

Pennell, perhaps unconsciously, reflects here a portrait of Afro-Brazilians more in line with the art of Johann Rugendas than with conventional abolitionist images. Rugendas, from Augsburg, joined an Austrian scientific expedition in 1822 and, as an early artist of note to visit Brazil, left drawings and watercolours that depict blacks, at times in communal spaces with whites, in a way that suggests a peasantry living in a harmonious environment, rather than plantation horrors. In this respect, there are echoes of Mrs Graham who shuddered at the sight of Bahia's slave market yet was taken aback by the relative freedom of slaves on the nearby island of Itaparica. Rugendas, who left Brazil in 1825, came down on the regime's side by declaring himself in favour of a gradual form of abolition.

Did Pennell ever wonder as to the comparative evils of Brazilian and British slavery? He had no experience of the Caribbean plantations and could only have heard reports about the appalling events of 1823 in Demerara-Essequibo, the British colony bordering Brazil. Yet he had met the travellers passing through Bahia who had visited both regions and usually considered the British system more exploitative, more ruthless. Another difference was manumission, the freedom obtainable by

---

* Pennell's report includes profiles of two of the freed African families. One, Manoel de Santa Anna, was aged about 60, married and with four living sons and a daughter, the youngest of about 19. He was too frail to continue fishing, but two sons were fishermen, one was a carpenter and one a soldier. None was married. His unmarried daughter had a son by another fisherman. Manoel rented an acre of land attached to his cabin where his wife attended to a small stock of fowls (FO 84/71/140).

slaves in Luso-Hispanic societies.[5] Among the illuminating stories of Bahia's *libertos* is that of Ana Marie dos Prazeres. In her will, drawn up in 1826, Ana Marie testified to having been transported in her youth from the Mina coast, a source of Gbe-speaking captives on the western edge of the Bight of Benin. How she earned enough to buy her freedom and proceed to a degree of wealth is not known: unmarried, she still bequeathed to her two children a house, money, clothing and household items. Most striking among her possessions, however, were gold and silver jewellery and tokens of Catholic piety, including a crucifix. A regular at Bahia's church for black worshippers, the Nossa Senhora do Rosário dos Pretos, she requested a Catholic burial and for a Mass to be said for her soul. So did many other *libertos*; Ana Marie dos Prazeres was rare for her wealth, but not for devoutness.[6]

There could be no remedy for slavery other than abolition, but for Pennell the most compelling priority was to alleviate the worst of an original, fundamental, atrocity. The voyage. The transportation of petrified humans in hellish conditions that traumatised all and killed many before futures of any kind could begin. Whatever the treaty's outcome, the Brazilian government seemed prepared at least to see those conditions reformed and, having campaigned before on this front, Pennell returned to the matter of admeasurement – the number of captives who might legally be loaded according to a vessel's capacity. On 27 March he wrote to Bahia's new president to remind him that the emperor's decree of 1824 continued to be openly violated.

A few days later, he met the president, Dom Nuno Eugênio de Lóssio e Seiblitz, and spoke in forthright terms: the illicit trade north of the line was spoken of so openly – it was 'too extensive and too notorious' – he must, surely, know what was going on. In reply, the president 'acquiesced in the truth of this', Pennell reported, 'but nothing passed to induce me to believe that any zealous measures will be taken for its suppression'.[7] He had, in effect, been waved away.

Matters were moving fast. In a mood equivalent to panic-buying, merchants had set up more voyages and were commissioning whatever vessels they could lay hands on. Pennell predicted the market was 'likely soon to be overstocked with slaves'.[8] And, as he anticipated too, returning slavers would be overloaded with utter pitilessness.

The first inkling of trouble came with the *Henriqueta*'s return on 26 March. She landed 523 living captives that day, just one short of her previous high mark, another satisfactory outcome for Cerqueira Lima. His exquisite Atlantic bird was bearing him fortune upon fortune – the *Henriqueta* now far the most profitable element of his fleet. However, João dos Santos also brought tidings disturbing to traders. He had sighted navy ships in a state of high activity in the Bight.

Further details emerged with the arrival of a schooner, the *Zeferina*, in April, with news that no fewer than ten vessels had been taken, among them Cerqueira Lima's *Independência*. Seven of her crew had been freed to return with the schooner, including the mate, António Pombo, who reported more grim news. On pointing out to his navy captors that the *Independência* had no captives aboard, they told him brusquely it made no difference; she was equipped for slaving and they now had orders to seize such vessels, with or without captives.[9]

Pennell raced off a despatch: 'This event has created great consternation. It is probable that all or nearly all the vessels which have recently sailed from here will also be captured.'[10]

He was not far wide of the mark. Between January and the end of April, the Navy had taken eighteen slavers, nine of them unladen. Fifteen were from Brazil, three belonging to Cerqueira Lima: the *Independência*, taken on 28 February, had been followed by *Carlota* on 14 March and *Bahia* on 3 April. None had captives aboard. The British and their Navy, clearly, had launched a new phase in what was seen as an economic war.

'The great gloom and dissatisfaction in this city' that Pennell cited in his next report was compounded by a blend of economic and political crises. Brazil's currency, the milreis, was on the slide. So was any remaining confidence in the Rio government: such was Bahia's sense of betrayal that Pennell likened it to a bomb 'which may explode at no great distant period and cause dismemberment of the Empire'.[11] For the time being, Cerqueira Lima's rage was focused on the British. Having recently won his first legal battle with the enemy, he announced he was going to launch a claim for further, even greater, damages.[12] At the same time, with prices at Bahia's slave market soaring, he turned to his flagship. João dos Santos had navigated her successfully on five hugely profitable voyages, had handled a rebellion at sea and seen off naval pursuit. From his every action, he evinced confidence. Together, he and his employer would continue to confound their persecutors. On 12 May, just six weeks after returning, *Henriqueta* sailed from Bahia again.[13]

Pennell went to work. He interviewed *Independência*'s mate António Pombo, extracting from him an admission that she had indeed been captured north of the Equator off Accra, and fired off a letter to the state president, pointing out that not only had Cerqueira Lima's schooner been in illegal waters, but so had the *Zeferina*, which brought back the crew along with 246 captives.[14]

The following day Pombo came to Pennell's office, saying he had made a mistake and spun an absurd story of having been on *Zeferina* when she loaded her captives 'at Malembo'. Pennell took up his pen to the president again: 'I shall not animadvert on what Mr Pombo calls his mistakes, but they appear to me to offer an additional motive for Investigation.'[15] A few days later, on 2 May, Pennell attended a hearing ordered by the president at which Pombo and four other sailors from *Independência* and *Zeferina* swore on the Bible to the truth of his later account.

Along with corruption, new depths of depravity were coming to light almost daily. A schooner, the *Nova Virgem*, arrived with 350 captives on board, 92 more than the number permitted even by the usual distorted standard of admeasurement. A still greater atrocity appeared in the bay within days. The brig *Tibério* had embarked no fewer than 654 Africans, of whom 134 had died.

In an increasingly sinister environment, the consul had one honourable and conscientious ally. The *intendente da marinha*, or marine steward, had been privately expressing his disquiet about such violations for years and – while imploring Pennell not to reveal him as a source – kept the consul informed.[16] He it was who disclosed these latest horrors. The usually sanguine Pennell was distraught.

As a junior figure in the diplomatic hierarchy, he had been recently warned by Canning against being intemperate and told not to 'enter into any controversy with the local authorities', so his approach was moderate.[17] In a letter to the vice president on 31 May he essayed a simple humanitarian approach, reminding him 'with deep regret' of previous cases of gross overloading, while pointing out that allowing the perpetrators to escape without penalty had only permitted further 'melancholy sacrifice of human victims'.[18] Privately, he paid a visit to his ally, the *intendente*, urging him 'not to allow the facts to be disfigured or smothered'.[19]

The vice president's reply amounted to a long-winded rebuff. Boiled down, it informed Pennell that 'no investigation can be granted on such public rumours'. As for the claim that virtually all Bahia's vessels were sailing north of the Equator, this was mistaken: their owners had 'affirmed . . . they were there for the purposes of carrying on a licit commerce in Gold and Ivory'.[20]

At this point Pennell started to seethe. He was used to official deceit. What he found hard to countenance, he told Canning, was

> that 134 human beings have lost their lives by violence or suffocation and that no individual or constituted authority appears to be called upon in instituting a legal investigation into so calamitous an event.[21]

Warming to his theme, he railed at the 'perverse blindness or diseased optics of the local authorities' over events 'which to the unjaundiced eye are as clear as the unclouded sun'.[22] The simple fact, he told Whitehall, was that Bahia's government believed even existing treaties could be legitimately ignored.[23]

With tensions and hostility on the rise, Pennell found himself more isolated and exposed to abuse than ever – and not just from local citizens. It often came from the English traders, who were happy enough to have seen abolition in Britain's colonies but fearful of the cost to them were it to be imposed on Brazil. They now made Pennell the butt of 'much sarcastic remark on my <u>philanthropic</u> exertions'.[24]

Brazilians' belief that their economy was being 'molested by the violence and wickedness of English cruisers' is not hard to fathom.[25] The anomalies of British policy were also obvious to campaigners at home, who, almost two decades since the Act of Abolition, had seen no law passed to liberate the 700,000 men, women and children still enslaved in the West Indies colonies. The crusading Thomas Fowell Buxton and others fulminated while, in Parliament, West Indies merchants and planters continued to hold sway through MPs loyal to their interests. George Canning, although piling pressure on Brazil to accept abolition, had been decidedly ambivalent in pushing through an Act for colonial emancipation. In April 1827, he became prime minister and was succeeded at the Foreign Office by the Earl of Dudley, who happened to own three plantations in Jamaica.[26] Lord William Douglas, one of the serving Lords Commissioners of the Admiralty – and therefore an overseer of the Preventative Squadron – had slaving possessions in Tobago.[27]

More widespread was a sense of apathy among the population as a whole about the conditions of slaves' lives, an attitude reflected in a popular verse:

I pity them greatly, but I must be mum,
For how could we do without sugar and rum?

Thanks to his contacts with local English traders, Cerqueira Lima knew that Britain's ruling class was protecting its interests and its population remained generally indifferent. He had allies too, for it appears a trader source told him about a cabal in Sierra Leone connected with the auction of captured slave vessels at Freetown who, for a fee, could manage the outcomes. Cerqueira Lima's go-between assured him they would see *Carlota* restored to her rightful owner.

Other factors reassured Bahia's kingpin he was winning. British seamen had signed on his vessels in the past, the *Carlota* certainly, and more may have followed. The desertions from British ships noted by Mrs Graham – of men lured by offers of windfall pay – had become increasingly common at Brazilian ports.

The large number of ships arriving from England makes the extent of participation by British hands impossible to calculate. But one of the most renowned vessels in maritime history may well have been caught up. In June of that year, a navy sloop sent to chart a passage around Cape Horn put in at Rio. She had lost six men to desertion on last anchoring here ten months previously, so Commander Pringle Stokes of the *Beagle* was on alert. It made no difference. Another nine hands were recorded as 'Run'. On her next return, a further three men deserted. As the *Beagle* had a complement of just thirty plain seamen, these were serious losses, and all eighteen featured in a 'List of Run and Disgraced Men' compiled for the Admiralty, including William Phillips, captain of the foretop, and James Grant, a bosun's mate.[28] It is not stretching speculation too far to suggest that some of the most senior hands on the *Beagle*'s first survey voyage went on to Brazilian slavers.

After months of frustration, the tide of Cerqueira Lima's fortunes turned. As so often, it was signalled by the appearance of the *Henriqueta*.

She came to anchor on 30 June after an absence of just forty-nine days, by far her swiftest voyage yet, carrying another 544 living humans, constituting her largest cargo. Word quickly spread around Bahia that Dos Santos had taken 'precautions' to avoid the navy cruisers – a reference to the latest subterfuge of sailing under US colours – and managed to embark this large number of captives in 'only a few days in the dangerous latitudes' – in other words, in the Bight.[29] For the master, and Cerqueira Lima, it represented a triumph.

Pennell had followed the *Henriqueta*'s every passage. From the attention he drew to her in his reports it was as if she had become emblematic of this conflict. Four days after her return he sent off another despatch, appending a full list 'of the unproved but undoubted illicit voyages of this vessel' since 1824:

> It is estimated that the profit on these six voyages amount to about Eighty Thousand Pounds and that her last voyage alone <u>more</u> than compensated for the loss of three vessels recently captured belonging to the same owner.[30]

Events were moving fast. A week later, Pennell was astonished to see one of the captured vessels coming into Bahia. The *Carlota*, it was soon reported, had been condemned by the Mixed Commission court at Freetown in Sierra Leone, where adjudication by British and Portuguese judges now took place, and auctioned off in the usual way. While Pennell was not fully in the picture, he did discover that she had been bought 'at a very low price' by an agent acting for Cerqueira Lima.[31] In fact, she had been picked up at auction for just £315 (the equivalent of about £18,000).[32]

More disturbing to Pennell was the news delivered by the *Carlota*'s master. The squadron at Sierra Leone had received orders that 'no further captures should be made of vessels unless with slaves actually on board'. Small wonder, he reported, 'this news has given great satisfaction to the illicit slave merchants here'.[33] The bitter irony that his new superior, the recipient of these despatches, was himself a slave-owner – the Earl of Dudley having just succeeded Canning at the Foreign Office – may well have been unknown to him.

Cerqueira Lima's triumphalist mood carried him straight back into another legal battle. Within days, Pennell, who now avoided 'all personal intercourse with this Gentleman', received notice of a new claim on the

British government – based on a list of seven vessels taken by the Navy. Three were owned by Cerqueira Lima, including the *Carlota* which he had just recouped, and four by fellow traders. They demanded £337,500 in damages, or about £19.3 million.[34] That makes for a striking comparison with the £315 he had paid to reclaim *Carlota*, plus the agent's sweetener.

The claim flabbergasted even Cerqueira Lima's fellow traders, as Pennell reported to Whitehall. The consul's response was a protest to the vice president over

> the enormous sum totally irreconcilable with the tonnage of the vessels in question which, if paid, would realize to the owners a profit beyond what the most sanguine avarice could have anticipated from their unmolested voyages.[35]

In vain, Pennell reminded the authorities of the emperor's one-time revulsion at the slavers' *sórdida avareza*. Cerqueira Lima had convinced the state administration: Bahia was being subjected to 'odious dictation' by Britain; he and his fellow traders, he averred, 'were treated like negroes'.[36]

His claim was dismissed by the Foreign Office as 'grossly and systematically fraudulent'.[37] Undeterred, Cerqueira Lima placed the case in the hands of his lawyer brother, Manoel, who perceived still greater benefits in the offing if more slaveship owners around the country could be co-opted in a campaign on the assurance of vast wealth at the bullies' expense. Over the next year, the Cerqueira Lima brothers compiled a landmark case against the British government founded on the Navy's seizure of thirty-three Brazilian slavers, twenty-four of them from Bahia. Cerqueira Lima was the most prominent of the owners, followed by Joaquim José de Oliveira, also a major trader. Another claimant was Manoel Cardozo dos Santos, brother of the *Henriqueta*'s master, who had profited sufficiently from serving in Cerqueira Lima's fleet to buy his own vessel, the *Hiroina*, also seized without captives on board.[38]

The total amount claimed by Manoel de Cerqueira Lima came to about £600,000, of which 20 per cent was on behalf of his brother. However, as Manoel was to receive 25 per cent of the sum sought by the other vessel owners, the Cerqueira Lima family stood to gain by almost £250,000.[39] These amounts represent the equivalent of roughly £34.4 million and £14.3 million today.

The case evolved into a prolonged legal saga. In one sharp rebuff in 1829, Brazil's ambassador to London was informed by the Foreign Office that the claim was based on 'fraudulent pretences'.[40] Yet nothing discouraged the Cerqueira Lima brothers in this prodigal venture. Five years later, despite further rejections at various levels, Manoel would take his claim to London.[41]

Abuses by Bahia's slavers touched new heights that year. Greed, as ever, was the driving force, but it combined now with the prospect of an impending treaty and recent capture of vessels on an unprecedented scale. Harrowing evidence passed on by the court at Freetown epitomised the sort of cases Pennell had been highlighting for years.

On 10 April, a week after the seizure of Cerqueira Lima's *Bahia*, a brig owned by one of his rivals was sighted farther down the coast in the Bight of Biafra. A party from the frigate *Maidstone* brought the *Creola* to and came on board to a sight overwhelming even for these hardened hands. At 85 tons, she was licensed to carry just 214 captives yet, as the court at Freetown found, 'the rapacity of the inhuman Master [had] induced him to cram nearly one hundred more into her'. The conditions in which many must have died on the voyage to Bahia were aggravated by the brig's poor sailing qualities – her 'craziness', according to one seafaring witness – and a slave-deck less than 3 feet in depth.[42] That the human toll was limited to nineteen before she reached Freetown was deemed a deliverance.

What the judges termed 'the studied barbarity' on *Creola*, along with the fact that her master, Manoel José Guimarães, and owner, Antônio de Albuquerque, were free to continue in their crimes without any threat of prosecution, was the cause of growing anger at Freetown.

While comparing degrees of inhumanity may be thought egregious, Dos Santos's seafaring ability and *Henriqueta*'s speed had preserved life at higher rates than often prevailed in transporting the enslaved. She had landed a total of 3,040 living Africans on her six voyages so far. The number of captives grew steadily across five of these, rising from 504 to 544 as Dos Santos's confidence and control of his vessel grew. Degrees of suffering are unquantifiable, but the indications are that there had been no significant toll from disease or overloading on those five voyages. The exception was her hellish third passage: the uprising on board from which only 441 survivors had emerged.

In the meantime, Pennell's predictions that returning slavers would be grossly overloaded and lead to a surplus in the market had proved correct. Notwithstanding the tonnage of vessels seized off Africa that year, he reported, Bahia was 'so much overstocked' that 1,311 captives had been transported onward to Rio.[43] It was no different there, the British clergyman Robert Walsh noted. 'There is such a glut of human flesh in the markets, that it has become an unprofitable drug.' As a result, he added with some satisfaction: 'Many speculators have been ruined by their unholy importations.'[44]

Age and stress were starting to tell on Pennell, now 62 and feeling the strain of local enmity. He enjoyed the care of one enduring friend, Dr Robert Dundas, superintendent of the British hospital, who had previously treated him for his gout and an agonising stomach ailment that had once threatened to carry him off. Although he had recovered, Pennell's condition towards the end of that fateful year was described by the doctor in a report to the Foreign Office as 'alarming'.[45]

What sustained him was conviction in the righteousness of the cause. And his final despatch of 1827 reported a breakthrough. After more than three years of having his petitions to Bahia's leaders over the imperial decree on admeasurement waved away, the new president had agreed it should be enforced – even though, he confided, it would 'cause much ill will towards him'. This, Pennell added, 'gives me the greater satisfaction as all my efforts with his predecessors were ineffectual, altho they have been <u>frequent</u> and <u>urgent</u>'.[46] No report was now complete without an observation on his arch-enemy. Pennell went on that he had visited his old ally, the *intendente da marinha*, who would be handling the reform. In the case 'of a vessel called the *Henriqueta*', it meant that instead of being licensed to carry up to 600 captives she would in future be limited to 490.

Pennell's service as a voluntary, self-funding diplomat had long been taken for granted. Quiet dedication had finally impressed the Foreign Office where it was decided that, health permitting, he would be made chargé d'affaires at Rio.

Bahia's overstocked slave market did not deter Cerqueira Lima. He had come up with a new strategy, linked seemingly to the rise of a new crop. Brazil had been slow to learn from Cuba's example but, in the years ahead, coffee would overtake sugar as its leading export. For now, plantations were popping up around Rio de Janeiro, and whereas sugar producers had long sought full-grown men to perform their labours, favour was being registered for youth.[47] It is also possible that the gender imbalance so glaring among the enslaved population was being reconsidered, along with a belated recognition that families created healthier communities.

Early in August, preparations were in hand for *Henriqueta*'s third voyage in a year. Dos Santos's orders were to sail for Lagos and there fill her lower deck in a way that stretched her capacity to new limits. There were two further stipulations. He was to acquire a significant proportion of captive boys and girls.[48] And they were to be taken not to Bahia, but to Rio.[49]

She sailed on 12 August with a crew of familiars. Dos Santos's trio of senior men included a Lisbon-born pilot Miguel Luis Vianna. There too was Cerqueira Lima's appointed healer, the former slave Sangrador Naraizo.[50] The hands – twenty of them Portuguese, twelve African – went to their stations almost by instinct. Ropes were hauled, canvas rose and flared. The *Henriqueta* picked up, cleared the bay and raced away into the Atlantic.

So she ran, as swiftly as ever, north across the Equator in six days, on to 4° 39' N and 2° 16' E by the eighteenth day, at which point she had covered 2,521 nautical miles.[51] Here topsails were furled and she slowed until coming to off Lagos on 2 September.

Negotiations passed with unparalleled smoothness. Tobacco and aguardente were offloaded within a day, and hours later were being replaced with humans. Whereas she had once anchored for months, in two days *Henriqueta*'s lower deck was more tightly packed than for any previous voyage. In addition to crew, her 90-foot length and 27-foot breadth contained 569 captives. More than a third of them were children. All were branded.

The 85 boys were aged 16 or under, the youngest a trio of 8-year-olds just over 4 feet tall named as Ochah, Chuokee and Lannosoo, with their respective brand marks described as 'face and left breast', 'right shoulder' and 'cheek and back'.[52]

At least four of the women – Oloke, Olojoe, Ahgotay and Morai – came aboard feeding babies and with brands 'all over'. Their babies were exempt from branding, but the 111 girls aged 14 or under were not. Twelve were aged just 8, including Loowo – 'cheeks and left breast' – and Mammesuloo – 'left buttocks'.[53]

On 5 September orders came to make sail. Again, the pieces moved slickly into place and by midnight a fresh south-easterly breeze had carried *Henriqueta* 80 miles towards the Equator and safety. The moon cast an illuminating beam on the sea when, soon after midnight, a lookout brought Dos Santos word of a strange sail.

He came up to see a large man-of-war to windward. She could only be a British frigate. There was no cause for alarm. His sweet *Henriqueta* had outrun one of these blundering hulks before, and she would do so again. With the gleam in his eye of a player at Bahia's gaming tables, Dos Santos set a course to cross the frigate's bow.

INTERLUDE

A bolition and emancipation: the two words tend to be closely associated in accounts of the campaign against slavery; yet in history they were much distanced. By 1827, twenty years had passed since the Act prohibiting the trade of slaves in the British Empire, but the influence in Parliament of West Indies plantation owners kept at bay any prospect of their workers' liberty. The endeavours of the Anti-Slavery Society came up against political forces, economics and, moreover, insistent claims that even talk of emancipation was dangerous. Just look at Demerara, said the naysayers.

The territory of Demerara, running along the northern coast of South America, had been founded by the Dutch in the 1740s and seized by the French before being taken by Britain in 1814 and absorbed into a regional empire cultivated for sugar by slaves. Demerara's crisp, golden produce had a special allure and its rich soil was bountiful. Then, in August 1823, stirrings among the enslaved led to uprisings that culminated in a confrontation between the military and protesters demanding that they be granted three days' rest in a week and the right to attend church on Sundays. They were fired upon, with the loss of between 100 and 150 lives. Subsequent trials led to ten 'rebels' being hanged, decapitated and their heads displayed on spikes.[1]

In the aftermath, it emerged the protesters had been roused by word that English leaders wanted to free all slaves but were being thwarted by the plantation owners. Missionaries were blamed for spreading news of Thomas Fowell Buxton's speech to Parliament in May declaring slavery 'repugnant' and calling for its gradual abolition 'throughout the British colonies'.

The central figure of the day at Westminster was George Canning. As a foreign secretary during the war with France, who was seen as the most brilliant statesman of his time, Canning had arguably an even more difficult line to walk in a time of peace. A shifting world order involved renewed dealings with old foes and allies, while a growing clamour for reform raised huge challenges at home. The question of emancipation, for example, had to address not only enslaved Africans but also legal discrimination against Catholics. While he continued to place pressure for abolition on Brazil and Spain – both France and the United States stayed well beyond reach for diplomatic reasons – Canning drafted orders for 'amelioration' of the conditions for slaves in the British West Indies. Any meaningful implementation, however, was opposed by the planters' lobby, who seemed to believe that a lighter hand on those they enslaved would be as incendiary as debating emancipation.

In 1826 Buxton went back into battle in the Commons, brandishing an anti-slavery petition signed by 72,000 Londoners, supposedly the largest yet laid before the House. Canning expressed regret that colonial assemblies had not made more progress in introducing amelioration but said they must be allowed another year. Buxton and his fellow abolitionists like Zachary Macaulay fumed. In private, Canning expressed support for reform. In his actions, he remained opposed.

Any real progress was bound to be prolonged in an era prior to clearly defined party power, and when many establishment figures were unwilling to acknowledge the wickedness of enslavement, let alone accept the financial burden of emancipation. Canning was seen as a liberal capable of drawing together Whigs and those Tories who had split from their reactionary 'Ultra' faction. Yet his own true convictions were indiscernible. One of his closest friends was Charles Ellis, head of the London Society of West India Planters and Merchants.[2]

The year of 1827 was a watershed. Barely had Canning taken office as prime minister than the strain of work led to his death, ushering in further factionalism, including a lurch back to High Toryism under the Duke of Wellington, who subscribed to the view that talk of emancipation had inflamed 'the temper . . . of the negroes' and declared: 'We must not plunder the proprietors in the West Indies in order to acquire for ourselves a little popularity in England.'[3] The victor of Waterloo was a prime minister to make abolitionists quake. Planters and their supporters raised bumpers.

Crisis in the emancipation movement had meanwhile been underlined when Buxton was seized by 'a fit of apoplexy' and collapsed. What appeared the imminent death of their most eloquent spokesman – the prime abolitionist, William Wilberforce, had already left Parliament for health reasons – left campaigners in 'a season of almost complete inaction'.[4]

Deploying the Royal Navy to suppress the trade had proved, from the outset, similarly divisive. Although it had the potential to serve the planters' interests – by reducing the supply of labour to rival producers – the operation was costly and attracted continual bouts of political hostility. The Admiralty, it has been suggested, had only agreed to send vessels to West Africa in the first place in 1807 in order to protect other forms of British trade and to deter French incursion in the region.[5] Their lordships did then still have a war to contend with, but even after the peace, and the creation in 1819 of a permanent squadron, their reluctance to assign sufficient or appropriate vessels to the task was obvious. If anyone had suspected that it would take another fifty years for its objective to be attained – the end of human trafficking from West Africa – resistance to the navy operation would have been even fiercer.

Leaving aside the still-evolving political climate in what has been termed the Age of Reform, the campaign was undermined by one persistent flaw – the failure of the naval hierarchy to recognise that this was a quite different kind of war at sea from the one still trumpeted by the nation. The Royal Navy, it was self-evident, had no rivals. It had become, like the monarchy, an institution of state subject to veneration. Faith dictated there should be no tinkering with the fusion of manpower and technology that had obtained this global supremacy.

Nowhere was the obstinacy of that credo more evident than in ship design. While officers and men continued largely to serve with the skill and dutifulness that had been crucial in the past, they were constantly let down by ships and vessels – from frigates to sloops and brigs – that were inferior to the quarry they challenged. Worse, the lessons at hand to be learned from failure were resolutely ignored.

What is so striking about this perversity, as will be seen, was that it flew in the face not only of the objective sought by the State and the Admiralty, but also of a matter both saw as quite as important as ending slavery – that of simple financial logic. The fact was, a fast-sailing slaver was to be bought for a fraction of the cost of building one of the cumbersome brigs turned out by England's shipyards.

In September 1827 one crisis at least in the war against slavery had passed. After weeks when friends and supporters despaired of his life, Thomas Buxton was back from the dead. The 'season of almost complete inaction' was over.

And thousands of miles to the south, *Henriqueta* set sail from Lagos on her seventh homeward voyage, bearing 569 captive men, women and children.

Part II
BLACK JOKE

CHAPTER 8

COMMODORE COLLIER'S PURCHASE
September–December 1827

The commodore was roused from his cabin just before 2am. A lookout had spotted a strange sail under the bright night sky and here in the Bight of Benin, some 80 nautical miles due south of Lagos, that signalled the likelihood of a departing slaver. Francis Collier came smartly up to the *Sybille*'s quarterdeck where the officer of the watch had already made all sail in pursuit of the dark shadow gliding distantly on the lee bow.

Collier had no illusions about the likelihood of success. The raked masts and arched sail visible above the horizon reflected a quarry familiar enough, even to an officer who had taken command of the Royal Navy's Preventative Squadron only four months previously, and that low, sleek outline signified a vessel too fleet to be within the grasp of a 44-gun frigate nearing the end of her lifetime. Barring intervention by the elements or fate, the chase – a brig as she was discerned to be – would hold to her south-westerly course and, with the wind in her favour, soon sweep from sight.

No anticipation of failure was evident from *Sybille*'s activity. For weeks men had been kept at their stations by a commander renowned for taut discipline – tacking and shortening sail as they moved up the Gulf of Guinea, firing the guns, and wielding cutlasses and small arms in boarding exercises – along with taking the occasional flogging; eleven men had felt the cat on their backs in the past three months.[1] Now they went gamely about their tasks, spreading canvas and hauling rope, while also observing that the brig, being on the lee bow, had the further advantage of sea room to the west. Though *Sybille* was set to the north-west under a full press of sail in a race to interception, the brig was surely bound to stay on her course and show them a clean pair of heels.

What followed was never set down in detail: Collier sent a report to the Admiralty typically sparing in describing his own deeds, and *Sybille's* log is similarly sparse. But an hour into the chase her quarry tacked to the south-east in a bold – or possibly derisive – shift to get to windward of *Sybille*. In doing so, João Cardozo dos Santos, the *Henriqueta's* master, had anticipated that with the wind at their back she could race across the bow of another clumsy pursuer before he set a new course, south for the Equator. Experience of leaving navy frigates in *Henriqueta's* wake had inflated his confidence to the point of wild misjudgement.[2]

At 4am, some two hours after the sighting and just as the brig crossed her bow, *Sybille's* long 12-pounders flamed out of the darkness from the forecastle. In a moment, *Henriqueta's* rigging was shredded. She slowed, all the attributes that gave her advantage swept away, her sails in tatters, her beauty lost. At 5.40 the frigate drew near and hove to beside her. Boarders came up the side wielding guns and swords. They met no resistance.

The lieutenant leading the boarding party approached her master. Both were young, William Turner aged 25, João dos Santos a year his junior. But while Dos Santos was a case-hardened veteran sailing with his seventh and largest load of captives yet, Turner found himself assailed by the stench of a slaver for the first time. An exchange between them established the facts: the brig was the *Henriqueta* of Bahia with 569 humans caged below; Dos Santos produced his Malembo passport but on being challenged did not dispute that he had just sailed from Lagos.

Dos Santos and his company were taken on to *Sybille* as prisoners. A prize crew took their place led by Frederick Mather, a master's mate, aged 34, and an unusual figure in the Royal Navy, having risen from the lower deck to pass his lieutenant's exam. Still awaiting promotion, but with none of the family connections common to the officer class, he now faced the challenge of sailing *Henriqueta* and all those in her to Freetown. Going below to examine conditions, he was presented with a harrowing insight into Dos Santos's method of preserving order: among the press of bodies reeking in the dark, many of the males lay in a motionless stupor; they had been sedated with aguardente. Eight were so drunk they died.[3]

As night fell that 6 September, Collier savoured his first prize since taking command at Sierra Leone in May. His appointment reflected an Admiralty desire to inject vigour into the squadron and the significance of this capture would assure their lordships of their prescience. The *Henriqueta* was notorious at Freetown, an object of beauty shrouded in evil, her escapes the talk of the squadron, but she had also won a dark renown in London thanks to William Pennell's despatches.

Collier's reserved modesty and strict disciplinary style apart, he had a warm regard for his young officers and among *Sybille*'s lieutenants Turner and Henry Downes would have joined him over a bumper in the stern cabin, there to reflect on the doctrines of their faith. On this occasion it was gunnery, that special tenet of Britain's naval supremacy, that had won the day.

At some point, João dos Santos was summoned to the table. Although mortified at the loss of his fortune-maker, he had no cause for undue alarm. His blue-uniformed interrogators were cool yet polite and under prevailing treaties between Britain and Brazil he faced neither detention nor punishment. Sooner or later he would reach home where he had accumulated enough money to buy his own brig. He was, after all, only 24, and this misfortune might yet open the way to riches rivalling those of his mentor Cerqueira Lima.

For three days the frigate and her prize remained in company, *Sybille* escorting *Henriqueta* while repairs were made to her sails and rigging. They worked south-by-south-east towards Princes Island where fresh provisions could be obtained and the brig set on her way to Freetown. Rain and cloudy weather followed them but there was no sign of the tornados encountered in these waters, just a modest breeze, when the island was sighted on 9 September.[4]

Here *Henriqueta*'s crew were transferred to the sloop *Esk* along with orders that they be sent on any suitable Brazil-bound vessel to be encountered. This was a standard procedure that rid naval officers of responsibility for their prisoners yet led to bizarre incongruities. The *Henriqueta* is a case in point: *Esk*'s log suggests that Dos Santos and his company were shifted into a pair of Brazilian vessels found near Lagos late in September, which were hardly likely to be innocent traders. So it proved: while Dos Santos seized the chance for a homeward passage to Bahia, at least one of his hands, Augustine José, was discovered on another slaver captured only a month later, having never returned to Brazil.[5]

The next day extra provisions came across to *Henriqueta* from *Sybille* before they parted – the frigate to resume cruising off Lagos, *Henriqueta* to start due west down the Gulf of Guinea. This voyage of roughly 1,200 nautical miles, although straightforward enough on a chart, was a severe test for the man in charge of a vessel beating to windward against a strong easterly current – all the while grossly laden with humans in need of fresh air and sustenance.

Frederick Mather faced, moreover, a new test of his seafaring skills. He had not just to keep these hundreds of tormented souls alive but, for all their sakes, to control them. Of these voyages to Freetown one observer wrote:

> The slaves, who have suffered comparatively little during the short time they have been in possession of the slave-captain, find their wretchedness daily increasing [and] are apt to attribute it to their new possessors, the English . . . The appalling misery is aggravated by a long working to windward, by intense heat and the state of the slave decks.[6]

The captives had now somehow to be reassured that what awaited was not death or further suffering but a form of freedom.

The vessel coming to anchor off Freetown on 27 September was described by one there that day as 'the *Henri Quatre* [sic] a beautiful brig . . . from the Bight of Benin with 548 slaves'. Intrigued, James Holman went aboard to find 'a multitude of slaves crowd[ing] her deck in a state of nudity'. Holman, a hardy, indefatigable traveller, had encountered many curiosities and horrors while wandering the world yet inspecting a slave vessel left an indelible mark, 'the spectacle humiliating, the immediate effect on the olfactory nerves oppressive'.

> The pressure of this dense mass of human beings was suffocating, the crowd so great that one poor slave who had fallen overboard in the night on the voyage was never missed until the following morning.[7]

There too was 'the officer who had charge of the vessel, confined to a small space in the after-part of the deck near the tiller'. Frederick Mather's lengthy apprenticeship on the lower deck had, it transpired, served them all as well as could have been hoped. Voyages from Lagos to Freetown were notoriously awkward, taking up to thirty-five days to cover those 1,200 nautical miles.[8] Mather had guided *Henriqueta* to safety in twenty-three days by seafaring skill and human management – the unshackled captives crowding her upper deck signifying an allowance of freedom on a passage that ended with a relatively high survival rate. Aware of his own peril, Mather had signed a will to benefit 'my beloved mother Mrs Elizabeth Mather now residing at Castle Gate, Nottingham'. For the time being, he had endured.

In the normal course of events, the captives would have remained on board for the judicial process to be completed by the court of Mixed Commission at Freetown. These hearings, established by treaty and overseen by adjudicators from Britain and Brazil, were usually a formality, evidence of slave-trading being in most cases incontrovert-ible. But only then could captives be officially freed and the vessel bearing them condemned to be put up for auction.

On *Henriqueta*, however, the decks were in a deadly state. A surgeon coming on board for an inspection found the captives needed imme-diate disembarkation. Two died before they could be moved, four more on coming ashore. The 542 survivors were delivered to the care of the colony's Liberated African Department.[9]

An official report, in highlighting that the brig's owner was 'the noted Slave Dealer Joze Cerqueira Lima of Bahia', praised Mather implicitly for 'a good passage of twenty-three days during which, notwithstanding the crowded state of the slaves, only twelve of the unfortunate beings died a natural death'.[10] The case illustrated never-theless the difficulties of beating to windward down the Gulf of Guinea. *Henriqueta*'s twenty-three-day voyage to Freetown may be compared with the twenty-eight days she took to cover more than twice that distance in crossing the Atlantic to Bahia. And the overall toll was higher than twelve. In all, with the eight who died from alcohol poisoning and one lost overboard, twenty-seven had perished. Far more terrible outcomes were common: a few months later, another captured brig, *Clementina*, lost 156 of 271 men, women and children while sailing to Freetown.

The scene that greeted the survivors coming ashore would have seemed strangely familiar. This was, after all, Africa, with a shoreline laced by rivers and swampy inlets and beyond it a blazing green space rising into a hill shaped like a crouching lion which had inspired Iberian mariners to call the peninsula Sierra Leone. Creeks, mangroves and mosquitoes affirmed where they were while other black figures bustled about the beach and the settlement beyond. Yet a strange aspect was beheld there as well – large, towered and spired structures from another world: among Freetown's features were St George's church and the clocked town hall.[11]

Dazed, the men, women and children, all 542 of them, were taken to a dusty red compound near the waterfront called the King's Yard, one large building surrounded by sheds, which may have served its purpose in the colony's early days, but with facilities 'not sufficient for more than 150' inhabitants (as ministers in London were informed) was in dire need of improvement.[12] Here the new arrivals were fed, given basic clothing and shown how to make what comfort they could in these surroundings.

Conditions at the compound made it imperative that their fate be resolved promptly, and a week later, on 6 October, the court of Mixed Commission found *Henriqueta* had been legally captured and declared 'the said Natives of Africa to be emancipated, and to be employed as servants or free labourers'.[13] By then one of the men and three older boys had decided to make their own way elsewhere and escaped the yard.[14] The remainder were lined up in their hundreds with interpreters to have names, ages, height and brand marks recorded in meticulous detail.

Among the eighty-one women were the young mothers, Aghotay, aged 28 and 5 feet 4 inches, with her six-month-old baby, and three others with children at their breasts, Oloke, Olojoe and Morai. There too were 111 girls, from 8-year-olds like Lowoo to the 14-year-old Kallehtoa. Next came eighty-five boys – among them Ochah, aged 8, with cuts on his face and left breast, and Woroo, all of 16 years. They were followed by the 261 surviving males, the tallest of them Cholay, at 5 feet 10 inches. Pages of these details, set down in a copperplate hand, would be sent back to London, where it is hard to imagine they received a second glance.[15]

Quite what the term 'emancipation' presaged for *Henriqueta*'s survivors was always going to be uncertain. The territory of Sierra Leone purchased by British abolitionists forty years earlier as the world's first settlement for freed slaves was a noble endeavour that had never quite gone to plan. Grand ambition, as ever in colonial ventures, was matched by neither funding nor resources, let alone comprehension at

Westminster of the challenges at hand. What has been defined as a laterite peninsula 25 miles long and 10 miles wide was set to join the largest communities of Africans forcibly displaced by the Atlantic trade, exceeded only by Rio, Bahia, Havana and Pernambuco.[16]

Colonial administrators were few in number and faced the additional trial of persevering against weather, disease and regional conflict, all of which exacted a fearful toll. Governors turned over at such a rate – it was said by the wit and Anglican clergyman Sydney Smith – that there were always two, the one who had just arrived and the one who was just departing. Along with those who retreated in dread or despair, a significant number died from fever. One, Charles MacCarthy, was killed and beheaded in a war with the slave-trading Ashanti kingdom.

Like so much of Britain's colonial past, the humanitarian aspects of Sierra Leone's founding and administration have been subject to recent reassessment. One detailed study has concluded: 'The antislavery humanitarianism of the elite abolitionists was an ideology incubated in the context of aristocratic privilege and evangelical moral panic, combined with a deeply held belief in the moral necessity of hard work.'[17] The same values, it could be added, prevailed largely among the ruling class towards Britain's commoners. Treatment of freed Africans may be seen in the context of a criminal code that made hanging routine and saw transportation to the far side of the world as a fitting punishment for loose women and juvenile thieves.

Freetown, located at the tip of the peninsula, blended structures of Georgian design with a corner of Africa described by one newcomer as 'houses and huts of every shape, of every material, surrounded by gardens crowded with orange and lime trees . . . the market a moving mass of screaming, quarrelling and bartering people . . . pigs, cows and goats roaming the streets'. From here, the travelling cleric Harrison Rankin looked back on a hinterland of evergreen hills as 'groups of maidens descended from the mountain paths bearing on the head calabashes with red and black pines, bananas, watermelons, mangoes'.[18]

The departure of a governor from Freetown. The frequency of such events disrupted administration.

The first black settlers in what was called 'the Province of Freedom' were a few hundred formerly enslaved black Britons transported from London in 1787 with the support of the abolitionist movement. They were followed by some 1,100 former American slaves who had either supported the British or been freed from plantations during the War of Independence and were initially taken to the colony of Nova Scotia before being resettled in Freetown from 1792, where they continued to be known as the Nova Scotians. A third community were the Maroons, black families who had successfully broken away from colonial rule in Jamaica, establishing their own settlements until a conflict in 1796 brought retribution: although promised a pardon on surrendering, they were banished – also to icy Nova Scotia; there they remained until the majority accepted an offer of resettlement at Freetown in 1800. The two main early settler groups, the Nova Scotians and the Maroons, retained distinct identities and, numbering some 2,000 in all, occupied their own quarters of the town.

Seminal change came with the Act of Abolition and deployment of the Royal Navy. By 1822 almost 8,000 Africans had been landed from captured slaveships. Five years later, at the time of *Henriqueta*'s arrival, their number had more than doubled, to some 16,575.[19] Known as 'recaptives', they occupied villages scattered behind the town, named symbolically after the colony's aspirations. Regent took pride of place, naturally, with Wilberforce and Wellington on either side at an appropriate distance from one another. Gloucester and Leicester were on nodding terms, while Hastings was duly positioned to the south. Each village had a white manager, sometimes a missionary, responsible for order and education.

Most newly arrived males were given an English name, along with a few tools, the means to cook, help to build a hut and a small plot. They also received a daily allowance of 3d, or thruppence, for six months before being left to their own devices.[20] Rankin observed that as plots were no more than half a rood – one-eighth of an acre – they 'suffice for subsistence but preclude extensive agriculture'.[21] Apprenticeships and labouring offered alternatives and could produce wildly varying outcomes, ranging from virtual slavery to the rise of private enterprise.

The fate of women could be random too. A handful emerged as stand-out figures, notably the formidable Betsy Carew. A Hausa woman rescued from an unknown slaver, she married a Maroon butcher and transformed their joint fortunes by selling meat to the Army. 'Possessing no resources but her own industry and talent,' Rankin wrote, 'this remarkable woman has risen to opulence, owning land and property, and having a considerable interest in shipping.'[22] For the great majority of women, marriage or domestic service was the likely outcome.

Finance was fundamental, however, and dealing with the *Henriqueta* case, it was reported to Whitehall, would require 'an increase in our expenditure to the amount of about £500' on top of resources already strained by the surge in freed captives.[23] Shortly before his death in 1826, Charles Turner, one of the four men to serve as governor that year, reported that 'with no one to teach them agriculture' the land was not yielding enough to feed a rising population.

Bringing together men, women and children from diverse ethnic groups, who shared no common language and were living up to 1,500 miles from their homelands, posed another challenge. Yoruba speakers made up the majority of freed captives and were more readily able to find a sense of identity. On being brought to the village of Bathurst, one recalled:

> Here we had the pleasure of meeting many of our country people, but none were known before. They assured us of our liberty and freedom; and we very soon believed them.[24]

But just a year earlier, the manager of Regent village reported that a number of inhabitants had 'forsaken their houses and lots' to 'separate into their different tribes' and 'reside in a state of wilderness and uncontrol'.[25] Over the years, many of those said to have thus 'absconded' fell back into the hands of slave traders operating along the colony's borders, often through the agency of fellow recaptives. 'Most of these inhuman villains are manumitted slaves themselves,' Turner wrote, 'in several instances relations or countrymen of their unfortunate victims.'[26]

What happened next to the men, women and children from *Henriqueta* lay in the hands of Thomas Cole, long-serving head of the Liberated African Department, and in that respect at least they appear to have been fortunate. Over a decade of assigning futures to thousands of confused, traumatised humans, Cole had handled his overwhelming duties while retaining a care for individual cases, from a woman 'found insane wandering about in a most destitute state', to the man 'of miserable and deformed appearance' who came pleading to his door. These were just two among the many he had declared 'invalids' entitled to a 2d daily support allowance.[27]

The great majority of *Henriqueta*'s male recaptives were duly sent to cultivate the villages – mainly Regent, Waterloo and Wellington. Boys went with them too, either to schools or to be indentured as apprentices. But twenty-six of the men went to the military, either the Royal African Corps or the 2nd West Indies Regiment.[28] The latter were not the first rescued Africans to be sent as soldiers to the Caribbean and would be far from the last.

Single women arriving at Regent and Hastings came with letters from Cole to village managers that they should receive the allowance of 3d a day until they could be married 'to men of their own nation, taking care that the men have suitable dwellings and are capable of maintaining a wife'.[29] Records show that in the months ahead marriages were made with farmers, labourers, soldiers and a fisherman.[30]

Aghotay and her baby, along with the three other feeding mothers, were sent to Wellington with the same 3d allowance. As for the girls, the youngest, such as 8-year-old Lowoo, were entrusted to the care of Waterloo's women. Thirty of the older girls went to Mrs Davey's mission school at Bathurst, the nursery of a famous Freetown citizen, one Samuel Crowther. Those considered above school age were to be indentured to 'respectable inhabitants', with an admonition that

> Great care must be observed that the character of the master or mistress for steadfastness and industry is such as to insure [sic] the apprentice's proper treatment. In the meantime children are to be placed in the schools.

Among those registered as masters and mistresses of *Henriqueta*'s apprentices were David Garrick and Betsy George – recaptives themselves.[31]

What became of them remains a mystery. But among those landed that year was a Yoruba-speaking youth from an unnamed Brazilian brig which had left Lagos – the same port as *Henriqueta* – to be intercepted by an unnamed navy vessel. Years later he began to set down a narrative relating how, on landing at Freetown, he had been named Joseph Wright and sent to a Methodist school at York village. Joseph was candid about his initial scepticism of the gospel: 'I liked to hear reading [but] I did not embrace or believe from my heart when first I read the word of God.'[32] In 1834, doubts set aside, he embraced the faith, and went on to train in England as a missionary himself. To suggest that the Rev. Joseph Wright, the first native African ordained in the Wesleyan Church of Sierra Leone, had been on *Henriqueta* may be fanciful; but it is not impossible.[33]

Missionaries were zealous in spreading the word at Sierra Leone, and their evangelising won other significant converts that year.

The boy Ajayi, it may be recalled, had been among 187 souls rescued by the *Myrmidon* off Lagos in 1822. His reception at Freetown was not painless. Having been taken to Bathurst, Ajayi and other recaptives were told they had to testify against their slaveship master. The business of the Mixed Commission court was, naturally, a mystery to Ajayi and his fellows who refused to have any part of it until 'we were compelled to go by being whipped'.[34] Yet within months he had adapted to his new life, learning to read and being singled out for his acute intelligence. Baptised Samuel Crowther, he sailed to England with his mentor at Bathurst, Thomas Davey, and for some months attended Islington's parish school.

By the time of *Henriqueta*'s arrival, Samuel Crowther was back at Freetown, the first student to be enrolled at the new teacher-training college of the Church Missionary Society (CMS), where he shone as a linguist. Through the Daveys he met a young woman recaptive, Asano, rescued by HMS *Bann* and renamed Susan Thompson. They married and flourished, he as a teacher and Anglican minister, she as a school-mistress, and together as the parents of three children. 'The day of my captivity,' he reflected, 'was to me a blessed day.'[35]

The Crowthers became among Freetown's most influential citizens and were bound to have encountered the thirty girls from *Henriqueta* sent to their old school. But Samuel and Susan did not stop there. In time, they would return on a mission to the land where they had been enslaved.*

The *Henriqueta's* destiny seems, in retrospect, to have been obvious. Capturing a vessel renowned for manoeuvrability and speed presented Collier with a rare chance to turn those gifts to good use in a campaign impeded by his larger, slower and clumsier ships – and even those insufficient in number. Here was a heaven-sent opportunity to set a thief to catch a thief, as the old proverb had it.

Why the Admiralty should have opposed this perfectly logical strategy was a mystery attributable perhaps to a blend of naval chauvinism and deep suspicion of innovation. As early as 1810, Commodore Edward Columbine had used a captured schooner as a tender, supplying provisions to the squadron's ships.[36] But from the outset their lordships were adamant that prizes – as condemned vessels were known – could not be used in chase and action. This was despite a tradition of the Navy putting indisputably superior French frigates to such a service – Collier's *Sybille*, captured in 1794, being just one example.

The agent of change was Collier's predecessor, Charles Bullen. He it was who took the *Hoop*, an American-made schooner flying Dutch colours in 1826, bought her at auction out of his own pocket and renamed her *Hope*. Stern orders came from the Admiralty that while she might be used as a tender, 'no vessel other than one of His Majesty's Ships [can] act in the search or capture' of slavers.[37] Bullen responded that she was simply to provide 'a shelter and comfort [for] officers and crews'.[38] In reality, *Hope* validated another old proverb, that old poachers make the best gamekeepers. She freed more than 850 captives in just seven months. By comparison, HMS *Bann*, most renowned of the

* Ordained a minister in London in 1843, Samuel Crowther went on to join a CMS mission to Abeokuta, inland from Lagos, preaching and teaching in Yoruba. He was celebrated back in London, introduced to Queen Victoria and Palmerston, and consecrated Bishop of West Africa in 1864. He published the first dictionary and grammar of Yoruba. Susan opened schools for children at Abeokuta and Lagos. Both died in what had been the Yoruba country, she in her seventies, he in his eighties.

squadron's British-made vessels, rescued 1,100 captives over two years before retiring exhausted.[39]

In turning a blind eye to their lordships' admonition, Bullen was the first commodore to set the squadron on a course of reform. But he had also attracted suspicion. Among *Hope*'s captures was the brig *Príncipe de Guiné*, another flyer and the property of 'Chacha' de Souza of Ouidah. She was also bought at auction by Bullen for the squadron – but served only briefly. Before handing over command to Collier in May 1827, Bullen sold her and *Hope* to a Portuguese agent at the nearby islands of Cape Verde. Both were immediately put back to slaving. The cost to Bullen of sailing them home had decided him to sell here, 'as a colonial official might dispose of his horses', in the words of one study.[40] There was still a dark irony that the *Hope*, an agent of rescue, should have been returned to her previous vile traffic.

These transactions came to the attention of a new governor at Freetown, Sir Neil Campbell, whose report to Whitehall suggested strongly that he did not approve of Bullen's dealings:

> If the Officers of HM Squadron sell their Prizes (after being condemned at this place and used for some time as tenders) at Cape de Verdes it evidently furnishes the immediate means for the Slave Trade in the vicinity of this Colony.[41]

The Admiralty promptly urged that Navy officers were 'not to purchase vessels of the description alluded to as tenders, but if they do it is to be under a clear understanding they are not to sell them again unless it be into the King's Service and not to individuals in Africa or America'.[42]

Most condemned slavers were bought by Freetown merchants, loaded with local produce and sent to England where they were sold at a profit.[43] Prices paid were conspicuously low, a fraction of the cost of new brigs or schooners in England or America. That only added to the logic of buying up faster vessels for the squadron. But auctioning had kindled another dark trade. Shady agents and go-betweens had seized their chance, snapping up bargains on behalf of Brazilian traders. As has been seen, Cerqueira Lima had recouped *Carlota* after her auction for a mere £315 (about £18,000 today).

Collier was determined that such should not be *Henriqueta*'s fate, and the wind had just shifted in his favour. Admiralty intransigence was softening, thanks to the now-incontrovertible evidence of the benefit of captured vessels to the campaign.

Three weeks after declaring her captives free, the court of Mixed Commission condemned the *Henriqueta*, making her the fourth of Cerqueira Lima's vessels to be ruled an illegal trafficker that year. On 10 November she was presented for public auction and snapped up for £330 by Kenneth Macaulay, one of Sierra Leone's few long-term surviving white inhabitants, a prominent trader and member of the governor's council.[44] Within months she was at sea again, this time on the opposite tack under the ensign of the Royal Navy.

The basic facts of the *Henriqueta*'s transition to the *Black Joke* are not in dispute. The details, however, are unclear. It is possible that Macaulay bought the infamous brig to ensure she did not return to Cerqueira Lima's hands. A genuine opponent of the trade and with a rare devotion to his adopted land, Macaulay was well aware of the nefarious networks here serving Brazilian interests. At the same time, like Freetown's other white residents, he was never known to disdain an opportunity for profit. As head of the trading firm Macaulay and Babington, he spent recklessly and had already made and lost a few fortunes while establishing himself as the leading prize agent for naval officers. If colonial Africa could ever have claimed its own nabobs, Kenneth Macaulay was one.

It is also feasible that Macaulay was acting all along on instructions. He was Collier's agent, handling his prize-money proceeds from the sale of captures – and *Henriqueta* may have come to Freetown with a note that she should be purchased on his behalf.

Either way, she certainly figured in Collier's plans from the time he anchored back off Freetown on 25 November. In the eleven weeks since her capture, he had continued cruising the Bights with all the zeal for which he was noted, holding within range of the coast yet covering between 60 and 150 miles a day, twice encountering tornados and, in chasing every sail that came in sight, boarding five vessels. Only one proved a loaded slaver – *Diane* with eighty-seven captives.

For an officer of Collier's history, it was a poor return. He had been appointed to the Preventative Squadron after a successful sea and land operation against pirates in the Persian Gulf. But in essence he remained a product of the heroic age – a midshipman on Nelson's flagship at the Nile and one of the great man's protégés. Africa presented him with duty of a quite different kind. *Sybille*'s logbook still speaks of the old naval order. In the space of a week, one seaman had been flogged for disobedience, another for insolence, and one had fallen to his death from the tops.[45] Of that other past, however, of fleet battles, troop landings or intense single-ship actions, there was no sign. Instead, Collier's early letters to the Admiralty raised a range of frustrations and challenges. One was the impunity of French slavers: a dozen of their vessels had been intercepted in the past six months carrying more than 1,500 captives. Top of the list, though, was the squadron's fundamental inadequacy.

> [Even] the gun brigs have but little chance of catching the slavers as they now employ the fastest American-built vessels. Both *Conflict* and *Clinker* have frequently chased them without effect and there is now no chance of catching them in the rivers as they embark their slaves a few hours before they weigh.[46]

Opportunity, in the shape of *Henriqueta*, lay at anchor nearby as Collier came ashore at the end of November and hastened to meet her new owner, Kenneth Macaulay. By Christmas Eve matters had progressed to the point of a note recorded in *Sybille*'s log: 'Held a survey on the *Black Joke* Tender.'[47] The outcome was reported by Collier to the Admiralty on the last day of 1827, the dawn of a new year perhaps portending his hopes.

I have purchased the brig *Black Joke* for a tender and have drawn on the Commissioner of the Navy for the sum of £900. She is a very fast vessel mounting two short 12-pounders and one long 18-pounder and appears well adapted to the purpose intended . . . She can act as Commodore Bullen's tender did and vessels taken by her will be condemned to HM Ship *Sybille*.[48]

The name assigned by Collier to the brig that transformed his squadron has given rise to some ribald speculation, as the phrase can be linked to a lurid ballad of eighteenth-century London, cited by Francis Grose in his *Classical Dictionary of the Vulgar Tongue* of 1785, about the female pubic region – 'her black joke and belly so white'. The question is whether an officer of Collier's rigour would have resorted to such foolery. He left no word of his own on the subject, but this was not the first time a naval vessel had been called *Black Joke*; an armed cutter of that name was deployed during the wars with France. The most likely candidate, though, emerges in the form of the *Liverpool Packet*, herself a former Baltimore slaver, captured and turned privateer in the war of 1812 when she took thirty-three American vessels and was nicknamed the *Black Joke*.[49]

A question may linger over *Henriqueta*'s transition to naval service. Macaulay had paid £330 at auction yet received £900 from Collier, so there was more than a hint of profiteering. But that was the nature of business in Freetown. Most whites stayed just long enough to make what fortune they could before escaping. Macaulay's finances were chaotic and he retained a vision of what the colony might achieve. He inherited the abolitionist dreams of an older relative, Zachary Macaulay, one of the Clapham Sect who campaigned with William Wilberforce and served two terms as an early governor of Sierra Leone, in the course of which he amassed a vast personal fortune through colonial contracts.[50] Kenneth was aged only 16 when he arrived in Freetown in 1808 as a clerk in the Liberated African Department, rising to head Macaulay and Babington, while spraying money about on grand projects and entertaining to the extent of rendering himself bankrupt. He had also stood in as acting governor in 1826 after the death of the incumbent Charles Turner.

What set Macaulay apart from most white inhabitants, however, was his attachment to the place. Among a population that fluctuated but was always small – in 1822 it stood at 128, in 1833 just 84 – he had stayed on for twenty years, despite bouts of yellow fever.[51] Macaulay had, in that quaintly outdated colonial term, 'gone native', with seven children by freed African women. That year he wrote an impassioned defence of Sierra Leone against critics in Parliament and the press who wanted it to be abandoned as a costly death trap for Britons. He also took on six men from the *Henriqueta* as apprentices, which gave them a better chance than most for a new start.[52] Macaulay's private life, along with his belief that the colony's 'moral and religious instruction' could turn recaptives into 'persons of property and respectability', strike a jarring tone today. He still comprehended why 'the African has, by his experience of European oppression and cruelty, been rendered suspicious'.[53] He would die in Freetown as he had lived, bequeathing his property and name to a long line of African descendants.

For his part, Collier took satisfaction in the deal. The £900 price (about £51,600 today) was still low for a vessel with the potential to transform the squadron, as well as the not-inconsiderable matter of his own prize money.[54] Moreover, unlike Bullen, he had been able to draw on navy funds to foot the bill.

The *Black Joke* would still be referred to as a tender. As such, she was notionally attached to supply Collier's flagship. In reality, as even the Admiralty now implicitly acknowledged, she would be released – set free to cruise independently in battling the very atrocities she had enabled.

CHAPTER 9

EXORCISING DEMONS
January–April 1828

His Majesty's brig *Black Joke* weighed and made sail from Freetown for the first time on 5 January 1828 in almost leisurely fashion. Temperatures were rising to the extremes of tropical Africa as lightly dressed hands went about their duties and the barest breeze ushered her 7 or 8 miles out from the peninsula's mountainous green lion. Her crew had come across from *Sybille* just days earlier, and a great beast the old 44-gun frigate now appeared from this low, gently curving deck. A change of regime too was signalled as the sun set on a glowing golden sea, and the brig's commander ordered sails to be shortened so a cask of rum could be opened in celebration.[1] That night the *Black Joke* was raucously baptised into the Navy.

For a few days she remained in company with *Sybille* and the sloop *Esk*, working south-east along the coast while her new crew acquainted themselves with her ways. Commodore Collier watched approvingly from *Sybille*'s quarterdeck as sails were briskly raised and shortened. Assurance that he had been right in entrusting his prize to Lieutenant William Turner was not long in coming.

Naval officers usually rose through a process known as 'interest' – cultivating family or other influential connections. Collier himself was a beneficiary, being the son of an admiral who died before he could direct the lad's course but was not forgotten thanks to a barrage of letters from his mother reminding Nelson how her 'dear boy . . . had the good fortune . . . to have stood near you in the never to be forgotten Victory of the Nile'.[2] Although a disciplinarian of the old school, Collier cared for those under his command and had a particular eye to advancing worthy young fellows who would never have the same chances he had enjoyed.

Turner appears to have had good reason for gratitude. In *Sybille's* muster, he was the most junior of her four lieutenants yet had been singled out by Collier to lead the party boarding *Henriqueta*.[3] Long had he awaited his first command. Born in the Hampshire village of Bedhampton to a prosperous Portsmouth wine merchant with maritime connections, Turner entered the Navy as a midshipman at the end of the Napoleonic War, part of a generation to have bypassed the heroic age entirely; Turner himself had never seen action. Service in the Preventative Squadron may have seemed a questionable alternative to life in rural Hampshire, but opportunities were few and the officer who passed one up was unlikely to be offered another.

Gratitude to his commodore notwithstanding, Turner had a quite different disposition in command. Collier's responsibility for a squadron demoralised by failure and at constant risk of tropical disease brought out the steely element in him. Floggings had continued on *Sybille*, with up to forty-eight lashes inflicted on eight men in the weeks after *Henriqueta's* capture, including two for attempting to desert.* Turner, on the other hand, had been presented with opportunity – a thing of beauty renowned for manoeuvrability and speed, 'her lines long, straight and clean, her sheer very slight, her lower yards greater in length than half the deck'.[4] He took to her as if liberated, and with the lightest of hands.

* ADM 51/3466, Log of the *Sybille*. Although a disciplinarian, Collier was certainly no tartar. While captain of the *Cyane* in 1812, he was struck by a seaman named Oakey who was sentenced to death. As Oakey was about to be hanged a letter came from the Prince Regent stating that, at Collier's request, the sentence had been commuted to transportation.

The *Black Joke*'s first company numbered fifty-five, all men drawn from *Sybille*'s muster yet in every sense a motley crew. This author has argued before that the Georgian age boasted no more egalitarian space than a naval vessel and *Black Joke* was a case in point, her length of just 90 feet and breadth of 27 feet containing young gentry from London society along with convicted criminals and African tribesmen.

Turner's immediate juniors were four master's mates – men who, like *Henriqueta*'s pilot Frederick Mather, had passed the lieutenant's exam and were awaiting promotion but occupied another social spectrum entirely. The youngest was 20-year-old Edward Butterfield of Chelsea, son of Rear Admiral of the Red, William Butterfield. Two years his senior, Alfred Slade came from another forces' lineage, being the youngest offspring of Lieutenant General Sir John 'Black Jack' Slade, a controversial cavalry hero of the Peninsular War and soon-to-be baronet. Though born into privilege, Butterfield and Slade would spend the rest of their lives fighting the slave trade at sea.

The hard labour ahead lay in the calloused hands of a notably diverse band of white and black seamen.[5] It was not just race that defined them, but varying degrees of experience and delinquency. The whites included a few younger naval seamen like William Wicks, aged 27, from Norfolk, and the veteran William Crouch, still agile enough despite his 36 years to serve as captain of the maintop in *Sybille*. However, the danger of service off Africa was enough to deter all but the most desperate hands, and on learning that they were bound for the Bight of Benin, forty-nine men had deserted before *Sybille* could sail from Portsmouth.[6] Their places were taken by fellows who had acquired their skill not with the Navy but in breaking the law. Convicted smugglers were being offered service in Africa as an alternative to years in another deadly environment, Marshalsea prison.[7] Over the years, smugglers became a mainstay of the squadron. On *Black Joke*, they were from the outset. Whether youngsters, like 18-year-old Thomas Atkinson of Liverpool, or ancients, such as Richard Holt, he all of 51 years, smugglers had a natural aptitude for handling small vessels close to shore.[8]

Most of the Black Jokes – navy seamen shared as a company the name of their ship – would have embarked with views typical of the day about 'savages', which raises an interesting question over their relations with the brig's other cohort, especially as anyone serving in Africa soon discovered that the black mariners known as Kru were skilled seafarers with a proud tradition of their own. From their early dealings with the Navy, providing services to and from the shore in canoes, the Kru had evolved into an essential component of the squadron – serving on board every vessel. Along with cultural knowledge that proved invaluable, they were more agile, sturdier and, above all, better able to survive local conditions than their white shipmates. Kru lived and served side by side with Jack Tar and, quite simply, without them the campaign would have foundered.

Along with officers and seamen, *Black Joke* had a bosun's mate named William Poulter responsible for routine order, four red-jacketed marines to enforce it, a carpenter, a cook and two ships' boys learning the ropes, Charles Cass and George Martin. Aged 14, Martin was the youngest member of the squadron.[9]

The challenge remained formidable. Collier's predecessor Charles Bullen had been the squadron's most successful commodore so far, with a record of sixty-seven slavers captured and more than ten thousand Africans freed during his three-year command.[10] Those figures still stand up poorly when compared with the number trafficked. In 1826, some 48,487 captives were recorded as being landed in the Americas and Caribbean. In 1827, it was 44,721. Both these figures exclude scores of registered voyages for which no captive count exists, so the two-year total doubtless exceeded 100,000.[11] Transatlantic slave trading had reached levels as great as the all-time high between 1780 and 1800 when Britain remained the leading slaving nation.[12]

The *Black Joke's* first cruising ground lay off the Gallinas estuary, a swampy, pestilential stretch of coast 100 miles or so south-east of Freetown. Why Collier chose to set her forth here when the trade had shifted more than 1,000 miles eastward to the Bights may be attributable to pressure from colonial authorities. Relations between commodores and governors, fraught with conflicting perspectives, were rarely harmonious. Collier had been urged by the latest incumbent to station a man of war in the vicinity of Freetown, even though, as the commodore pointed out, 'for every 5 slaves embarked [here], 200 are shipped from the Bights'.[13] As the new commodore, Collier perhaps wanted to show willing, to reset dealings with Freetown.

The *Black Joke* functioned broadly under an age-old naval regime. Men were divided into larboard or starboard watch, one of which was on duty at any time of a day broken into four-hour spells. Collier had issued instructions that 'the people' be allowed 'an hour and a half to their dinner and half an hour to breakfast and tea', which was standard procedure, but whereas on *Sybille* men were exercised at the great guns and with cutlasses, *Black Joke*'s activity was measured under canvas. Off the Gallinas, she swayed fleetly, constantly: 'Made, shortened and trimmed sail', as it was noted.[14]

Her logbook, the record of daily life, is a curiosity – incomplete and with significant gaps. Turner's command, however, is fully recorded, and the entries speak of a company kept in sharp trim and revelling in the gifts of a vessel blessed with seafaring magic, of cruising at ease under shortened sails while eyes ranged from river mouths to horizon until the sight of 'strange sail' set men racing aloft to hoist canvas 'in the chase'. Activity turned to repose when darkness fell: Turner encouraged recreation, when men might gather in song seated on the deck; and he eschewed use of the cat. Light-handed discipline was a mark of *Black Joke*'s regime from the start and should be considered a factor in the evolving character of harmony noted by those who sailed in her.

Five days out of Freetown, still in company with *Sybille*, they were cruising off the Gallinas where two rivers and sundry creeks fed out of the mangroves into lagoons shielded from the sea by a high sand bar when their first test presented itself.[15] Sighting a strange sail, Collier signalled *Black Joke* to give chase. Canvas billowed, jibs set her racing and with a following wind she ran down and boarded the stranger within two hours.[16] As it turned out, the *Corsair* was a British brig on legitimate trade to Accra. But *Black Joke* had hit her stride and the following day was a turning point.

On the morning of 11 January, the hands were at breakfast when a cry came down: 'Strange sail on the starboard bow.' They stood some 30 miles offshore from the Gallinas estuary, at 6° 49′ N and 12° 9′ W, so there was little doubt as to her purpose. Mess tables were hastily stowed as the signal to chase came from *Sybille*.[17]

Details are sparse, being limited to the bare details contained in the log, but it appears *Black Joke* had to come about. This, on top of the fact that the stranger was a fast schooner, indicated a prolonged chase. As darkness fell they were still in pursuit, now of a shadow. But *Black Joke* had the wind and, it was noted, 'the vessel herself seemed sensible of being in pursuit as she threw the white spray fiercely from her weather bow and recklessly plunged into another wave'.[18] So it went on until dawn when the wraith took shape – and Turner exulted. There, on the larboard bow and within range of *Black Joke*'s long 18-pounder, ran the Spanish slaver *Gertrudis*.

At 6.50 the gun thundered out. *Gertrudis*'s master was unable to respond, having, by one account, cast her cannons overboard in the night to hasten their flight.[19] An hour later *Black Joke* hove to beside her and a boarding party took possession of the schooner, bound for Cuba with 155 captives.

The master was taken prisoner with his twelve-man crew. In his place was installed Edward Butterfield, the youngest of Turner's mates but the one most able to guide *Gertrudis* to safety; the admiral's son had been with the squadron for three years, since the age of 17, and was more experienced than anyone else on *Black Joke* to navigate these waters in a turbulent season. Barely had Butterfield and the prize crew come aboard than they were tested by what Turner termed 'a Tornado from the north-east'.

Up on deck, men braced themselves. A flash of lightning would be followed by the crack of thunder, 'like heavy artillery, the ship trembling under the violence of each shock'.[20] Below, the souls brought on to *Gertrudis* just days earlier and already in terror were cast into a form of hell in this low, dark space, lurching, buffeting, turning on itself. Screaming, wailing, bodies were trapped, some crushed by the weight of those slammed against them. Glimpsed through the grating above, they presented a vision of the damned.

This time the tornado proved blessedly brief. At 8 that evening: 'Calm and cloudy. Parted company with Prize. Made, shortened and trimmed sail.'[21] Over the next two weeks Turner continued to tack off the Gallinas, sighting *Sybille* and *Esk* and making one pursuit that fell short when, with jibs filled to bursting, the standing martingale was carried away.[22] As water was running low they started back towards Freetown against breezes from the north-west. Two days out, another tornado blew up with thunder and lightning. Just as rapidly, it swept away.

On 25 January they anchored off Freetown to find *Gertrudis* safely berthed. Despite their sufferings, every one of the 155 captives had survived to be delivered to the Liberated African Department. In its terse brevity, Turner's log had recorded a turning tide in the voyage launched at Baltimore eight years earlier. *Black Joke*'s first capture began the exorcism of *Henriqueta*'s demons.

For all the inhumanity that it opposed, any account of the Preventative Squadron needs to guard against what has been termed the 'white saviour' narrative. Officers like Collier battled against impossible odds with hopelessly inadequate resources. They served conscientiously while facing considerable risk and, for long periods, ignorance or indifference at home. But they were there not as volunteers. They were under orders. And many of the officers who had been on half-pay since Bonaparte's defeat needed whatever commission was on offer.

If further incentive was needed, it came in prize money. Rewarding a ship's company for capturing an enemy was another naval tradition which, in Africa, meant making prizes of captives. The Abolition Act of

1807 introduced a bounty of £20 for every liberated male captive, £15 for a woman and £5 for a child. As the cost to government of this 'head money' rose, it was reduced in 1824 to £10 for each man, woman or child.[23] The proceeds were distributed on a descending scale from captains to seamen, as we shall see, but to take one example, Frederick Mather, who had navigated *Henriqueta*'s 542 survivors, received £114 as 'a lieutenant's share' in prize money.[24] Edward Butterfield was due about £31 for delivering *Gertrudis* with 155 captives. (These amounts are the equivalent of £6,540 and £1,780 today.)

Then again, agents took their share and were known to delay or even fleece a recipient of his dues. Commanders also ran the risk of damages for wrongful capture, as shown by the various legal claims of Cerqueira Lima and others. One case that year involving two Bahia slavers, *Vencedora* and *São João Voador*, caused the Mixed Commission to agonise over 'the sum to be awarded' when claimants 'perjure themselves to augment the amount of their damages to an inconceivable extent'.[25]

An individual's fate was, moreover, always subject to random fortune. In the case of Frederick Mather – who had landed at Freetown with the assurance not only of prize money but, finally, promotion to officer rank – that soon soured. Within months he was afflicted by 'obstinate constipation & obstruction' and found 'entirely unfit for further service'.[26] His promotion to lieutenant was never confirmed and he sailed home an invalid, possibly to the care of a devoted mother in Nottingham.[27]

Whatever the financial benefits, officers and men constantly confronted by harrowing forms of suffering were deeply affected, in some cases traumatised. The 'mental imbecility' diagnosed in Edward Wood, a gunner's mate discharged from the squadron that year, may have been just one such consequence. Seamen were not the only white outsiders to go mad in these parts. As will be seen, naval surgeons, officials and even a colonial governor were diagnosed as 'deranged'.[28]

Senior officers stated emphatically and repeatedly in their reports home that the slave trade was 'more horrible than those who have not had the misfortune to witness it can believe'. Or, as another wrote:

Indeed, no description I could give would convey a true picture of its baseness & atrocity.[29]

He made a significant point. This was an age when atrocities might be, and were, recorded in their factual detail while their nature remained impossible to visualise. In the campaign to eradicate slavery, a whole world separated those witnessing the violation of humanity at first hand and those at a distance who comforted themselves with words and gestures, or dismissed it out of hand.

Among the common hands, responses were more complex. They too were here out of need, facing either poverty or prison at home. Some may even have sailed in slavers themselves. But they took a pride in their trade, in the exhilaration of riding the waves, in a tradition that had made Britain the first seafaring superpower. They were, as one account of the squadron put it, 'inflexibly xenophobic, unthinkingly racist yet dying in their thousands to save individuals with whom they had nothing in common but humanity'.[30] And working alongside African seamen with a self-respect of their own rubbed off. None were saviours. All were fellow humans.

The Kru had engaged with European mariners since the sixteenth century. As master boatmen of formidable physique, they became essential early on to all traders on this estuarine shore, including slavers, being noted for 'the robustness and fleshiness of their bodies, and also for great agility'.[31] As participants, they escaped enslavement themselves; and unlike other West African people, they acquired mobility and choice.[32] This distinctive culture aroused interest, as one English traveller observed: 'They spend much of their time on the water and live chiefly on fish and rice.'[33] The notorious slaver Théodore Canot called them 'amphibious', while a naval surgeon, noting their migrant adaptability, spoke of 'a remarkably strong, active, hardy and intelligent race of men. They are, in fact, the Scotsmen of Africa.'[34]

The founding of Sierra Leone in 1792 opened new opportunities for Kru in the form of paid contractual work, first with English traders, then the Navy. From a homeland some 400 nautical miles to the south-east near Cape Palmas, canoes would be piloted to Freetown under a headman bringing his cohort to present what he called his 'book' – a tin box containing references from previous employers – and work would soon be forthcoming. After the Navy's arrival, a settlement in the capital known as Krootown became a recruitment centre.[35]

With its rambling sheds and a population that fluctuated constantly due to migratory cycles, Krootown retained the cultural distinctiveness of its inhabitants. Tribal ritual spurned Christianity along with any education in reading and writing. Kru were identifiable from a blackened scarification of the forehead. They consorted with local women but did not marry, remaining followers of a headman whose authority extended to handing out punishments and the distribution of wages. It was then, with status raised and bearing European goods, that they might return to their homeland to reintegrate and marry. In the words of one colonial governor:

Distinction, respect, power among his own countrymen as soon as age permits it, are the objects of every Krooman; he is trained up to the habit of looking forward to these as all that is honourable or desirable.[36]

Kru named Ballah, Sambah and Jacki were contracted to the colony as porters, longshoremen and stevedores.[37] The Navy, defeated by tribal nomenclature, had devised its own system of identities. Headmen retained their standing, being granted titles like King George. Their people came on board with a variety of names. Salt Water, Sea Breeze and Pea Soup were not unique, and Bottle Beer was quite common. Some may have reflected notions of character: Peter Warman, useful in conflict; William Gumption, no slave he.

Their wages were comparatively generous and studies of the Kru indicate they took to naval customs enthusiastically. The gold braid of officers was lusted after and shipboard ceremonial enjoyed by men familiar with ritual. Associating with white shipmates led to a rising trend in having an anchor tattooed on forearms.[38]

In almost every respect, these patterns point to similarities between black and white seamen, between Kru and Jack. Both were members of a commoner corps in authoritarian worlds, yet with a proud culture based on seafaring and defined by self-respect and peer regard. Ashore, they were outsiders who sustained their identity in isolation and only truly became themselves again once they returned to the sea.

Their main differences were swimming and drink. Jack was famously shy of the water, reasoning that in the event of shipwreck, swimming would only prolong suffering and it was better to break into the hold for rum and a last carouse. Kru, on the other hand, were said to swim 'like porpoises' and never really took to grog; although allowed two-thirds of the rum ration, they usually sold it to Jack.[39] These preferences were noted by a visitor to Freetown who observed a seaman on the street 'roaring incoherently and unable to stand' without being propped up by his grinning Kru companion.[40]

The value of Kru to the squadron was widely acknowledged. Being paid in line with naval rates raised their incomes well above what could be earned on merchant ships or ashore. As headmen, the likes of King George received the pay of a hand rated Able (33s 6d a month) or Ordinary (25s 6d); their people were mostly rated Landsmen, at 22s 6d a month. While their main duties were to transport men and goods out to sea and bring rescued captives ashore, they also took to new tasks: Jack Haulaway proved handy at raising canvas, Wil Centipede agile in the rigging.

They served as pilots too. The traveller Harrison Rankin, arriving in a navy ship guided to anchor by a Kru pilot, was astonished 'to find a black treating a white man with aristocratic independence'.[41] His tone may sometimes jar with sensibilities today – the Kru were 'good fellows and fine specimens of the animal man' – but Rankin engaged with Africans, took an interest in their world, and left pithy, at times moving, observations of the colony. His account of a Kru sailor visiting liberated

Africans he had superintended on a captured slaver might serve as a postscript to the *Gertrudis*:

> No sooner was the good-humoured, merry face of the hideous Bottle of Beer perceived than a general rush took place from all quarters of the yard. All gathered round, laughing and shouting his name. The women and children pressed upon him; at least a dozen seized him by the hands, arms and knees; a little girl climbed up his back . . . Even the invalids, hearing the name of their friend, rose from mats and tottered from sheds to meet him. He had been kind to them when kindness had little power to lessen their misery.[42]

Through what proved to be decades of futile efforts to suppress the slave trade, the squadron continued to provide similar glimpses of humanity.

The *Black Joke* spent six days at anchor while the hold was cleared and provisions were taken on, including 120 pounds of fresh beef and kegs of salted pork. Although Kru were allowed ashore, Collier had placed strict restrictions on leave for naval hands after a drink-related disaster involving *Henriqueta*'s prize crew who visited 'grogshops selling the very worst spirits'. He reported furiously: 'One man died from drinking, another fractured his skull, the remainder are living objects of wretchedness.'[43] There was no such concern about the quality of drink at sea: *Black Joke* also took on 35 gallons of rum in eight casks.[44]

On the evening of 31 January, a line of narrow canoes appeared, paddled by black men, 'glistening bodies either entirely naked or with the smallest handkerchief tightly bound round the middle'. Coming alongside, they 'scrambled up the chains and sprang on deck as if intent on taking forcible possession'.[45] The *Black Joke*'s Kru complement varied but from this point – her first fully independent cruise – they numbered almost twenty. Three came on as headmen, rated Able. They were Jim Freeman, Peter Warman and Jim George. Among their followers whose names may light up the imagination were Half Dollar, Jack Snapper and Ben Johnson.[46]

Miscreants or not, Englishmen did not go naked and *Black Joke*'s smugglers were all Englishmen. In their canvas trousers and cotton shirts they were still a disparate band, with a number of elders. Thomas Bailey, aged 52, from Chichester and William Fielder, 50, from Portsea, as well as the 51-year-old Richard Holt, were among that generation of old hands who had served during the Navy's apogee of glory in war with France and turned to their illicit trade in desperation, having been cast overboard after the peace of 1815 when a mass pay-off reduced naval manning from 147,000 to 23,000 within four years.[47] Merchant shipping too had been ravaged by the post-war slump, forcing younger men of seafaring families to join an industry running French brandy across the Channel under the noses of Customs. William Wells, 18, from North Shields, and John March, 26, from Portsea, fit that profile.[48]

Under the temperate hand of Lieutenant William Turner, they sailed again on 1 February. This time, though, the *Black Joke* had been despatched to the same dark heart of enslavement that had once been her trading ground – the Bight of Benin.

Pursuits and storms aside, it was not a coastline to excite interest. 'A low, flat country distinguishes this part of Africa,' one officer wrote, 'and tires the voyager by its unvarying tameness till the Calabar river is reached when the magnificent Cameroon mountains tower from their huge base into the skies above.'[49] *Black Joke*'s daily routine while passing down 1,200 miles of swampy shore was enlivened with exercises at the 18-pounder and small arms, but also led to her first casualty when one of the smugglers, 23-year-old William Cross from Suffolk, went overboard and drowned before a boat could be put out.[50]

Close-shore cruising did at least mean fresh food and water were at hand. On 20 February they came to off Accra to take on twenty-six sheep and sacks of fruit and vegetables for cruising off the Bight. Here, a few days later, began weeks of tacking to and fro across the horizon from Ouidah and Lagos. In that respect, the manoeuvre that largely defined the squadron's operation resembled the wartime tactic of block-ading French ports to prevent enemy ships coming out.

A daily routine kept the hands busy at setting, trimming and short-ening sails, interspersed with bouts of hectic activity brought on by seasonal storms. In the early hours of 10 March, for example: 'Furled the topsails to a heavy tornado from the NE. Cloudy with rain. Opened a cask of rum.'

Activity of a more welcome kind came later that day when a strange sail was sighted 2 miles to the west and, propelled by *Black Joke*'s topgal-lants, they chased it down in four hours, firing muskets to bring to a Spanish schooner, *Vigilencia*. Neither now, nor the following day, with the interception of a Brazilian vessel, *Gabrita*, could just cause be found for detention; but the energy of two successful chases was shared by the Black Jokes, along with more rum.

She had been back at sea for two months when activity turned to action. It began at 2am on 2 April with a sighting west of Princes Island. Oddly, the stranger did not try to flee and instead tacked towards them. As Turner noted, she was formidably armed too, with fourteen guns including 24-pounders against his solitary 18-pounder.

Disparity in their firepower clearly emboldened the Spaniard – for such she proved to be – who fired a shot to windward in warning before coming up to stand on their starboard beam.[51] Having cleared *Black Joke* for action, Turner sent across a boat with Edward Harvey, a master's mate, and two men, to make a standard inspection of her papers.

Watching as they came beside the Spaniard, Turner stiffened. Harvey and his fellows were being 'hurried out of the boat'. Once on deck, Turner observed, they were manhandled and treated 'like prisoners'.[52]

The boat came back in the hands of a Spanish mate who confirmed Harvey had been detained and demanded Turner's papers. 'Naturally I declined.'

While the two vessels idled at a distance, rising voices could be heard from the Spaniard. The boat crossed again, this time with a note from

Harvey reporting that she was the *Providencia*, a letter of marque autho-rised by the King of Spain, and her captain suspected *Black Joke* to be a South American pirate. Turner's presentation of his own papers did not resolve matters.

There is no clear account of what triggered the guns. Confusion was part of it. But the *Providencia* was no slaver and, it turned out, had been intercepted by *Sybille* a few days earlier. Her company were infuriated by British interference, especially now that they had the greater fire-power. Harvey was caught up as they milled around the deck 'in a great state of insubordination'. The captain, in danger of losing control, had Harvey write another note urging Turner to send fifteen more men in exchange for fifteen from *Providencia* while they sailed together to Princes Island to let tempers cool. However, Turner reported, it came 'with a threat of firing if I did not comply . . . I of course rejected the proposition and detained two of his officers and one of his seamen, being equal to the number he had kept of mine.'[53] The *Providencia* opened fire in the mid-morning, damaging *Black Joke*'s rigging but without inflicting casualties. With the men already at their stations, Turner was able to raise enough canvas to carry her round on to their antagonist's bow. It was a brilliant manoeuvre, bringing *Black Joke*'s sole 18-pounder into play on its pivot and leaving all *Providencia*'s guns pointing hopelessly out to sea.

Over the next hour, the Spaniard's sails were shredded by a mixture of grape and roundshot. Unable to bring their own fire to bear, her crew turned hostile to the English in their midst. Harvey was obliged 'to put myself under [the captain's] protection, two or three of the men having run at me with knives during the firing'.[54]

At 1pm *Providencia* hoisted a flag of truce. One of the men detained on *Black Joke* urged that he be allowed to return to her and assure the captain that she was indeed a British naval vessel and no pirate. Harvey and his companions were then boated back. At sunset the two brigs parted, as Turner reported from Princes, 'he to the south, and I made the best of my way to this anchorage'.

The *Black Joke*'s first full-on engagement may be seen as a misadventure based on confusion that had accomplished nothing in terms of the squadron's objectives. That was not the view presented by Collier in a report to the Admiralty stating that he had suspected *Providencia* in their earlier encounter 'of being a pirate' and her captain's resort to firepower had confirmed this. Turner and Harvey were lauded for their 'exemplary conduct'.[55]

Whatever the specifics, not many actions in history showed a single naval vessel prevailing against a foe with fourteen times as many guns. As *Black Joke* passed gingerly to the island for repairs, Turner knew he had a company with the measure of her, who could stand up to overwhelming firepower and carry the day.

CHAPTER 10

'A COSTLY GRAVE FOR BRITISH SUBJECTS'
April–July 1828

Princes Island nestled in an oceanic corner of West Africa, a mountainous speck that rose imperiously from the dark heart of the Bights. For the squadron it was a point of rendezvous and a source of essentials like food, wood and water. It was a place of beauty too: one officer wrote of anchoring 'under a huge, flat-topped mountain which rises perpendicularly on every side almost from its base'; another noted 'the diversified grandeur and wanton, luxuriant magnificence of this gem of the ocean'.[1] Above all, though, it was a haven, where men jaded by weeks of fruitless cruising under tropical skies came ashore to the pleasures tendered by a castaway queen.

Princes was the domain of Madame Ferreira, a lady of dark hue, ample proportions, welcoming disposition and 'though not of dazzling beauty, certainly of an attractive order'. Madame was the wife of the Portuguese governor, who was rarely to be seen, and the hospitality she offered uniformed British visitors at their spacious villa overlooking a sandy beach at West Bay was at least in part due to his surreptitious trading practices. She showed great partiality for the new commodore and such were the essential provisions supplied by Princes that Collier turned a blind eye to the island's enslaved population. A regular guest, he was also happier to have his men go ashore here for local comforts than at Freetown with its deadly grogshops. As has been noted, strange acquaintanceships were born in the desperate loneliness of the West Africa station.[2]

What passed on *Black Joke*'s first respite at Princes went unrecorded and it was in any event brief. Four days served for her canvas and rigging to be patched up and by mid-April she was back cruising off Lagos. The following weeks illustrated the frustrations as well as the challenges of tacking along even a limited stretch of coast while pursuing every sail to come in view. The Bight of Benin ran almost 350 nautical miles from Cape St Paul's to Cape Formoso, with seasonal storms and hazy skies that reduced visibility at the day's start and end, while the air sulked with sultriness.

In four days from 20 April, three strangers were sighted: the first went off into the darkness and was not seen again; the second raced on through a squall yet was finally brought to after five hours by warning shots and proved to be an American brigantine bound for Bahia – without human cargo; the third eluded them for only two hours and, it turned out, was an innocent trading barque from Liverpool which had fled in terror of *Black Joke*'s sleek and distinctly un-British outline.[3]

Activity came as a blessing. More familiar were spells when time passed with no sight beyond a distant shore and all around the vastness of a sea which 'often for days together remained a profound calm till the water itself assumed a leaden hue', and the mere sight of a shark's fin drew excitement. 'Indeed,' observed one officer, 'the conduct of the cruiser and shark seemed somewhat similar, both were loitering about in the hope of picking up something.'[4]

Dawn came on 15 May with a thunderous squall briefly illuminated by lightning. As it passed, the daily routine commenced:

Wore & set courses & topsails on the caps. 9am Mustered by divisions. Loosed sails to dry. People employed as most necessary. Killed two sheep. 10am Stowed small sails.

The stranger was sighted late that afternoon, standing almost 14 miles in the north-west. The distance was formidable but her position due south of Ouidah indicated she was up to no good; men raced aloft to make all sail.

Through the night they ran on. At first light she was sighted again, now 10 miles off. Turner crowded on more sail with royals and flying jib. By noon they had closed to 5 miles. At 5pm the chase could be discerned as a brig and an especially swift sailer too but weighed down by an immense load and showing signs of panic, as indicated by an abrupt change of course to shake them off.

After a full twenty-four hours they had closed to within 3 miles yet with darkness descending for a second night. At this point Turner's determination not to lose sight again of what could only be a heavily loaded slaver emerged: there was a risk to setting foretop studdingsails when a tornado might sweep out of nowhere in minutes, but in this instance piling on extra canvas outside the mains was worth it.

They came alongside as night fell – to another heavily armed quarry mounting eight guns. This time there was no broadside. The finale was recorded by Turner in a manner typical of an officer noted by Commodore Collier for his clarity and brevity:

> 9.50 Hove to. Boarded and captured the Brazilian brig *Vengador* with 645 slaves.[5]

The significance of *Black Joke*'s second capture cannot be so casually passed over. More Africans had been rescued from *Vengador* on 16 May than from any of the 390 slavers seized by the West Africa Squadron in its twenty-two-year history. The figure of 645 captives found in a single vessel would endure as a chilling record until 1834.[6] If it were still needed, here was the most compelling validation yet for deploying captured slavers in the cause of humanity.

For now Turner's priority was preserving as many of these lives as possible – a duty rendered all the more taxing because of the pure hell revealed on *Vengador*. Some sense of the scene that greeted the boarders may be gathered from statistics: as another American-made brig, the former *Henriqueta* was similar in dimensions, yet her worst overloading of 569 captives had still been 76 fewer than the number found forcibly pressed within *Vengador*'s 100-foot length and 25-foot beam. The power of words to describe the scene escaped those present that day; but we may recall the witness to another captured Brazilian slaver struggling to comprehend

> how it was possible for such a number of human beings to exist, packed up and wedged as tight as they could [be] crammed in cells three feet high . . . The heat so great, the odour so offensive, it was quite impossible to enter, even had there been room.[7]

The duty of navigating this floating death cell to Freetown – for fatalities were a certainty – fell on Edward Harvey. Having held his nerve in the *Providencia* action, the ambitious young master's mate was deemed worthy of the responsibility, and the prize money that would be due once this perilous exercise had been accomplished. The maladies lurking on *Vengador* prescribed that the prize crew also be of robust health, and among those chosen was the 18-year-old smuggler William Wells.[8]

Turner would remain at hand, to assist in the event of tornados or other crises. *Black Joke* was to be a guiding light, quite literally: a blue torch burned at her stern every night for *Vengador* to follow.[9]

During the fraught weeks they spent beating to windward down the Gulf of Guinea, Turner uncovered some of the dark secrets of *Vengador*'s past. He already suspected her previous identity – may indeed have been fairly sure – and when her master Miguel Netto was brought to the cabin for questioning, he confirmed that she was previously the notorious *Príncipe de Guiné*, captured two years earlier by Commodore Bullen with the then-record number of 608 captives, only to be sold by Bullen on his departure and find her way back to the trade.

One other intriguing fact came to light: this same brig, once the property of 'Chacha' de Souza and reputed to be as fast as if not still faster than *Henriqueta*, had now come into the possession of a certain José de Cerqueira Lima of Bahia.

Turner's succinct record of the passage speaks of a shepherd with a constant eye to his flock. That need, to keep *Vengador* in sight, meant the Black Jokes were busier than ever in the rigging, shortening sail for the prize to catch up as they moved ahead, then raising canvas again to stay with her. At times the two brigs would approach to within hailing distance for the cry: 'All well!'[10]

Fair progress had been made over five days when a signal came that not all was well: the bloody flux had appeared on *Vengador*. Whether tormented captives were being allowed up on deck in batches is not clear; the outcome could certainly have been more terrible. But symptoms had spread to some of the prize crew. Two sufferers were boated across by Kru, to be replaced by two other unnamed hands and the carpenter, who was sent to repair a badly sprung gaff.[11]

Bodies were now having to be unceremoniously dropped over *Vengador*'s side, including those of children. Seamen were hardy types but not immune to the cries, suffering and deaths of the very young. Four days later, assistant surgeon Coates went across from *Black Joke* to render what treatment he could. Two more of the prize crew, including the youth William Wells, had to be removed, this time for reasons related to trauma rather than physical health.[12] Just then a fresh following breeze came up and they started to quicken along.

The *Black Joke* came to off Freetown in the first week of June with *Vengador* following in the wake of her torch. Twenty-one of those destined for slavery had died on the passage. But that had been made in three weeks, thanks to Turner's management, and 624 living men, women and children were still delivered to the care of the Liberated African Department, the largest single intake in its history.

No crew member had died. William Wells made some kind of recovery; but the agony witnessed on *Vengador* carried a disorder of its own. Wells had seen too much. On 17 June he disappeared ashore and did not return.[13] In deserting, he had turned his back on six months' wages, and prize money to boot. Whether the young man from North Shields ever returned to his home is not known.

There could be no such escape for *Vengador*'s captives. From the fetid sweltering inferno below where, for almost a month, their squeezed bodies had been twisted into coils – 'heads and necks bent down by the boarding above' – naked men, women and children were brought up, handed a fragment of cotton covering and conveyed ashore in canoes by Kru. Over the days that followed new forms of dread and trauma were experienced. In the words of a witness to one such transition: 'No joy at the fact of liberation was perceptible' among those gazing about their new surroundings. Indeed, such was a state of general confusion that, in some cases, 'a strong desire of return to the ship was expressed' – as if reaching out for the lives that had been taken from them. More captives would die before life for the majority resumed in a different form.[14]

The ritual of condemnation and emancipation by the Mixed Commission was at least prompt and from 16 June they began to line up before a clerk at the King's Yard for each individual's details to be taken down. Of the 624 captives who had come to Freetown, only 607 were listed so another 17 had either died or fled in the hope of escaping this unfathomable world; some might even have been kidnapped for resale by other former captives.

First in line at the yard was Iffay, a 24-year-old man, just 5 feet tall, tattooed on the right side of his chest. The last of them was a girl, Yahdeepay, aged 10 and with cuts on her cheeks.[15] The entries, in the same hand that had recorded the captives brought ashore from *Henriqueta*, would have taken days to set down as heights and brand marks were examined and a translator questioned each subject and passed on names to the scribe. Their ages were estimations. Almost all the 274 men appeared to be in their twenties and were less than 6 feet tall.

First on the list of ninety-five women were the six young mothers, among them Adoobee with a 10-month-old baby. How they had survived *Vengador's* conditions cannot be imagined, any more than wondering how many of this particular category of sufferers had died and been cast into the sea. Seemingly the youngest of the women was 15-year-old Lahmee, with 'cuts all over'.

What stands out on the list, though, is the proportion of children. Among the 142 boys were a significant number, like Daddah, aged between 6 and 8. The 96 girls were mainly 9 and above, but also included the likes of 7-year-old Obookaleh and Agai, aged 8. Most were noted as having 'cuts on face'. As Bahia's leading trader in humans, José de Cerqueira Lima evidently continued to focus on youth.

Of their state, physical and mental, little can be said. Yet among the women, from feeding mothers like Adoobee to the younger Fahnookay, scars ran deep. Harrison Rankin, the wandering scribe who spent days observing the occupants of King's Yard, wrote:

> The women sustain their bodily sufferings with more fortitude than the men and seldom destroy themselves; but they brood more over their misfortunes, until the sense of them is lost in madness.[16]

There are no records or statistics adding substance to Rankin's haunting conclusion that 'insanity is the frequent fate of women captives'. It may be no coincidence, however, that a hospital was established at the village of Kissy that year for 'the sick, distressed Liberated Africans from the villages and for such newly arrived people from slave vessels'.[17] Kissy hospital became, in effect, sub-Saharan Africa's first lunatic asylum.

Children, on the other hand, Rankin believed, 'soon recovered from their sufferings, and their elastic spirits seemed little injured'. The 238 children from *Vengador* aged 14 or under were distributed around villages, from Hastings to York and Regent to Waterloo, some to mission schools. Had the 6-year-old Daddah been blessed with fortune, he might have followed in the footsteps of Laiguandai, another boy of his age and origin, who landed around this time, learned to read and write, was given the name Peter Wilson and taken into the paid service of a colonial official where he met and married a woman named Eliza. Peter later set down an account of his life published in the village where they ended their days.[18]

Another possibility is that Daddah went on to serve an apprenticeship, in which he would notionally have received training in a trade that would stand him in good stead. Rankin noted that indenturing had produced carpenters, tailors and masons, and he spoke to one tradesman who said he thanked his liberators, despite the fact that 'the white man is so ugly to look upon'.[19]

But indenturing had a questionable record overall. Many apprentices ended up as tyrannised domestic slaves to masters and mistresses who had handed the authorities a fee for their services and drew from that a certain logic. As Rankin put it:

> Any resident, of any colour, may enter the King's Yard, and select a boy or girl. He pays ten shillings and the child becomes his property under the name of apprenticeship for three years ... Domestic servants are in the habit of buying them and of employing them in the heavier drudgery of housework.[20]

Rankin was still more disapproving of the colony's conscription system. The Royal African Corps had landed in Sierra Leone as a white military unit but, as attrition took its toll and new recruits were needed, officers would call at King's Yard and draft the sturdiest males into a service which ultimately carried many off to the West Indies.* In Rankin's eyes, black men used to 'swaying their limbs in perfect freedom' found a heavy scarlet uniform 'grievously impeding'. He went so far as to declare the fatigues of drill and parade more contrary to African

---

* Of some 99,752 captives brought to the colony in the half-century from 1807, an estimated 5,169 males were enlisted in the Army (Anderson, *Abolition in Sierra Leone*, p. 98).

tradition than 'the labours of a plantation' and quoted a freed black man as saying: 'Soldiers are slaves.'[21] Yet they did receive pensions and, as archive records show, some lived on in retirement at Wellington, Waterloo and other villages.[22] African soldiers served under the same conditions as their white fellows – men themselves hardly treated by Britain's ruling class as fellow citizens. One eminent historian of empire has written: 'In some respects . . . white soldiers overseas shared levels of unfreedom with black slaves.'[23]

Just how rescued Africans might be resettled was always going to pose an overwhelming task. As Rankin noted: 'To restore each slave to his original tribe would be impossible. To land all upon the territory of any native chief would be to renew the miseries of bondage.'[24] That year, Thomas Cole of the Liberated African Department faced a challenge unprecedented in his twelve years at Freetown, due to the human numbers landed from captured slavers.

Of the 274 men on *Vengador*, 142 were sent to the villages – each with new clothes, a mat and blanket, supplies of jerk beef and cereal, and a ticket for the 3d daily allowance. The other 132 were assigned to the military – compared with the 26 from *Henriqueta* – the majority to a West Indies regiment.[25]

The crisis did spur one innovative idea. In July, Cole sent village managers a plan to break the mould of subsistence farming. In every settlement, he wrote, a recaptive experienced in cultivation was to have ten men placed in his care, each of whom would be assigned an acre of land to tend while receiving the usual allowance for three months. This would grant 'industrious farmers the means to extend their agricultural pursuits on a much larger scale' while 'giving instruction to newly arrived liberated Africans'. Products thought most likely to profit the community were coffee and cotton, with lesser parcels of land given over to arrowroot, ginger and vegetables. Seeds and plants were distributed accordingly.[26]

Arrowroot and ginger became useful exports but commercial agriculture long remained stagnant in Sierra Leone.

There had been other low points in the colony's ramshackle history, but the period between 1827 and 1829 was especially fraught. Governors continued to drop like flies. After the death eight months earlier of Sir Neil Campbell – he having survived for almost a year – an army officer, Lieutenant Colonel Hugh Lumley, stood in briefly, to be succeeded by another army type and explorer, Dixon Denham. He had been in office for just over a month before dying of a fever on 9 June, the week of *Black Joke*'s return.* That brought Lumley back again, but it appears he was already ailing; two months later his body would join the rising number of those interred at Circular Road cemetery. Samuel Smart, an official virtually unknown beyond Freetown, duly wrote to the Foreign Office that the position 'has devolved upon me'.[27]

In London, voices that had long opposed the whole idealistic foundation of the colony regained stridency. One MP declared it ridiculous that the budget for Sierra Leone was being renewed, 'given the havoc of the climate on European health'. The high Tory mouthpiece *John Bull* milked Sydney Smith's old witticism, stating that governors were being sent out 'like despatches, in triplicate'.[28] On receiving news of Campbell's death, *The Times* thundered:

> To send Englishmen to such a pest-house [is] to yield to the mixture of quackery and hypocrisy which has instigated a certain class of people in this country to press upon Government the retention of a costly grave for British subjects by nicknaming it a school for the civilisation of negroes.[29]

So hostile was the political mood it seemed the colony might be abandoned.[30] Property values in Freetown collapsed. Much like the world of the East India Company, Sierra Leone's dangerous climate and

---

* Denham had accompanied Hugh Clapperton on the first expedition to trace the source of the Niger in 1822 and, after their falling out, did his best to blacken Clapperton's name – it was he who accused Clapperton of 'impropriety' with an Arab servant – while lauding his own lesser achievements.

distance from regulation had always left it exposed to underhand busi-ness practices. That year, with trade in decline and some white inhabit-ants facing ruin, a onetime trend became common practice: more slaver vessels were being captured, and more opportunists were buying them up at auction to sell back to Brazilian traders.

While auction malpractice gave rise to frustration in the squadron, the Navy faced some embarrassment itself. When Turner came ashore in June it was to ensure the condemnation of his prize, *Vengador*. She was about to be auctioned, as was the *Esperanza*, a schooner recently taken by *Sybille*. Yet both vessels had been sold by Collier's predecessor, Charles Bullen, to save himself the cost of sailing them home; as seen above, *Vengador* was previously the *Príncipe de Guiné*, the *Esperanza* none other than his own tender, *Hope*.

Among those present at the auctions was a mysterious Englishman recently arrived in Freetown. John Brockington landed from a Brazilian brig, claiming to be a partner of the American consul at Rio and bearing large quantities of coffee and sugar.[31] A more familiar figure was William Henry Savage, a local tycoon. Born in England to an African father and English mother, Savage had come to Freetown early on as a school-teacher before losing his post in a cost-cutting purge, forcing him to turn to more questionable lines of employment. Living outside the colony, he made a fortune using slave labour to trade timber from nearby territory and on returning to England obtained appointment in 1821 as a notary public. Back in Freetown, he now represented the owners of captured slavers at hearings before the Mixed Commission, arguing that 'vessel and cargo' should be restored to them.[32] A highly controversial figure, he was also, it has been claimed, a target for racial hostility.[33]

Bidding for the two vessels was intense. Prices when the hammer came down indicated that arms were still going up after the estimates had been passed. Among the bidders was Kenneth Macaulay, purchaser of *Henriqueta*, a man usually on the trail of a profit but also desirous of preventing these vessels returning to the wrong hands. The *Vengador*, however, was knocked down to Brockington for £920.[34] The *Esperanza*

1. Shipyards at the American port of Baltimore produced small, fast-sailing vessels that outran traditional British designs and were prized by slave traders. It was here that the *Henriqueta* was launched in 1824.

2. Two-masted brigs like the *Henriqueta* were ideally suited to the close coastal manoeuvring required at West African slaving ports such as Ouidah where captives were brought out by canoes.

3. Warriors from the kingdom of Dahomey were sent in raiding parties to neighbouring regions where men, women and children were seized and marched to the coast for trading to slavers.

4. On being brought aboard a slave vessel, male captives were shackled and driven below. Africans had come to believe their captors were taking them away to be eaten.

5. The lower deck of a Spanish slaveship. Captives were not always kept in shackles, as this painting by a naval officer shows, but their confinement was designed to maximise numbers and minimise resistance.

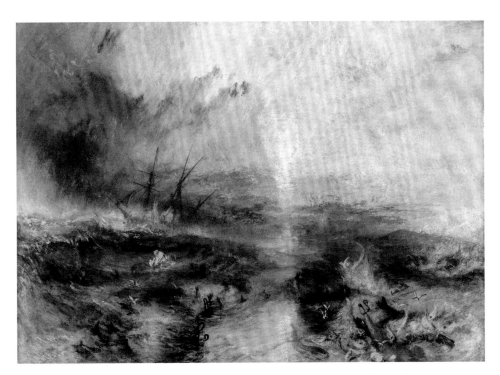

6. William Turner originally entitled his abolitionist masterpiece *Slavers Throwing Overboard the Dead and Dying – Typhoon Coming On.* Similar events were witnessed on slave vessels trying to escape the Preventative Squadron.

7. Children were traded in great numbers in Brazil due to the low birth rate among enslaved men and women. The British artist Augustus Earle painted a range of such scenes while living in Rio de Janeiro in the 1820s.

8. Bahia in northern Brazil was the home of José de Cerqueira Lima. Ownership of the *Henriqueta* and other slave vessels made him a wealthy and influential tycoon in the first transatlantic capital founded by Portuguese colonisers.

9. Captives being thrown from boats as a slaver makes ready to escape an advancing navy cruiser. The speed and manoeuvrability of these vessels posed the Preventative Squadron's greatest challenge.

10. Navy officers fresh from victories in the wars with France found little glory to be won with the squadron. Among them was Commodore Francis Collier, seen here as a boy midshipman behind the cannon and near his mentor Nelson at the Battle of the Nile.

11. Smugglers made up a significant and skilled group in ships of the squadron. On conviction they had been offered the option of service at this dangerous station instead of gaol or transportation.

12. The African seafaring Kru people were essential to the anti-slavery campaign, sturdier and more able to survive the conditions and fevers that carried off many of their white shipmates.

13 & 14. Two portrayals of the *Black Joke* taking *El Almirante*. As a converted slaver, the *Black Joke* had already proved herself the Preventative Squadron's most successful cruiser when news of this capture brought her fame in Britain, inspiring artists such as Nicholas Condy and William John Huggins. Her pursuit of the Spanish brig through the night was dramatically imagined by Condy. The closing phase of the action is accurately evoked by Huggins.

15. The harbour at Freetown. The colony of Sierra Leone was born as an abolitionist dream but faced various crises in the 1820s with the growing number of rescued captives, poor resources and fever outbreaks.

16. A wine cooler presented to the *Black Joke*'s commander, Henry Downes, on capturing *El Almirante*. The trophy was fashioned from timber of the Spanish slaver.

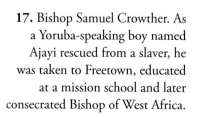

17. Bishop Samuel Crowther. As a Yoruba-speaking boy named Ajayi rescued from a slaver, he was taken to Freetown, educated at a mission school and later consecrated Bishop of West Africa.

was bought by Savage for £710. By the time accessories were added – some paid for by Brockington – she had realised a total of £1,285.[35] Both amounts far exceeded the average for schooners and brigs of less than £400.

At this point Brockington grew anxious. Perhaps sensing some intervention to thwart him, he raced aboard his new vessel urging that she set sail immediately, even though she had insufficient hands. As Collier later reported to the Admiralty, *Vengador* had departed

> under English colours with Mr Brockington on board . . . Such was the hurry to get her away that one of the most respectable merchants here Mr McCormick [sic] sent his own brother on board to make up the numbers.[36]

John McCormack, an Irishman from Lurgan, was indeed a well-regarded member of Freetown's white community with a successful timber business that paid its Kru labourers and had attracted to the colony three of his brothers, one of them, William, a seaman.[37] He also had a child by an African woman, had lived in Africa for most of his life and would rise to positions of legal authority in the administration. But the economic crash had brought him to the verge of ruin. Lured by handouts from Brockington, he may have reasoned that he was, after all, doing nothing illegal. He had also bought *Black Joke*'s first prize *Gertrudis* in February for £620.[38] Both *Gertrudis* and *Vengador* would be sold back to Brazilian slavers by Brockington.

Legal or not, naval men like Turner observed these proceedings with bitter frustration. When Savage placed at *Esperanza*'s helm José Rios, master at the time of her capture and a known slaver, he felt compelled to intervene. As the most senior officer then in Freetown, Turner sent a boarding party across from *Black Joke* and 'seized [*Esperanza*] for being illegally navigated'.[39]

Savage protested. *Esperanza* had already been licensed to sail by governor Lumley and, Savage insisted, it was only his intention 'to take away [her crew] from this place under an expressed and written direction from the Brazilian ambassador'. He turned to Macaulay for 'a particular favor', suggesting that 'as agent to Commodore Collier your opinion must have great weight with Lieutenant Turner'.[40] At a meeting between the three men, Savage swore that he had not bought *Esperanza* as a slaver but for his own legitimate purposes. A declaration to this effect was addressed to Lumley – now in his death throes – and Macaulay.

'As I was not here,' Collier wrote to the Admiralty, 'circumstances induced Lt Turner to let her go.' Whether Collier's presence would have altered the outcome is debatable, for as matters stood there was no legal obstacle to anyone – even active slave traders – bidding at Freetown auctions. Turner, determined to preserve the Navy's distance from a shady shambles and save himself from any claim for damages, received from Savage 'bonds of indemnity as [*Esperanza's*] owner'.[41]

Turner's suspicions were confirmed soon enough. *Vengador* with Brockington on board was back in Brazil within weeks while *Esperanza* was recorded a few months later as sailing 'from the Bight of Benin with upwards of 300 slaves'.[42] As Collier summed up the fate of the squadron's prizes in his final despatch that year:

> Most of the slave vessels that are captured and sent here for condemnation are again purchased by agents and sent to the Brazils.[43]

While Sierra Leone's future hung in the balance – as it did until 1830, when a campaign to have the colony handed over to recaptives was defeated in Parliament – mistrust only deepened between those battling slavery at sea and those entrusted with resettling its victims in the far more equivocal state ashore.

Navy officers never took to Freetown. Strained relations with colonial officials, the danger of infectious diseases, even the whiff of corruption – these all played against the instincts of men comfortable in their own small, tight and, above all, controllable environments. Moreover, the colony was distant from the squadron's main theatre of operations in the Bights and posed the additional challenge of unfavourable sailing conditions to return there. The island of Fernando Po, it had been argued, was far more suitable for the Navy, with a prime anchorage at the corner of the Bight of Biafra. In 1827, the Admiralty had sent out a brilliant maverick, Captain William Owen, in the frigate *Eden* to establish a settlement there.

Seamen had little liking for Freetown either. Ports usually offered the allure of licentious pleasures, a frolic ashore combining women and drink. But thanks to the lethally potent brews of the 'grogshops' detested by Collier, men were now rarely given shore leave. And, unlike most ports used by sailors, it was noted that local women would not come out to anchored vessels, being perhaps wary of seagoing as a whole.[44] To these ordinary hands – unable to get their hands even on pay or prize money until returning home – it seemed that besides brief visits to Princes Island, gratification was being kept at a distance. Their vexation is to be seen in what became a rising trend in floggings for drunkenness.

Capturing the *Vengador* with her record number of captives was, on paper, a windfall for all concerned. Even at the recently reduced rate of £10 'head money' for each rescued man, woman or child, the total due from government amounted to £6,240 (the equivalent in purchasing power today of £358,000). That would not go directly to *Black Joke's* commander and crew but was in theory to be shared around the squadron, which did at least even up the random fortunes of common endeavours. The prize system itself had been reformed in 1808 to allow the lower deck – seamen and marines – half the entire proceeds. Captains now received one-sixth, and officers and petty officers lesser portions. But its real benefits to men of the Preventative Squadron are something of a mystery, as the usual bureaucratic failures were compounded by malpractices and the absence of any reliable administrative system. No records have survived detailing the distribution of prize money from *Vengador* besides a note that Edward Harvey received £161 (or about £9,200) as a 'lieutenant's share' for navigating her in *Black Joke's* wake to Freetown.[45]

At bottom, the distribution system remained inequitable, with vast disparities between the earnings of Collier and those of his officers, let alone common hands. The commodore's pay-off ran into thousands of pounds, Turner's into a few hundred, while William Wicks, a seaman rated Able who returned to his native Norfolk in 1830 after surviving almost three years in Africa, had earned in all £88 1s 10d. After deductions for tobacco and a few advances which he managed to splurge ashore, Wicks walked away with £63 1s 1d (or about £3,610 today).[46]

A comparison may be made with one of *Black Joke*'s Kru headmen. In contrast to the legendary profligacy of seamen ashore, it was noted that the Kru had a 'steady view to the acquisition of wealth'.[47] So when Jim Freeman left the squadron after a similar spell of duty to Wicks, he received his £65 1s 2d pay-off in full.[48] The only difference in the original amount was because the Kru did not receive prize money.

That was an injustice Collier, to his enduring credit, did his best to remedy.

One year in, he had the measure of his command and an eye for reform. The squadron's health had held up reasonably well so far, with just a handful of deaths. However, as he explained to the Admiralty, seamen could not endure the conditions here as Africans did. In the first of a series of despatches urging equal treatment for black and white hands, Collier wrote that he and his fellow commanders were agreed that the two-thirds proportion of rations given to Kru was unfair.

> For people who really work as hard as these men do it is not sufficient. The use they are to the squadron is incalculable as it is quite impossible that Europeans could stand the sun, rain and fatigue these Kroomen go through.[49]

Collier warmed to his theme. One captain, he went on, reported how his Kru hands 'have frequently made good-humoured representations when they have not had enough to eat', saying: 'Black man works more than White man but gets less.'

Seamen's skills were undermined by the poor state of their vessels.

On this occasion, his petition was successful. 'With unaccustomed generosity,' it has been noted, 'the Admiralty authorised Collier to issue such increased allowance as he considered necessary.'[50] The campaign for prize money continued.

The fundamental problem remained that Collier's squadron was simply not equipped to do the job it had been charged with. Resources of a frigate, two sloops and three brigs, all of them elderly, were never going to stop the scores of lean, rapid slavers plying the Atlantic and, however forthright Collier's despatches, their lordships would not strengthen his hand. He certainly did not pull his punches on the latest encumbrance to be bestowed upon him: the 12-gun brig *Plumper* had replaced *Conflict* – no athlete she, but worthier than a brig condemned by officers as useless in the chase and, moreover, in a disgraceful state with rotting timbers; Collier informed the Admiralty that *Plumper* was 'the most useless and inefficient vessel I have ever met in HM service'.[51] As it transpired, her commander Edward Medley was equally inept, having been set aside on half-pay in 1815 with a recommendation that he never be reinstated.[52]

Many years later, reflecting on the prolonged campaign to suppress the Atlantic trade, Lord Palmerston, foreign minister during that era, would comment caustically on the Admiralty's habitual negligence:

> If there was a particularly old slow-going tub in the Navy she was sure to be sent to Africa to try and catch the fast-sailing American clippers.[53]

In that respect at least, *Black Joke* represented a rare light of hope for Collier and his people. And it may account for the way they took her to their hearts.

CHAPTER 11

RISING TO RENOWN
August 1828–April 1829

Turner saw his time with *Black Joke* coming to an end. Together they had rescued almost 800 captives in six months while confronting and overwhelming far superior firepower, much to the benefit of morale and the commodore's delight. News of their latest exploit in capturing *Vengador* had reached Collier, whose despatches assured Turner that promotion was imminent. But although captaincy was the prime desire of a whole generation of long-waiting lieutenants it would end Turner's association with his bewitching flyer. He would take command of a ship. She would be passed to another young officer deemed worthy of opportunity.

They were back cruising the Bight of Benin off Ouidah when around noon on 6 August the *Sybille*'s distinctive outline was spotted to leeward. As she drew near men were seen lined up on the flagship's upper deck and spirits rose when 'we received three cheers from [them]'.[1] The *Black Joke*'s smugglers responded in kind. That evening Turner went across to dine in the great cabin.

Along with congratulations, Collier had tidings of *Sybille*'s recent activity – and of a tragedy. After weeks of fruitless questing they had sighted a schooner near Badagry, starting a chase that ended in disaster when the slaver under Spanish colours ran ashore in heavy surf and broke up. In what were deemed dangerous conditions, *Sybille* tacked away. Hundreds of lives had almost certainly been lost. A few days later she intercepted a Brazilian vessel *Josephina* and this time seventy-seven captives were rescued and taken to Freetown.

With Turner's promotion now only awaiting confirmation by the Admiralty, the talk turned to *Black Joke*'s armoury. Lack of firepower had not restrained him thus far and Collier lauded his willingness to take on dangerous antagonists. A lesson had nonetheless to be taken from the *Providencia* action. With her single bow-chaser, *Black Joke* had prevailed against a 14-gun foe only by adept manoeuvring and her next encounter could misfire disastrously. More slavers were arriving heavily armed. Pirates, too, were now swarming along the Gulf of Guinea. At Collier's instruction, a 12-pounder carronade was brought across from the frigate.[2] Mounted on a traversing carriage, it would enable *Black Joke* to fire to port and starboard.

They parted the following day with Turner bearing despatches for the sloop *Primrose* cruising off Lagos. These were moments to savour – the billowing crack of canvas above, a hissing at her low sides and a broadening trail in her wake – while, he noted with pleasure, 'fetching to windward and running down the coast under topsails and foresail'.[3] Collier's letters were delivered to *Primrose*, an invigorating chase ended with the release of a vessel on legitimate trade, and all the while mundane routine was interspersed with boarding exercises as cutlasses were wielded and pistols brandished by the brig's crew of miscreants.

Late in the afternoon of 27 August they were approaching the shore and had trimmed and stowed small sail when a lookout reported three strangers standing off Ouidah. There could be little doubt they were slavers, most probably Brazilian, and in an age-old naval ploy to deceive potential foes – a *ruse de guerre* – Turner raised Brazilian colours.

The consequences erupted at sunset in a ballet of delicacy, blood and fury – one that would resonate down Admiralty corridors.

Phillip Prouting's origins were not those typically associated with buccaneering. The Hampshire fishing village of Emsworth where he grew up dated from Roman times and nourished a small, well-settled community of oystermen who prospered on the reputation of their flavoursome harvest. The Proutings were a fishing clan and Phillip, born in 1802, was baptised at the medieval church of St Thomas à Becket at Warblington that had long served local seafarers.

How Prouting came to sail for South America is unknown: he was not of that Emsworth generation once plagued by press gangs from Portsmouth just a few miles to the west; but, as has been seen, the end of the long wars with France had left seafarers of all kinds destitute and Emsworth's oyster riches were being ransacked by fishing invaders from other ports. In the 1820s, Phillip Prouting joined what became an exodus of seamen across the Atlantic, where Britons had sought fortune and plunder since the time of Sir Francis Drake.

Rewards for many were to be had at this time in the naval conflict between Brazil and the emergent republic of Argentina – or the United Provinces of the Río de la Plata as it was. Whereas Brazil had a powerful navy, the former Spanish colony with its capital at Buenos Aires was desperately recruiting seafarers of all kinds, initially to man small vessels in a vain attempt to prevent a Brazilian blockade of Río de la Plata, and, when that failed, to loot and disrupt Brazilian commerce.[4] Although privateering, as this practice was known, had a tradition which embraced the likes of Drake and Henry Morgan, two elements were essential to distinguish it from piracy: privateers had to be licensed by a recognised state and could only attack an enemy. Among those to have crossed that line was William Kidd, hanged at Execution Dock back in 1701.

Phillip Prouting's passage from oysterman to buccaneer began in Buenos Aires. It may be assumed that he had won some credentials in the war before Don José Arriola and seven other local citizens bought the schooner *Presidente* and appointed him captain to plunder vessels under the Brazilian flag.[5] The *Presidente*'s early history is shrouded in haze, but Prouting was 25 when her licence was approved by the Buenos Aires regime in May 1827, authorising him to recruit what became an almost entirely British company and bestow rank on those of his choice.

It is recorded that she captured various Brazilian vessels, reaping rich rewards which were laid in the hands of Haddock and Dinzey, English agents on the Caribbean island of St Bartholomew.[6] Darker accounts of 'outrages' also emerged. Prouting was reported to have been fined by the island's authorities for trying to sell captives from a Brazilian slaver.[7] Not only enemy vessels were being attacked. A petition from London merchants at what had become commonplace looting 'of British ships . . . by vessels of war sailing under the Buenos Aires flag' led to the Navy being put on alert 'for seizing and sending [them] to England for trial'.[8]

The last word on Prouting from Buenos Aires was of *Presidente* sailing for the Caribbean at the end of 1827 to enlist a new crew as 'nearly all his officers and men had left him'. This was clearly successful because a few months later he was seen 'on the coast of Africa' with an exceptionally large company of 95 to man the schooner's 14 guns and crew her prizes.[9] The seizure here of an English trader, the *Perfection*, would later be attributed to *Presidente* as a capture requiring a prize crew that reduced her company by twenty men.[10]

Their first known African foray occurred in August when, on successive days at Ouidah, Prouting's men boarded two slavers – *Campeadora*, a Spanish schooner, and *Hosse*, a brig owned by 'Chacha' de Souza but registered under Portuguese colours. Both their crews were taken on to *Presidente* and placed below in irons.

Prouting's involvement in slaving is open to question as both vessels were captured before being loaded. Their trading goods of tobacco and rum were intact, though, and as well as booty he now had three well-armed vessels, all capable of scouring the Bight for further spoils. Thus were matters poised on the evening of 27 August.

At about 4pm Prouting sighted what he took to be another sumptuous prize, a brig of sleek beauty approaching from the south. One of his prisoners, Juan Evangelista, master of the *Hosse*, later testified to having warned that, although flying the Brazilian flag, she was no slaver but an infamous navy cruiser called the *Black Joke*. Prouting reportedly replied: 'I don't care a curse. As soon as they come near me, I'll fight them like hell.'[11] According to another account he said: 'She is a damned fine brig, has but one gun, will do very well for us, and I must have her.'[12]

Up on *Black Joke*'s quarterdeck, Turner saw three vessels coming out from Ouidah, 'all tacking occasionally, beating to windward', and at first took them for the slavers he had intended to deceive by flying the Brazilian flag. Yet one was leading the way and their true purpose became clear when at 6.30 'she fired a shot at us and showed Spanish colours'.[13] In the gathering gloom, *Black Joke* lowered her Brazilian colours and raised the flag of the Royal Navy, then tacked to within hailing distance where Turner called out three times. Answer came in the form of a broadside.[14]

Vastly outgunned, Turner's strategy now turned on luring his main adversary, *Presidente* – 'the topsail schooner', he termed her – from her consorts. 'I continued to stand off the land wishing to draw her from the others, she being evidently a superior sailer.'[15] He took a brief rest below before the officer of the watch came down to report 'she was close upon us'.[16] 'At 11.30, I had the satisfaction to see her on our weather quarter, her consorts out of sight. I immediately tacked when she bore up & made all sail. We did the same.'[17]

With *Black Joke* now in pursuit, they danced on through the night. On *Presidente*, Prouting seemed heedless of the fact that they had a navy vessel on their heels. He fired up his company with assurances that she was a privateer carrying gold from Brazil and ordered the militia commander, a Spanish mercenary named Rodríguez, to prepare for boarding.[18]

Turner had his own boarding plans in hand. The crew was divided into four parties to be led by Turner himself, Harvey, Butterfield and Slade, bearing pistols, cutlasses and knives. Here, finally, Collier's exercise regime would be fully tested. Of rest there had been none when the first light of day came up to reveal *Presidente* a short way ahead. 'Seeing she could not get away,' Turner reported, 'she rounded and fired a broadside.'

As *Black Joke* came alongside, her lone carronade thundered, muskets blazed. *Presidente*'s boom was shattered. A man at the wheel went down. So did Prouting, 'hit by a large shot'. A wave of more than forty bellowing men brandishing their weapons surged across on to *Presidente*'s deck, smugglers to the fore followed by the forbidding spectacle of advancing Kru. Just two boys and a helmsman remained on *Black Joke*.

The struggle was brief. Among the bodies scattered on a deck left swirling in blood, Turner found Prouting 'killed by a roundshot which cut him literally in two'.[19]

His next shock – a 'deep sorrow' – was discovering that their antagonists were Englishmen. Five others were dead, twenty wounded. One Black Joke had been killed in hand-to-hand action, John Williams, a gunner's mate from Carnarvon.[20]

There was little time for reflection before the other two vessels came in sight led by *Hosse*. Turner pulled down his colours to deceive them into thinking he had struck and, as he related, 'she came up and we took possession'.[21] Prouting's third vessel, *Campeadora*, promptly made off. No more blood had been shed.

As the cloud of confusion settled, a few facts came into focus. Not only were most of the seventy-one prisoners Englishmen, but 'many of them had served years in the Navy'.[22] Among them were John Clements, ranked lieutenant by Prouting, who had taken command on his death, and George Byron, another lieutenant, placed in charge of *Hosse*. The seamen included a black hand named John Hudson who was wounded in the action and taken across to *Black Joke* where, the surgeon reported, 'I was obliged to take an arm off'.[23]

What passed between Turner and the prisoners was not set down. Clements and Byron might have argued – as indeed they later did – that the whole affair was down to misapprehension, to a belief that being under Brazilian colours *Black Joke* was a legitimate quarry, and that her raising of the navy ensign had gone unseen as dark came on. Then again, the *Presidente*'s commission produced by Clements had expired three months earlier, and neither *Hosse* nor *Campeadora* were Brazilian vessels. Moreover, enough Buenos Aires privateers had gone piratical for there to have been little doubt in Turner's mind that *Presidente* was just one more.

His sorrow may still have been compounded by knowledge that these men – like his smugglers – had been cast away by the Navy after service in war and were now liable to be repatriated for trial as pirates and executed. John Hudson would not be spared for having lost an arm. They were duly consigned below in irons.

Another quirk of fate not lost on Turner was how life had set him and Phillip Prouting on their divergent courses. Prouting – 'an Emsworth man' as he discovered – had been born just a couple of miles from his own native Bedhampton, and in the same year as him, both destined to be seafarers, one with the fortune to pursue honour, the other driven to plunder, and all converging here on the bloody deck of a pirate ship.

The aftermath was messy, prolonged, and left a range of questions unresolved.

Turner accompanied his two prizes to Princes Island and a rendezvous with *Sybille* in the first week of September. Collier reported to the Admiralty: 'I feel quite at a loss to express in adequate terms my satisfaction at the conduct of Lt Turner and his gallant crew.'[24] Turner's own account, praising in turn his trio of master's mates, Harvey, Butterfield and Slade, for leading their boarding parties 'in the most gallant style', was enclosed. Further tributes were extended to *Black Joke*'s company of Kru, whose services the commodore had noted before, and her smugglers.

At this point *Black Joke* sailed for Ouidah to resume cruising while the two prizes started west for Freetown bearing seventy-one prisoners. Strains between navy men who had found themselves on opposite sides firing at one another gave rise to a claim of 'cruel treatment' and of several prisoners being flogged.[25] The drama did not end there: *Presidente* lost her main mast in a tornado, was swept on to a reef and left 'a complete wreck'. It was something of a miracle that everyone on board got off and survived six days as castaways before being rescued and taken on *Hosse*.[26]

Off Ouidah, meanwhile, *Black Joke* had returned to action. On the afternoon of 14 September she was lying some 120 miles south of Ouidah when, Turner noted: 'Saw a sail on bow. Made studding sails in chase.' In doing so they fell in with the 18-gun *Primrose*, she having already been in pursuit for six hours. They still came up on the slaver together, as Turner recorded: 'Hove to in co *Primrose* and captured schooner *Zepherina* with 218 slaves for Bahia. Sent Mr Slade on board as prize master.'[27] Credit was given to *Primrose* as the senior vessel, though it is questionable whether the slaver would have been taken and her captives saved without *Black Joke*'s intervention. Three weeks later they outstripped *Primrose* again, only to board a quarry that turned out to be French.[28] The *Duc de Bordeaux* was one of a dozen French slavers allowed to proceed under treaty that year.[29]

Turner brought *Black Joke* in at Freetown for the last time on 4 November, a farewell accompanied by 'a heavy tornado with rain and thunder'.[30] Awaiting him was confirmation of his promotion. In the revelries that followed, Collier's appreciation for the rise in morale wrought by Turner and his brig was reflected in the presentation of a sword inscribed:

> A token of respect and regard from Commodore Collier, the captain, officers and ship's company of HMS *Sybille* to Capt Wm Turner for his zeal and gallantry while lieutenant commanding the *Black Joke* tender.[31]

Turner's legacy arguably went deeper. 'Zeal and gallantry' often amounted to naval clichés for exemplary service. Another ingredient, rarely mentioned and frequently absent but essential to success in a ship of war, was harmony. Two men had died on *Black Joke*, one in action, the other lost overboard. Yet in the ten months of Turner's command there had been no recorded floggings. His band of smugglers had found purpose in running aloft to crowd the upper yards, exhilaration in the shrouds, and perhaps even satisfaction at rescuing fellow human beings.

Logbooks can be indicators of health, efficiency and contentment: ships gained a reputation among seamen just as commanders did. On *Sybille*, Collier's regime had eased but use of the cat continued, mainly for drunkenness or neglect yet also on two men who 'ran' at Princes Island, only to be apprehended and receive forty-eight and thirty-six lashes.[32] On *North Star*, another frigate, two men had been given sixty lashes and another fifty lashes in a single month.[33] Turner's record, whether in action, in saving lives or in setting *Black Joke* on her voyage of redemption, was outstanding.

He was now homeward bound – and he would not be alone. Collier, in describing the arrival off Africa of 'the most determined pirates' from the Caribbean, who 'fly the flag of Buenos Aires but have never seen it', had identified a trend that the governor at Freetown ruled should be subject to law.[34] Forty prisoners from *Presidente*, including John Clements, George Byron and other British subjects, were sailing to England with Turner in HMS *Plumper*. His first duty on reaching home would be testifying against them.[35]

But the transformation begun by an English farmer's son and a dedicated company of white and black seafarers would continue. From a dungeon of suffering, the low, sweeping brig launched on the east coast of America five years earlier had become a symbol of inspiration to those who sailed in her.

The press seized on the story even before it reached the Old Bailey. Swashbuckling tales from the high seas always attracted readers and word of the prisoners' arrival at Portsmouth and transfer to the grim stage for public hangings at Horsemonger Lane galvanised the prints. *The Times* led the way with headlines – 'THE FORTY PIRATES' – and reports from preliminary hearings which left little doubt as to the accused's guilt.

The initial charges were for 'piratically attacking' *Hosse* and *Black Joke*.[36] Early on, the Admiralty's solicitor Charles Jones discerned a snag in the case of the *Black Joke*. Although flying false colours was common practice in navy ships there were tricky legal implications here because it could be argued that *Presidente*'s crew believed they were firing on a Brazilian enemy. Rather than enter these troublesome waters, the charge would be limited to the *Hosse* case – though here too there were potential catches: the schooner's owner 'Chacha' de Souza was a Portuguese citizen but was also known to be Brazilian as well as a notorious slaver; and *Hosse*'s purpose at Ouidah was hardly in doubt.

The trial opened on 6 April. One of the prisoners had either been released or died, but the accused still numbered thirty-nine and crammed the benches of the Old Bailey, from the most senior officer, Clements, to the one-armed and destitute black hand, Hudson, as the charge was read out:

> The *Presidente*'s commission from Buenos Aires was dated May 1827 and was only for a year. The capture took place in August 1828. It did not entitle the prisoners to capture and plunder vessels or property belonging to Portuguese subjects.[37]

The prosecution's case covered familiar territory. Turner's account of the chase and action set a dramatic tone but was no longer particularly relevant as the attack on *Black Joke* did not feature in the charges. The main witness was Juan Evangelista, master of the *Hosse*, who testified to her capture and how, on presenting his Portuguese papers to Prouting and pointing out there was no war between Buenos Aires and Portugal, 'he said never mind, he did not care about flags'. Evangelista went on to say he had warned that the brig *Presidente* intended attacking was the *Black Joke*, a navy vessel, to which Prouting responded: 'I don't give a curse.'[38] However, the witness's denial under oath of any involvement in the slave trade may not have helped the prosecution case, particularly when he was asked how he had recognised the *Black Joke* and replied: 'I had seen her before many times.'[39]

The prisoners also had one critical factor on their side. The shabby treatment of naval servicemen as a whole – officers and petty officers as well as seamen had been discarded – roused an influential circle of sympathisers, and the defence was in the hands of one of England's most brilliant barristers. Stephen Lushington, a liberal reformer and early opponent of the death penalty who also happened to be a devout abolitionist, had counselled against individual testimonies being given under oath as they would be subject to cross-examination. Instead, a joint statement was delivered in the name of John Clements, the senior officer. Skirting deftly around awkward themes, it amounted to little more than a declaration that, before entering the *Presidente*, 'all the officers and some of the crew had served in the Republican Navy' of Buenos Aires. As to their presence off Ouidah, it went on:

> Gentlemen of the jury, you know that on a voyage from the West Indies to Buenos Aires, owing to trade winds, vessels are obliged to come near to the coast of Africa. Brazilian slavers being constantly on the coast, we ran along it, it being little out of our course to Buenos Aires.[40]

This faintly ludicrous exposition of Atlantic sailing conditions (which carried an implication that the accused were liberators rather than pirates) would hardly have stood up to cross-examination. Under the same exemption, the prisoners avoided having to answer the essence of the charge itself. Their involvement in making an unlawful attack under Spanish colours on the *Hosse*, a vessel flying the Portuguese flag – however questionable its use may have been – was simply passed over. No information was ever forthcoming on their previous history, how they came to be in the Caribbean or their recruitment by Prouting.

Instead, they were represented as victims:

> We were put in irons, very cruelly treated and several of us flogged on the voyage to Sierra Leone. But conscious of our innocence, we have anxiously looked forward to this day of our trial.[41]

Lushington had not put a foot wrong in his efforts to spare these men the gallows and his final argument was inspired. Fundamentally, the case came down to the use of false flags – or, as Lushington put it in more diplomatic terms to the judge and jury, if 'certain aspects' of the prosecution's argument were deemed to have wider legal consequences, 'the commander and crew of every British ship of war during the late hostilities might equally be charged with [piracy] for seizing neutrals'.

He concluded: 'The consequences to the whole navy, My Lord, would be incalculably dangerous.'[42]

Lord Chief Justice Tenterden agreed: 'The point is certainly one of great importance.' He passed over reports 'of cruelties having been practised by the prisoners' on other ships, adding: 'Before us there is no proof of cruelty.' In a summary that virtually ensured the verdict, he went on:

> The circumstances might induce the jury to think the captain of *Presidente* had grounds for suspecting the *Hosse*, though under Portuguese colours, might be Brazilian property, and if the jury think so, the prisoners could not be found guilty of piracy.[43]

A verdict of Not Guilty was delivered directly.

The case caused a considerable stir at the Admiralty, which carried out its own inquiry into the use of false colours on *Black Joke*. Turner's avowal that he had raised the naval ensign before opening fire was not in doubt, however, and as that was the Navy's standard for legitimising this time-honoured ruse, its use continued – as it did into the twentieth century.

The acquitted men were duly released from the Old Bailey's gaol at Newgate, and promptly submitted a demand to the Admiralty 'for the restoration of their clothes and money' taken after capture. The same newspapers that had previously splashed accounts of their misdeeds adopted a more charitable tone. *The Times* reported: 'Many of the sailors [are] destitute. Their officers are standing by the men and are arranging for the evidence necessary for the claims which they have upon the Admiralty, Commodore Collier of the *Sybille* and Captain Turner, late of the *Black Joke*, for compensation.'[44]

The claims went nowhere. Turner had acted entirely within his remit, had returned fire only after receiving a broadside from *Presidente* and it suited the naval establishment to insist that the privateers had indeed turned piratical. Turner may still have reflected on the whole affair with regret: at least some of those to have ended up in the dock had been driven there by desperation, may even have believed they were engaged in legitimate activity. What became of them after being acquitted is unknown, but penury almost certainly awaited most.

As for the legacy of Phillip Prouting, little more can be said. A memorial was placed at the fishermen's old church, St Thomas à Becket in Warblington, stating that he had been 'unfortunately killed in action on the coast of Africa on August 29, 1828, in his 27th year'. It was later removed. For decades, attempts by relatives to trace Prouting's plunder stockpiled in the West Indies went nowhere. What became of it was known only to his agents at St Bartholomew. Resolution finally came forty-two years later when the effects of the 'late Commander of the Buenos Ayrian schooner *President* [sic] who died at Sea' were ruled to be worth less than £100.

Captain William Turner returned to his own family church, St Thomas the Apostle at Bedhampton, scarcely two miles away. He was due some respite and comforts of home but would not be spared duty in Africa for long. Officers skilled in cruising the Bights had never been more needed and Turner was to return with the squadron's next flagship.

In the meantime, the popular prints had alighted on a new yarn for readers. A dashing navy brig was reported to have confounded slavers with her latest deeds: the *Black Joke* had begun her rise to acclaim and renown.

CHAPTER 12

'SHE SEEMED TO EXULT IN WHAT SHE HAD DONE'
November 1828–May 1829

No one else had rejoiced more heartily at William Turner's promotion than his old rival Henry Downes. Envy would have been natural too, even resentment, for the two lieutenants had come out together in *Sybille* and as the senior man Downes must have felt crushed when *Black Joke* was first entrusted to Turner.[1] For almost a year Downes had observed her grace, noted her captures, her growing reputation, yearning for the moment that he trusted – that Collier indicated – would come. So it did, with Turner's rise and departure for England. On 18 November, Lieutenant Downes finally came aboard the vessel of his dreams.

Command of the *Black Joke* provided Henry Downes with an opportunity to redeem his reputation and repair a career thus far more notable for misfortune than high achievement. He had been born into estate and expectation, yet always seemed to be at the back of the line. As the fourth son of eleven children fathered by a wealthy Essex landowner, he was never going to inherit the manor, instead being sent to sea as an advantaged boy of 14 to become a midshipman. Such had been the start for many senior officers, but far from catching a following wind, Downes had been in doldrums ever since. He was involved in the disastrous Walcheren expedition to invade Holland in 1809, followed by shipwreck off Ceylon, before being caught up in one of the greatest scandals to disgrace a navy ship. Although finally promoted to lieutenant, he carried some of that taint with him and was paid off after peace with France.[2] There, ashore on the family estate in Essex, he lingered for more than a decade. By the time a return to service came, in the undesirable form of the Preventative Squadron, he was 37.

But recrimination was not Downes's way. He was a devout man who sailed with his Bible and saw duty in Africa as a mission.[3] In the eighteen months since arriving in *Sybille*, he had thrown himself into this service with dedication, along with a keen eye and notebook, taking an interest in African society matched by few of his peers. Being directly involved in handling captives, he had compiled 'a lexicon of the Accou language used by slaves taken in vessels from Wydah' that enabled him to discern those in need – 'Abi ha-mi' (I want to eat) or 'A-noo' (My belly sick) – as well as to issue warnings – 'Ahee da ca-eoi' (Silence or you'll get punished).[4]

Downes's faith and care should not have posed an obstacle to command, yet Collier had awarded *Black Joke* to Turner, junior to Downes by more than ten years as well as in standing. Perhaps, then, it came down to the *Africaine* affair. That had cast a long shadow, one which none of those involved had ever fully escaped.

Homosexuality's common association with all-male seafaring is not to be wondered at, yet records show court martials for the capital crime of 'sodomy with man or beast' to have been rare. While this was in part due to a tendency to overlook uncomfortable truths, events on the *Africaine* had evolved over years until reaching a point that a blind eye could no longer be turned.[5] Her return to England in 1815 from the East Indies Squadron precipitated a series of inquiries and trials that exposed an active homosexual group of at least nineteen men and four boys, including a midshipman and the captain's servant, in a ship's company of some two hundred.[6] Testimony to paedophilia as well as regular 'sodomy' and mutual masturbation orgies taking place in the seamen's quarters was given by a range of witnesses, so there could be no question of these activities being known only to a secret cabal. Indeed, evidence as to the extent of this homoerotic society so stunned those officiating at court-martial trials that a question arose. Was not *Africaine*'s officer class, and, above all, Captain Edward Rodney, in some way complicit?

Henry Downes's part in all this seems to have been just one more link in his chain of misfortune. He only came on the *Africaine* after his previous ship *Daedalus* was wrecked off Ceylon, when the ship's culture was already established, and, having just been promoted to lieutenant, stood fourth in a hierarchy where he was scarcely in a position to create waves. Moreover, when an act of 'uncleanness' on the lower deck was reported to him by a concerned seaman, William Brown, who had been with him on *Daedalus*, Downes informed the captain, so could hardly be accused of collusion himself.[7] At a subsequent hearing, Brown testified that before coming on *Africaine* he had been warned she was 'a Man-Fucking Ship'.[8]

Weeks of trials culminated in the hanging on *Africaine* of four men – one, John Westerman, still a teenager – on 1 February 1816. Others were gaoled or flogged. That same day, an inquiry began into the state of discipline under Rodney at which Downes was one of four lieutenants to stand by their captain, declaring 'no laxity had prevailed' (although Downes did note that Divine Service had been held only once in two years).[9] Rodney was duly cleared of culpability for *Africaine*'s 'depraved habits'. But his reputation was ruined. A son of the distinguished Admiral Lord George Rodney, he never served again. His officers, too, were left blighted by a shame the Admiralty did its best to erase.[10] The *Africaine* was broken up.

Thirteen years had since passed. On *Sybille*, Collier had a sharp eye for sexual vice himself, having just had two hands, John Whitecross and John White, punished with forty-eight lashes each 'for indecent practices' and a third with twenty-four for an unspecified offence involving a boy.[11] But any lingering doubts about Downes had been set to rest over the two years he had now spent in *Sybille*. He would manage *Black*

Joke in ways quite different to Turner, with more caution, less daring perhaps, but with an absolute commitment to delivering human beings from slavery.

Downes shared another asset with Turner: both may have owed their rank to social advantage, but that came from prosperity rather than blood, which distinguished them as a class from 'the taut-handed, kid-gloved, high-caste' type represented by Collier. As lieutenants, both excelled at motivation, forming bonds of familiarity with *Black Joke*'s hands of a kind usually confined to small vessels where, it has been noted, 'they became more like elder brothers than strict superiors'.[12] Like his predecessor, Downes would have no need for the cat.

They sailed together, *Sybille* and *Black Joke*, on 2 December. Once again, Collier would be at hand to watch a new commander find his way as they passed down the Gulf. Over the next three weeks they frequently came in sight of one another, but *Black Joke* was constantly racing ahead, breaking away on 17 December, for example, to deliver despatches to Cape Coast Castle – long the headquarters for British operations in West Africa – before returning to catch up with the flagship.[13]

Christmas Day was spent at sea, 120 miles south of Lagos in squally weather that carried away *Sybille*'s foretop but, once Collier had conducted Divine Service, festivities commenced and the slaughter of three oxen fed everyone heartily. One of *Sybille*'s marines, William Bambrook, evidently overdid the celebrations as he was given thirty-six lashes the next day for drunkenness.[14] Barely had he been hauled down with a bloodied back than a strange sail was sighted on the weather beam. It was left to *Black Joke*, naturally, to fly off in pursuit and report back that although a slaver, she was French.

Since taking command Downes had found little time for his usual daily Bible reading. ('The most profitable method of perusing the holy scriptures,' he once wrote, was to start at the beginning of Genesis, Psalms and Matthew, 'and read three chapters a day'.[15]) A primary concern was his crew. They were fine seamen, these smugglers, and working closely with them had confirmed his belief that they were decent fellows too, loyal to their ship despite having been let down by their country. Hands like Thomas Eason were the salt of the sea, with all the qualities on which Britain's maritime power had been founded.[16] But some were ageing, with three past 50 and, for reasons known only to the Admiralty, their duties were all the heavier due to a recent order that Kru hands were not to serve on tenders. Collier had partially turned a blind eye to this absurd decree while penning a protest to their lordships that 'her people have begun to suffer from being employed in duties that should only be performed by the natives' – a reference to the heavy work carried out in canoes; but for the time being *Black Joke*'s Kru numbered just four – King George, Tom Walker, Cut Money and Louis.[17]

Another concern had started to arise over *Black Joke* herself. It was known that as well as beauty, she was a thing of delicacy. A delight to the eye both in hull and rigging, she floated on the foam, as one mariner wrote, 'light as a seagull with long, slender wands of masts that swung about as if there were neither shrouds nor stays to support them'.[18] But Baltimore clippers had an innate weakness. They were lightly built and in haste: timber needed seasoning to be durable; British ships may have been cumbersome by comparison but, made of weathered oak, they endured for decades. The brig launched just five years earlier as the *Henriqueta* had no such lifespan in the mind of her creators. After weathering their first severe storm in the Bight together, Downes was relieved to set down in his little notebook: 'Brig well tried, stood on her Caps like a Briton.'[19]

She parted from the flagship early in January. Collier was dispersing his resources along the entire length of the coast, from *Primrose* patrolling the seas around Freetown in the west, to *Eden* the extremities of the Bight of Biafra in the east, with *Medina* and *Clinker* the waters in between.[20] A combination of brigs, schooners and frigates, each carried between twelve and twenty-six guns.

Downes's orders were to stand off Lagos with an eye to a large Spanish brig, *El Almirante* (the Admiral), well known to the squadron, which had been at anchor there for months due to the death of her master but now, from telescopic observations, was showing signs of activity. Being especially heavily armed, with no fewer than fourteen guns and an eighty-man crew, the Spaniard might have been assigned to one of the squadron's stronger combatants, but the fact was only one vessel had the pace of her. *Black Joke* would have occasional support from *Medina*, a 22-gun sloop cruising in her vicinity which also reinforced her ageing and Kru-diminished company with a mate and seven hands.[21] Collier would hold *Sybille* at a rendezvous north-west of Princes Island where she might be able to intervene while also being placed to intercept vessels emerging from Ouidah and Bonny.[22]

Black Joke had lingered alone off Lagos for two weeks when it was observed that *El Almirante* was loading captives. Downes sent in a note to her new master – a warning that 'all the English vessels of war are aware of you and cruise vigorously off this port'.[23] This apparent attempt to delay her sailing had no effect. At daylight on 31 January, a call came down from *Black Joke*'s masthead: a brig was standing to the south under a press of canvas.

The slaver had a distinct advantage, having awaited her moment to escape under dark so that she now stretched some 8 or 9 miles ahead, and *Black Joke*'s race to catch up soon slowed as the wind eased. At this point Downes ordered men to the sweeps.[24] These devices had not so far been needed but – as the long oars that gave a Baltimore clipper additional flexibility and added momentum when winds fell slack – they had enabled *Henriqueta* to escape a navy ship four years earlier, and they would prove crucial again now.

Hauling went on for more than four hours, a 260-ton vessel propelled by about 30 men in seasonal temperatures that reached 90°F, by which point they had advanced enough for Downes to make out that the quarry was indeed *El Almirante*. Three further hours' travail brought them within range to open fire from *Black Joke*'s bow-chaser. The slaver shortened sail, wore and replied with a broadside. At this point Downes concluded: 'It being sunset and not considering it prudent to sweep the *Black Joke* under the full range of his guns, I discontinued the action and kept close to him the whole of the night.'[25]

Yet despite the vast disparity in their respective firepower – an 18-pounder and a 12-pounder carronade against ten 18-pounders and four long 9-pounders – there was never any question of allowing the Spaniard to disappear. Throughout the night they were near enough to appear like dark apparitions, as 'we repeatedly passed each other within musket shot'.[26] Daylight found them becalmed, eyeing one another across more than a mile. And there they stood for much of the morning, each mustering resources and considering options. At 12.30 a light breeze came up from the west favouring *El Almirante* and her master Dámaso Forgannes made his move.

With the Spaniard advancing, Downes's strategy was to tack, manoeuvring with the wind so as to avoid coming broadside on. Even now, *Black Joke*'s every action indicated a willingness to engage: confidence in the essentials of gunnery remained at the heart of naval endeavour.

Self-belief was demonstrated when the slaver came in range and an opening volley from her larboard guns was answered by the Black Jokes: 'We gave him Three Cheers, hoisted the Union Jack at the fore, [Navy] Ensign at the main and kept the pivot gun and carronade at work at him.'[27] The damage inflicted was all the greater, Downes related, thanks to the *Black Joke*'s cook, an African named Joseph Francis, having stowed a chain in the carronade, 'which he vowed should pay a visit to the first craft we had any palaver with'.[28] *El Almirante*'s rigging was shredded.

Downes decided boarding to be his best option, even though outnumbered almost two to one, and at around 3.15, with their antagonist's mobility reduced, 'I put the helm up, trimm'd and stood directly for him'. Just then 'the breeze failed us'. Again, *El Almirante*'s broadside was brought to bear, and for fifteen minutes she blazed away. Had Downes not ordered everyone to 'lay flat as flounders', *Black Joke*'s casualties must have been severe. She still suffered, canvas holed by grapeshot – flying jib, foretop staysail, main top gallant.

Events under sail were always unpredictable. Shifts in the wind, however slight, a passing breeze or sudden slack – all had the potential to turn fortunes; and Downes owned that it was luck – in the coming of a light air, and *El Almirante*'s attempt to wear and retain the advantage – that enabled him to close on her stern and commence to rake her fore and aft.[29] 'Our position could not have been better, being within a biscuit's throw of his taffrail, and the pivot gun and small arms sweeping away every one who showed his head.'[30]

It lasted twenty minutes while a Spanish crew, quite familiar with the ghastliness of slave voyages, were confronted with new visions of suffering drawn from sea battles: amid flashing guns, blood and limbs and other body parts exploded across *El Almirante*'s deck; as well as the roundshot that had cut Phillip Prouting in half, men were being felled by musket fire and exploded shards of wood sent flying through the air by the 18-pounder pivot gun. They were lying there, silent or groaning, when, Downes recorded, 'one of the men got on the taffrail to say they had had enough'.

Trauma was shared by the 466 captives bracing below as the cannon fire, a shaking roar which none had ever heard before, thundered above. Some were wounded, others tried to escape. As *Black Joke* came up to board, an 8-year-old girl was seen to leap into the sea. Kru hands raced to the rescue and Downes was relieved to report: 'Two of our men jumpt overboard and fetched her alongside.'[31]

The sight on *El Almirante* that met boarders was none the less grisly for being familiar to old navy hands. Fifteen of her eighty-man crew had been killed, including the master Forgannes and two officers, and thirteen wounded. While their bodies were still being wrapped in scraps of canvas and cast off, one of the officers was found to be wearing a belt holding twenty gold doubloons and a ring on one finger. The finger was unceremoniously hacked off with a knife.[32]

It had been one of the squadron's bloodiest engagements. Further deaths followed among the slaver's crew. Six Black Jokes had been wounded, one mortally: John Johnson died a few days later. As for the captives, Downes's elation in the moment clouded initial assessment: his report, that 'being below they suffered but little; some were slightly wounded', proved too sanguine. Eleven died of wounds and their number would be further reduced before reaching Freetown.

They came to at the rendezvous in West Bay a few days later, *Black Joke* and her prize, to cheers from the flagship and others of the squadron. Once again, a delicate brig of a kind that had no part in British naval tradition had confronted and defeated a foe of vastly superior firepower. To Downes and others of his faith, it was as if she sailed with God's blessing. And despite having suffered damage to forecastle bulwarks as well as sails and rigging, her flags were still aloft and she retained in Downes's eyes a 'very <u>rakish</u>' beauty – so that 'She seemed to exult in what she had done'.[33]

The *Sybille* too had a capture at hand – a Brazilian brigantine *União* with 405 captives, which, for a vessel of her dimensions, was the most grotesquely loaded slaver Collier had yet seen. Briefly, he might have considered the traders to be on the back foot. He had just been able to report to the Admiralty a year of unprecedented success, with the rescue in 1828 of 4,566 captives, 'nearly double the number in a single year before'. Sickness in the squadron was reduced to its lowest level yet.[34]

As it transpired, the flagship and her tender had combined in delivering a further blow to slavers. Papers found by Downes in the master's cabin on *El Almirante* proved to be coded letters that, when matched with documents from *União*, became decipherable and revealed the route being taken by vessels to Havana. Traders in Brazil and Cuba were also being warned that, as the British had become more effective, only fast and heavily armed slavers should be sent to the Bights.[35] This intelligence was forwarded to the navy commander in the Caribbean.

Collier reserved his most glowing praise for *Black Joke*. Of the action with *El Almirante*, he informed the Admiralty: 'I never in my life witnessed a more beautiful specimen of good gunnery than the stern and quarter the Spaniard exhibits.'[36]

No language that I am master of is capable of conveying my senti-
ments of the gallant conduct of Lt Downes and the officers and crew
of the *Black Joke* who certainly have executed this service with
matchless intrepidity.[37]

Collier's shining tribute may have been intended in part to reflect the
squadron's achievements under his command, but it also showed a
desire to reward that officer generation who – unlike his own – had
missed out on glory yet were performing their duty with all the devotion but none of the recognition of Nelson's era. Along with the likes of
Turner and Downes, he would single out men further down the line –
master's mates awaiting promotion.

A further mark of Collier's decency in command was an eye to the
lower deck that sat alongside his taut disciplinary regime. *Black Joke*'s
smugglers were lauded to the Admiralty for conduct of 'the greatest
gallantry' throughout their service, but in particular the bloody actions
with *Vengador* and *El Almirante*. 'There is not a single instance,' Collier
went on, 'of one of these men being punished, or even being complained
of.'[38] Reduced though they had once been – to poverty and criminality
– these old hands had rediscovered spirit and pride through demanding,
skilled duties that rekindled their sense of worth.

Collier also resumed his campaign on behalf of the Kru. Having
won reform for their ration allowance, he took up the cause of
prize money. The Admiralty did finally agree to this radical request in
principle – or at least passed it to the Navy's treasurer – but securing
payment proved elusive, as is seen from a letter in which Collier raised
again some months later the subject of 'prize money claimed by
Kroomen serving in this squadron':

As there have been no arrangements for payments to these people
out here, may I request their Lordships will be pleased to take their
case into consideration and give such direction for the future
payments being made.[39]

Yet on Collier's own ship, rumblings of discontent persisted. Once the mood of a ship was established, she could be a stubborn creature and *Sybille*, for all her own feats, never quite shook off a disaffection that prevailed below. On 13 February, seven hands were tied up to receive between twelve and forty lashes, mostly for drunkenness but also disobedience and in one instance mutinous conduct.[40] Next up were Samuel Rogers, who got twenty-four lashes for contemptuous conduct, and a marine who received forty for stabbing a shipmate in a drunken spat. In the case of Richard Wilson, a few weeks later, it came down to thirty-six for insolence, while John Wellington earned another four on top of that for 'excessive insolence'.[41] Monotony and lack of shore leave were hardening the mood of insubordination. The *Black Joke*'s smugglers had at least the prospect of further activity to keep their spirits up as the squadron dispersed again.

The task of guiding *El Almirante* with her 455 surviving captives to Freetown fell to *Medina*.[42] As a 22-gun sloop and one of the squadron's more successful cruisers, she might have been preferred to remain prowling the Bight, especially with three captures of her own the previous year. But there was now no question over the commodore's choice of favourite.

At dawn on 14 February, Downes gave orders to sail. For the first time in his naval career, perhaps in his life, he had felt the tide running in his favour. Having seized his moment, he had Collier's assurance that promotion awaited. Yet a fresh concern clouded his view from the quarterdeck – the severe and unrelenting pain in his lower limbs. Gout may have been associated with bibulous aristocrats, but it thrived in the wet, salty conditions of a ship and had blighted the service of many a seafarer. Whether in his cabin or on deck, Downes was moving about gingerly.

Black Joke advanced with her customary fleetness – 170 miles towards Lagos from noon to noon before slowing. It had been agreed that her notoriety among slavers required a change of strategy so, instead of moving up to within sight of the port, she stayed well across the horizon while cruising to and fro. It may have been a mark of Downes's pain that for the time being his notebook fell silent.

Accra was among a number of ports along the Guinea Coast to have evolved from a slaving hub – it stood less than a hundred miles down from the infamous Cape Coast Castle established by British slavers – to a source of provisions, and one of significant importance to the squadron in supplying live cattle and grain. It served also as a rendezvous point, so it was no mere coincidence that when *Sybille* came to on 16 April, she found *Black Joke* at anchor.

Under normal protocol, it would have been incumbent on Downes to cross to the flagship – and a pleasure too, as he had further glad tidings for the commodore. As it would appear, however, his mobility was by now so reduced that Collier had to go onto the brig.[43] There, in the tight space of his cabin in *Black Joke*'s stern, Downes gave an account of the weeks to have passed since they parted.

It began uneventfully, he explained – days of tacking while keeping the men active at those boarding exercises of Collier's that had proved so rewarding. Their first chase started at sunset on 5 March and went on until after midnight when they came up and boarded what turned out to be one of those confounded Frenchmen. But then, Downes went on, while still laying to at dawn, they saw a brig and a brigantine to leeward. 'We made all sail after the brigantine and fired several shots at her but she did not shorten sail till grape began to whistle about her ears.'[44]

Young Edward Butterfield had led the boarding party on what turned out to be another brutally laden monster, the *Carolina*, carrying 420 captives to Bahia, which submitted with four of her crew so severely scorched by *Black Joke*'s grapeshot that they died.[45] One unexpected bonus, Downes added, was that the crew also included no fewer than sixteen Kru hands – unexpected because, although it was by no means unknown for Kru to be found on slavers, it was quite rare; and a bonus, he could have pointed out, because *Black Joke* was in real need of the gifts seen when two of his Kru had jumped overboard to rescue the child on *El Almirante.*

Here the cabin discourse might have reflected upon the lower deck's twin elements, and their quite distinct talents: Jack Tar for reefing and hauling, the man of rope and canvas; and Salt Water for his ease with the element itself.[46] Both were essential to the tender's continued endeavours and, Collier agreed, the sixteen Kru hands should stay with her in defiance of Admiralty instructions.[47]

Their meeting amounted to Downes's valediction. The *Black Joke* had delivered his brief moment of fulfilment: two major captures in a space of five weeks, including one of the squadron's few demonstrable triumphs; but their time together had passed as quickly as it had come. Downes left her that day never to return. On *Sybille* he was examined by the surgeon who found him: 'Afflicted with Rheumatic Gout aggravated by cold and serving in *Black Joke* and entirely unfit for service in this country.'[48]

Thanks to Downes's urging, Edward Butterfield would be promoted to lieutenant a few months later, still aged only 21. What defined Downes's command, however, was the bond he had sustained with *Black Joke*'s hands over the past five months. Seamen enjoyed a ballad and on their passage to Accra – and aware that Downes would not be with them much longer – one of the smugglers, Thomas Eason, a Wiltshire man, started to pen a eulogy:

> Come all you gallant sailors bold, and listen to my song,
> The truth to you I'll tell although not very long,
> It is of a noble brig, my Boys, the *Black Joke* is her name,
> Commanded by bold Downes, a man of well known fame.

Running to fourteen verses and relating the *El Almirante* action in the finest tradition of chauvinistic doggerel, Eason's song was presented to Downes before he sailed home.[49] He responded, paying tribute in kind with two verses which concluded:

Here's a health to all the *Black Joke*'s crew,
And may that health go round.
I hope they'll see many happy days
When they are homeward bound.[50]

Downes never went to sea again but his affection for the old hands endured. Along with Eason's verse and other mementos of *Black Joke*, he kept a list of the company present at the action with *El Almirante* which takes the form of a ship's muster, listing in order mates and seamen, marines, boys and Kru, and which, in recording various deaths with the relevant label 'DD', illustrates that he followed with care what became of them after he left.[51] It tells, as will be seen, a poignant, melancholy story.

Like his predecessor, Downes sailed home with a trophy from the commodore – one less dashing than Turner's sword, but no less fitting: a wine cooler carved from *El Almirante*'s timbers with gilded handles and a plated inscription: 'A Tribute of Admiration and Respect from Commodore Collier C.B. to Lieutenant Downes for his gallant conduct in command of H.M. Tender *Black Joke*.'[52] He was also to receive a pay-off of £275 2s 6d which, as the equivalent of about £15,800 today, was no great emolument for two years' service in Africa but would be supplemented by his half-pay as a commander, offering a comfortable retirement.[53] At this point, most relatively junior officers nearing 40 would have disappeared into obscurity.

But Downes's return to London generated a publishing phenomenon. The despatches from Collier recently alighting on the desk of John Wilson Croker had set the secretary to the Admiralty musing. The *Black Joke* had attracted unprecedented press attention for the Preventative Squadron thanks to the piracy trial just concluded at the Old Bailey. Here, surely, was another story to feed the popular prints – about the latest exploits of this indefatigable crusader against evil. In the margin of Collier's report on the *El Almirante* action, Croker wrote: 'Make a note for the Gazette.'[54]

On 17 April – less than two weeks after the piracy trial ended and while the acquitted privateers were still nursing grievances – the *London Gazette* ran an exclusive about the *Black Joke* and the 'zeal and courage of Lieutenant Downes and his men in a successful action against a vessel of very superior force called the Almirante'.[55] The next day *The Times* picked up the story, followed by the *Morning Advertiser*, the *Evening Mail* and regional titles across the country.[56] The *Black Joke* was launched into the annals of naval legend.

Far from disappearing into obscurity, Henry Downes emerged to a renown of his own, being invited into powerful circles that included the Duke of Wellington. During the founding of the Royal United Services Institute, initiated by the Iron Duke, Downes became a leader of the naval cohort and, as director, shaped its governance as 'a strictly scientific and professional society, and not a club'.[57] He had a fine house in Kensington's Ladbroke Terrace, but lived quite frugally with a single female servant, serving charitable causes in which visitors were invited to join while sharing a glass of wine in the sitting room. There, conversation might turn to an oil painting over the fireplace which Downes had commissioned from Nicholas Condy, a blazing canvas in which *El Almirante* is being absorbed in flames against a night sky under *Black Joke*'s withering fire, and the story could be retold while glasses were refreshed from the wine cooler fashioned from a piece of timber at the heart of the action that day.[58]

CHAPTER 13

PLAGUE AT SEA
March–December 1829

The huzzahs and praises attending *Black Joke*'s capture of *El Almirante* tended to blot out a dark aftermath – one easily overlooked by the outside world. As always with suffering, only those present were alive to what human agony entailed and, as in war, death statistics read in the press brought little real comprehension. When the casualties were among the common or lesser orders, there was little concern either. For witnesses it was different.

Spanish slavers bound for Havana, of which *El Almirante* was one, had the worst reputation for brutality. Nationality was no yardstick, however, and when it came to loading, Brazilian vessels could be just as atrocious: the *Henriqueta* herself had been carrying 569 captives, a number once inconceivable on a brig, and we may recall the state on another Bahia-bound slaver when more than 500 souls were released from below, an 'eruption of all ages and sexes, in a state of total nudity, swarming up, like bees from the aperture of a hive . . . so that it was impossible to imagine where they could all have come from, or how they could have been stowed away.'[1] Some insight into those conditions came when water was brought:

It was then the extent of their sufferings was exposed in a fearful manner. They all rushed like maniacs towards it. No entreaties, or threats, or blows, could restrain them; they shrieked and struggled and fought with one another for a drop of this precious liquid . . . There is nothing which slaves, in the mid-passage, suffer from so much as want of water.[2]

Accounts of *El Almirante*'s passage are sparse. Still carrying 455 captives, she was sailed by a prize crew of a mate and twenty men from *Medina* and accompanied by her on a relatively quick voyage of seventeen days to Sierra Leone. There was no record of illness or upheavals before they arrived at Freetown on 7 March.

Yet there they waited, for days, then a week, and then still more days, still at anchor in their prison. By now they had water and food and would have been allowed up on deck in groups. But they remained in intense confinement and *El Almirante* was infested. Dysentery, the slavers' plague, had her in its grip. Two weeks passed in which men, women and children died daily – whether they were dropped over the side or boated ashore for burial is unknown – before permission came from the colonial authorities for survivors to be landed.[3] By then, thirty-nine captives had died of disease at the edge of freedom.

An explanation of sorts was sent off to London a few days later: 'The slaves were not landed' because the officiating surgeon believed

> there was not any absolute necessity for it, and the number of those lately brought into this harbour being so great as to make it very difficult to find accommodation for them, even in cases of the most pressing urgency.[4]

The prosaic blandness of the phrase 'not any absolute necessity' as applied to the rising toll on *El Almirante* is only given some context by the case of the *Arcania* three months earlier; the condemnation of this Brazilian schooner was recorded in a despatch stating, without clarification, that the court had 'emancipated the surviving slaves, 269 in number, 179 having died between capture and adjudication'.[5]

Within days of being sent to Kissy hospital, seven more children from *El Almirante* died – four of them girls and three boys, aged between 6 and 9.[6]

Officials surrounded by constant torment, madness and death could be dulled into helplessness. The fact was that the Liberated African Department's resources were exhausted, so that while, on the one hand, Commodore Collier celebrated the year of 1828, with the rescue of 4,566 captives, 'nearly double the number in a single year before', on the other, those ashore dealing with 'the unprecedented number of slaves brought here' were unable to cope.[7]

Throughout Sierra Leone's history, it has been said in one recent study, inhabitants found ways to disrupt and resist. 'They refused to be a blank canvas onto which imperialist goals, ambitions and fantasies could be imprinted. As such, they presented successive governments and generations of abolitionists with a complex series of moral, political, ideological and practical challenges.'[8]

Local officials faced just such tests, only head-on. Thomas Cole, head of the Liberated African Department, had recently been confronted with a potential threat after an influx of Hausa captives, Muslims who resisted the proselytising of missionaries and removed themselves beyond the colony's boundaries. Rumours swirled that a large force had 'armed themselves for the purpose of coming down to plunder Waterloo, destroy the houses and murder all who offer resistance'. Danger passed but tensions endured.[9]

Cole battled on. He had overseen the transfer of village managership to men of African descent, mainly from the community of Nova Scotia settlers.[10] Now a new village, to be known as Murray and with space for 700 allotments, was laid in place within weeks and virtually all *El Almirante*'s male survivors were sent there.[11] The women went to Hastings and Regent with instructions that they were 'to be married to such of the men of their own country as can comfortably provide for them'.

When troubles came to light, Cole showed concern: a woman turned out by her husband 'because of her mind being occasionally disordered' was taken in hand; a girl apprentice found being ill-treated was removed from the care of one Susan Taylor.[12] The indenture system itself was coming under scrutiny as apprentices were not only being abused but sold on; many had vanished and, it was reported, 'it is much to be feared these unfortunate victims have been carried off into the adjacent countries'.[13] In one case, Cole wrote to the king of a frontier people as 'My Dear Friend', promising that if three children from Hastings were returned, 'I shall not fail to send you a compensation for your attention'.[14]

Not just the 'owners' of recaptives were tainted: after his death, it was discovered that a recent short-lived governor, Dixon Denham, had pocketed the 10-shilling fee paid per head for hundreds of apprentices, to the tune of £230 10s.[15]

Through all the suffering and chaos, one recent visitor to Freetown had been inspired by the place, moved by what she beheld and resolved to contribute to its future as best she could. It was the children who affected her most, their appearance on landing 'like moving skeletons' and the 'painful proportion of child deaths'.[16]

Hannah Kilham was a widow, a Quaker who had battled poverty in her native Sheffield, co-founding the Society for the Bettering of the Condition of the Poor, before embracing the anti-slavery movement and deciding she should go to Africa as a teacher. With a grasp of the Wolof language gained from two African sailors in London, she joined a mission to the Gambia country which lasted but briefly before her companions' deaths forced its closure.[17] Then, in calling at Freetown and on another visit in 1827, she noted with concern the number of children being indentured compared with those educated in village schools.

Hannah's loss of her only child, a daughter, at the age of 6, may have been a driving force. In three months at Freetown, she met officials and missionaries but also a range of inhabitants from whom she made notes on more African languages – Yoruba, Hausa, Igbo and Mende, among others. When she returned home it was to compile her *Specimens of African Languages* and raise funds for a school at which she intended to teach children in their own tongues while introducing them to English. Her published *Report on a Recent Visit to the Colony of Sierra Leone* concluded:

> My mind has for years been impressed with a conviction that our great duty towards Africa is to strengthen the hands of the people *to promote each other's good* . . . It is the Africans themselves that must be the Travellers, and Instructors, and Improvers of Africa. Let Europeans aid them with Christian kindness.[18]

Her plea did not fall on deaf ears. Two years later, Hannah Kilham would return.

Westminster's preoccupation with issues seen as far more pressing on the national interest had long undermined the foundations of a land where freed Africans might rebuild their lives, and the Foreign Office had been particularly ineffectual in recent years. The appointment in 1828 of the Earl of Aberdeen, a foreign secretary of rare grasp and global understanding, held out the prospect of change.

One consequence was the arrival at Freetown of George Jackson, a senior diplomat with experience in Berlin, Washington and St Petersburg. Jackson's appointment as commissary judge in the Mixed Commission on the stupendous salary of £3,000, half again as much as the governor, along with a vast outfit allowance, suggested a real shift in resourcing the colony.[19] All of which raised hopes among those working for humankind at sea and ashore.

Jackson could only have been unnerved at what he found. That Sierra Leone was not a posting sought by anyone of his background and pedigree is clear, and he had only accepted it after prolonged negotiations over pay and conditions.[20] Even so, the squalor of Freetown, a place without inns, clubs or theatres, only a moving mass of Africans and a population of fewer than 100 whites, none of his type, had come as a shock. Then there were the challenges inherent to his post.

The process of condemning captured vessels had been reduced to a mockery by the frequency with which they were purchased by slavers' agents. José de Cerqueira Lima continued to rebuild his depleted slaving armada and was about to have 352 captives delivered at Bahia by *Carlota*, the schooner named after his wife, which had been restored to him in just that way.[21] As things stood, there was still no legal obstacle to anyone bidding at these auctions.

It soon became clear to Jackson, moreover, that the connivance of Brazil's government in the deceit practised by its traders proved the treaty undertaking of 1826 to abolish the trade in 1830 was never going to be honoured. Jackson urged Aberdeen to apply diplomatic pressure, noting that ten of the thirteen vessels captured the previous year were Brazilian and adding: 'While I rejoice at the success of HM Squadron . . . I fear [it] must be regarded rather as proof of the perseverance of those engaged in this inhuman traffic.'[22] Jackson also raised the impunity of captured slaver masters who, instead of being banished to Mozambique as Rio had recently agreed they should, still returned to Brazil and within months were

again employed in their old vocation more actively than ever . . . with the experience and local knowledge they have gained which makes it more difficult for their opponents in the squadron.[23]

The arrival of *Black Joke*'s latest prize offered further insight into Brazilian methods. On her capture, *Carolina*'s master Francisco da Costa had admitted to Lieutenant Downes that her 420 captives had been loaded at Lagos. Brought before the Mixed Commission, he swore they had been legally taken on at Malembo, south of the Equator.[24] Such falsehoods were by now familiar and the judges had an ace up their sleeve in a liberated African named Ogoo, a native of Benin appointed to oversee those coming ashore who testified that almost invariably they were from his homeland.[25] Da Costa eventually admitted that the captives had been loaded at Lagos; the *Carolina* was duly condemned and her 391 survivors set free.

Jackson was unsurprised. 'The perjury thus exhibited,' he wrote to Aberdeen, 'is become too notorious to require any particular notice from us.' More disturbing was 'a new system of fraud', in which the Rio government was plainly complicit, designed to prevent vessels being seized without captives, despite being obviously engaged in slaving. Instead of a 'regular slave passport' authorising *Carolina* to load Africans at ports such as Malembo, 'the authorities at Rio scrupled not to grant her a commercial passport [for Lagos] which had the slaves not actually been found on board would have screened her from capture'.[26]

Jackson and Collier shared a common objective and it had all started promisingly. But it was not long before strains once more emerged between those battling the slave trade ashore and those at sea. It began with another of Jackson's letters to Aberdeen in which he accused *Black Joke*'s former commander William Turner of impropriety in removing sails from *Vengador*.[27] Strictly speaking, all contents of a captured slaver were to be left aboard until she was auctioned, but given the shortage of supplies for navy ships thousands of miles from home, a charge of plundering a prize for some canvas amounted to legal pedantry and failed to comprehend naval needs. What really angered Collier when the case was brought to his attention, however, was an airily unsubstantiated remark by Jackson – 'I have some reason to believe the practice complained of is of too frequent occurrence' – which, in the circumstances, amounted to a suggestion of corruption.[28]

As the powers ashore had utterly failed to prevent slavers getting their hands back on vessels only captured in the first place by the blood and sweat of naval endeavour, it is not hard to understand Collier's fury. (He might well have pointed out that the *Hosse*, taken the previous year by *Black Joke* in the *Presidente* action, had recently been captured again, this time by *Sybille*, after being picked up for a song at auction and returned to 'Chacha' de Souza.) Jackson also recommended that to prevent further plundering of canvas, an inventory 'of sails, stores etc' be taken of every captured slaver. The Admiralty agreed, despite Collier pointing out 'most respectfully to their Lordships' that these vessels were so crowded 'it is with the greatest difficulty even the slaves can be counted'.[29]

On the fraught question of improving survival on passages to Freetown, Jackson suggested that a surgeon should go on each captured vessel 'to make so close and careful an examination into the health of all on board as would enable him to give such assistance on the spot'.[30] He went on to propose that sufficient medicine to treat all captives be sent on every prize. Worthy though the notion was, it came from a landsman only recently arrived in Africa with scant insight into conditions on a slaveship. The *Sybille*'s surgeon, a man experienced in tending to sufferers, refrained from pointing out the impossibility of treating each individual squeezed into a wooden dungeon but replied that it would require a tenfold increase in supplies, which the Navy would not allow; and besides, supplies of clean water and warm clothing were a better remedy.[31] Collier merely reiterated his point about inconceivably cramped decks, observing that one of *Black Joke*'s prizes, the brig *Vengador*, had carried 645 captives and a crew of 47 along her length of just 100 feet.[32]

Relations were bad enough before Jackson raised an old chestnut questioning *Black Joke*'s legitimacy as an independent cruiser, writing to Aberdeen that 'authorising tenders to make separate cruizes, not only at a considerable distance from the ship but even on a totally different part of the coast, however expedient and desirable . . . appears to us to be at variance with the spirit of the treaties'.[33] This challenge to the very foundation of the squadron's recent success demonstrated the gulf between those expressing high-minded intentions while safely ashore and those charged with executing them at sea. Despite their common objective, they remained constantly divided by their respective elements.

Just as matters were coming to a head, the squadron was afflicted by a crisis far more serious than anything attributable to legalistic pedantry, and which could have threatened its very survival.

The *Black Joke*'s new commander came aboard with a record more impressive than that of either of his predecessors. Lieutenant Edward

Parrey had served on HMS *Shannon* in a furious action with the US frigate *Chesapeake* in the 1812 war and distinguished himself in Collier's previous command in the Persian Gulf, sustaining wounds in an action against pirates. Parrey's arrival in Africa with the schooner *Primrose* in 1827 brought him back under the commodore's eye and he was a natural choice to succeed Henry Downes when he limped away on 16 April.[34]

At this point, *Black Joke's* logbook falls silent or, more specifically, appears to have been lost, so there is a large gap in her daily record. However, other entries show Collier had brought together most of his squadron to blockade Ouidah, where at least eight Spanish slavers had arrived, while *Black Joke* continued cruising off nearby Lagos. Their designated rendezvous remained Princes Island.

This time success fell to *Sybille* with the interception on 29 April of a Spanish schooner, *Panchita*, carrying 291 captives. Three days later another Spaniard was boarded – without captives but of clear enough purpose for Collier to have her eight guns cast over the side and the prisoners from *Panchita* sent on board to return to Havana. At the same time a prize crew went over to the slaver. Their old shipmates watching her sail for Freetown would never see them again.

Health had always to be Collier's primary concern. Strict cleanliness was part of his regime, along with ventilation of the ship and good provisioning. In this last respect at least the squadron was fortunate, with ports such as Accra supplying live sheep and oxen, along with fruit and vegetables. Even so, almost 9 per cent of the squadron's number (81 out of 958 officers and men) had died of disease the previous year – the highest proportion in its history so far – and he had narrowly survived a bout with 'the severe fevers of the country' himself.[35] At such times, ships sailed to one of Britain's two South Atlantic refuges, St Helena or Ascension, lonely outcrops of surreal isolation which yet offered healthy climates, fresh produce, beer and spaces where 'the people can go ashore and enjoy themselves'.[36]

In July, however, Collier felt able to report with 'sincere satisfaction' that the squadron was 'in wonderful health'. The state of *Sybille* showed what could be done by holystoning decks and good diet, she having lost just one man to fever, along with two in accidents and one in action, since arriving.[37]

With the campaign at a rare high point, he also returned to speaking up for those hands who were only in Africa because of petty crimes from which they had long absolved themselves. On receiving a petition from *Black Joke*'s smugglers:

> I have been induced from their exemplary conduct to request that their Lordships permit their returning to England when their ship does as a reward for their gallant and good behaviour, and I should feel it likewise a favour upon myself.[38]

In retrospect, these despatches carry the ring of a curse. Even as Collier celebrated the fine health of his ship, poison was lurking below. Eight marines had recently come on board from the *Eden*, and two were exhibiting symptoms that could only have spread alarm across the lower deck.[39]

It started with diarrhoea and vomiting, not in themselves specific signals in an environment where dysentery was readily spread by contact with captives and malaria was common, though often not fatal.[40] The first signs that instilled terror were a man's drawn face taking on a yellow hue and his vomit emerging in a froth of black blood. Then his shipmates would recoil in dread. Yellow fever, or the 'yellow jack', was the plague of the Guinea Coast.

The first ailing marine died on 22 July, the second three days later. They were followed a week later by a boy named William Wainwright, in circumstances that for the time being enabled an orderly ceremonial noted in the log: 'Committed the deceased to the deep.' But with fear rising across the ship, Collier turned to the Bible: while Sunday worship had been irregular in the past, Divine Service was now being held on *Sybille* every week.[41]

It made no difference. From the third week in August, death was a constant presence. The commodore's steward, George Lewis, two seamen and another boy were cast over the side within five days. At this point Collier set a course for a rendezvous at Princes Island. There as they came to anchor was *Black Joke*, her beauty reduced to sheer disarray.

Frequent though tornados were at this time of year, *Black Joke* had been caught in a veritable hurricane that carried away her main mast and rigging along with two of her smugglers, Joshua Lacey and William Jack, both recorded in the muster as having drowned.[42] Seamen were a superstitious tribe and between fever and storms a dark cloud seemed to have settled on this corner of the Bight. Yet as men came across from *Sybille* and *Medina* to help carry out a week of repairs, raising a new mast and main top, she seemed to have escaped the yellow jack.[43]

Around this time news came that deepened foreboding. The captured slaver *Panchita* had been safely navigated to Freetown, only for everyone to be confined on board. The lack of basic accommodation ashore was well known but it now appeared Freetown was in the midst of its own epidemic. Yellow fever had spread along the coast, from ships to shore and back, and had the colony in its claws. Isolation failed to protect those on *Panchita*. The entire prize crew died, along with 33 of her 291 captives.[44]

All the while, bodies were being committed to the deep almost daily from *Sybille*. All eight of her new marines had died, along with a mate, Luke Allen, and a third ship's boy, William Russell, when Collier decided to abandon the blockade and sail for St Helena. 'The list [of men with symptoms] is hourly increasing,' he wrote to the Admiralty, 'and our main deck is now crowded with the sick.' He had considered staying on while taking command of *Black Joke*, but 'thought it might appear I was deserting my ship at a time when my countenance and assistance were most required'.[45] There is no reason to doubt Collier's sincerity. At this point *Black Joke* remained in good health while *Sybille* was simmering with unease and prone to violent outbursts: the marines, nominally in charge of enforcing order but perhaps unnerved by the fever's appetite for their kind, had become a distinctly fractious part of

More than a quarter of the squadron's force died in the fever outbreak of 1829.

the crew. On 23 August orders came to make sail. *Black Joke* was left to patrol Lagos on her own.

Men were still dying on *Sybille* but as she pursued her south-westerly course, running off 110 miles a day, the rate slowed. The last was another boy, William Young, at 7am on 10 September. Two days later they came to anchor off St Helena, with its mild tropical climate and rare comforts, for an extended spell of recovery. She remained there on 21 October, firing a 21-gun salute to mark Trafalgar Day which, in the circumstances, carried a certain hollow echo.

Much of what passed on *Black Joke* over the following months is a dark mystery. In the absence of her logbook there is no diary of daily events, and she is glimpsed only in occasional sightings from other vessels. These show that she continued to cruise the Bight, which, in the circumstances, was remarkable, for the records that do survive point to a nightmare unmatched since her days as a slaver.

In all likelihood symptoms had already appeared on her when the vessels started to go their own way from Princes Island on 23 August. Among the first to come down with fever was the poet of the lower deck. Thomas Eason had penned his paean to *Black Joke* in the aftermath of the *El Almirante* action when spirits were buoyant and prize money was in prospect. Eason was the first of her smugglers to be dropped over the side, his body stitched up in his hammock and weighted down with two 18-pound balls from her pivot gun.[46] That was on 30 August. There followed a pause. In the last days of September two hands died, including 14-year-old George Martin, a ship's boy and the youngest member of the squadron. By that point the yellow jack had taken hold.

On the first day of October, three men died. The following day, the oldest of *Black Joke*'s smugglers, Richard Holt, aged 51, and another hand were dropped overboard.[47] Others became restless, then despondent before vomiting blood. The loss at this point of a quarter of a company that only ever numbered about forty-four recalls a contemporary description of

> poor wretches lying upon gratings on the deck, some dying, some dead, some delirious, some screaming for water to quench their parched tongues . . . others calling on their wives and children to bestow on them their last blessings.[48]

But for her Kru hands it is hard to see how *Black Joke* could have remained active, let alone in pursuit of slavers. On 11 October, however, 100 miles north-west of Princes Island, they sighted a brigantine and, although in open sea at 1° 51′ N, 5° 51′ E, were able to bring her to. It was as well that the *Cristina* – Spanish and recently departed from the Bight of Biafra with 348 captives – offered no resistance.

The aftermath brought yet further drama and still greater tragedy. With the young mate Alfred Slade at the helm and a prize crew aloft, *Cristina* was being guided down the coast towards Freetown when another pestilence started to fester among the bodies below – not a fever, to which Africans were relatively resistant, but smallpox. On what turned into another hell afloat over their thirty-day passage, Slade seemingly lost his bearings as *Cristina* neared Freetown and went aground on a muddy bank at the Scarcies River mouth.

Details of what followed are scant. Slade reported that the crew 'used every exertion to get her off the bank' without success. As she filled with water, boats came across from a passing English merchant ship, *Sappho*, and carried the captives ashore. But *Sappho*'s master would have no further contact with diseased castaways and it was days before another vessel arrived from Freetown to ship the survivors. By the time they were landed, 116 of the original 348 captives had died. Another sixteen followed in the next few days. The remaining 216, it was reported, were 'taken to Kissy and placed in the hospital there'.[49] Kissy hospital, as previously noted, had been founded as an asylum for traumatised as well as ailing Africans.

Black Joke, in the meantime, had continued to battle her own demons. Four more hands died after *Cristina*'s capture, including her youngest smuggler, an 18-year-old Liverpudlian named Thomas Atkinson.[50] She came in at the Fernando Po rendezvous in mid-November where Parrey hoped to find care for her sick. Sixteen hands had died at this point. But such was her state that Collier – back from St Helena – ruled that 'landing men would have ensured almost certain deaths' among those already recovering there. Parrey was ordered to take her to Freetown.[51]

Here the extent of Sierra Leone's own epidemic became evident. The fever had seemingly been landed at Freetown in May from *Eden*, the ship that introduced it to *Sybille*. Among those afflicted was George Jackson. In June, the head of the Mixed Commission, 'completely horror struck with the ravages of the fever among the

European population', sailed home to England.[52] Other officials died. All adjudication was suspended. 'Every countenance you see wears the aspect of fear', noted one resident.[53] Another observed, 'the loveliness of the prospect was lost', adding: 'This is Sierra Leone, the Europeans' grave!'[54]

The 1829 epidemic illustrated the gap that would always divide whites who saw Africa as an alien world where a quick fortune might be made and those who came and stayed. Among the latter, Kenneth Macaulay, who had once profited handsomely yet also created an African world and family of his own, also succumbed to the fever that year. His company, Macaulay and Babington, had been dissolved, but he still left enough to his seven children to ensure the endurance of an influential Anglo-African clan.[55]

Another Africanist, Harrison Rankin, saw most whites in the colony as wearers 'of the gold brocade or the button of office' – men 'uninterested in its permanent prospects, unaffected by its progressive improvement' and intent simply on surviving long enough to retire on 'generous salaries'.[56] (Rankin did not shy from drawing a comparison between white and black migrants, noting that Kru too dwelt in Freetown only to reap the benefits before returning to their homeland.)

With the Mixed Commission in collapse after Jackson's departure and deaths of other officials, it was as well that William Smith was at hand. Born in Yorkshire in 1795, Smith had come to Africa as a young clerk and survived long enough to be appointed registrar to the commission. He too had a personal investment in Sierra Leone, with a 13-year-old son William by a woman of the Fante people who had accompanied him when he moved to Freetown from Cape Coast Castle.[57] In the months ahead, as the colony descended into a cauldron of feuding and disorder, Smith brought a steady hand to the commission, which had acting govenor Henry Ricketts at its head only briefly before he too sailed for home, ostensibly to escape the epidemic but in reality because he was found labouring 'under aberration of mind'.[58] In this environment, it was not only upon rescued Africans that madness was visited.

While yellow fever was the bane of whites – it became the source of the sailors' song 'Beware, Beware the Bight of Benin, For few come out though many go in' – Africans had been afflicted by the relatively new smallpox curse. Statistics in this instance are unreliable, including one of just 285 for deaths among recaptives that year, clearly a gross underestimate.

Whatever the causes of death, captured slavers continued to present terrible cases to the Liberated African Department. In August, a Brazilian schooner called *Ceres* was captured and despatched for Freetown. Of the 279 captives, only 130 survived to be resettled, the rest dying of dysentery due to brackish river water shipped by the slaver's master. Another shock awaited the Mixed Commission when it was found that *Ceres* was none other than the *Gertrudis*, the first capture made by the *Black Joke*. The deepest shame in this instance, however, lay with the local timber merchant, John McCormack, who had bought *Gertrudis* at auction for £620, either at John Brockington's behest or with the intention of selling her on to him. *Gertrudis* duly sailed to Rio where Brockington's agents, Messrs Platt, Millen and Reid, traded her on again.[59] (McCormack later sailed to England, for health reasons, but years later returned to Freetown seemingly a changed man, serving as a magistrate and founding his own church.[60])

Still nothing was being done to thwart malpractice at auctions. That same year, the well-known slaver Théodore Canot is recorded as having arrived from his trading base at Rio Pongos to buy a condemned vessel and recruit seamen from slaver crews awaiting repatriation.[61]

All the hope that had burned so bright at the start of the year was extinguished. The squadron had suffered the worst losses in its history, a grim record that would endure to its end. Collier's own morale was drained. Naval officers of his time were familiar with triumph, not disaster. As he came to the end of his third year running a campaign in which resources entirely inadequate to start with had been ravaged, where the Admiralty was deaf to the requirements for progress but

expected it nonetheless, and when what little support he received from
the authorities ashore had vanished with a tide of departing officials, his
faith in his calling was shaken.

The Preventative Squadron had a force of 792 officers and men at
the start of 1829. By the end of it, 202 – more than a quarter – had died
of disease.[62] Worst affected was the frigate *Eden*, she having lost 110 of
her company before finding relief at Ascension. Among the dead were
her surgeon and his two assistants; another surgeon was appointed but
service with the squadron left him with 'his intellect deranged'.[63]

In terms of numbers, *Black Joke*'s sufferings were not as severe. But
with twenty-three dead she had still lost more than half her company.
Among the last was Alfred Slade, who did not long survive the *Cristina*
disaster, dying of smallpox on 20 December along with another of the
prize crew.[64]

Alfred, it may be recalled, was a son of the army general Sir John
'Black Jack' Slade and had come to Africa with Edward Butterfield,
he the son of an admiral, both as hopeful young would-be officers,
both going on to join *Black Joke*. Still only 21, Butterfield had
already shown his fortitude in action and, far from losing heart,
threw himself ever more wholeheartedly into the campaign. Within
months his promotion was confirmed and with it a move to *Primrose*
as first lieutenant. For years he continued to battle slavery here,
before moving south of the Equator and taking up the fight with a
command off Angola. His early death ashore would be as shocking as it
was mysterious.

One of Freetown's busiest men at this time was a little-known individual known as J.R. Birchett. Every member of the squadron was aware
of his own peril and most had appointed an agent to handle their effects
in the event of death. While the late Kenneth Macaulay had acted on
behalf of officers, J.R. Birchett was the proxy of ordinary hands.

In the months ahead, Birchett processed the pay due to almost all
Black Joke's deceased smugglers, retaining what seems a dispropor-
tionate fee before passing the balance on to their beneficiaries. William

Poulter, for example, left £71 14s to his wife Ann, of which Birchett received £8 16s 6d. Of the £63 3s left by William Beale to his wife, Birchett pocketed £7 11s 6d. As the widow of the oldest man on board, Ann Holt of Winchester was more fortunate in having £2 5s deducted from Richard's legacy of £50 12s 8d.[65] In most cases, from wages of £55 6s (the equivalent today of about £3,160 for two years of service), Birchett took £1 15s 6d.

Some had named no beneficiaries, so the £26 13s due to Tom Walker, the only Kru death on *Black Joke*, and Thomas White's £47 6s, went to navy funds.[66]

Events that year offer a harsh reminder of hardship in the lives of common seamen. It bears repeating that decades of war had involved pain of its own kind but also brought virtually constant employment and a pride that culminated in victory. Men in the squadron served not out of desire but from need or, in the case of smugglers, to avoid prison. Bitterness ran deep, as is seen in a rising incidence of violence and indiscipline on *Sybille*. In the weeks after her return from St Helena, the mood darkened further with regular beatings for insolence and neglect as well as drunkenness. On 19 December, a hand named William Naples was given forty-eight lashes for 'throwing his bed overboard and contempt to a superior'.[67]

Although the state of *Black Joke* cannot be assessed in the absence of the logbook, it is hard to conceive that she now sailed with any of her old *esprit*. What the evidence does make clear is that her physical state – never sturdy – had declined. When next she came up with *Sybille* at West Bay in January 1830, carpenters and sailmakers had to go across from the flagship to carry out extensive maintenance.[68]

Just eight months had passed since the heady days when Thomas Eason wrote his homage to 'a noble brig, my Boys, the *Black Joke* is her name'. Eason was at the bottom of the sea, and Henry Downes's addendum tribute to her company now echoed with saturnine mockery:

Here's a health to all the *Black Joke*'s crew
And may that health go round.
I hope they'll see many happy days
When they are homeward bound.

Safely at home himself, Downes was nonetheless affected. It bears repeating that he discovered and recorded in his notebook the death of each man who had been with him on *Black Joke* and, in the years ahead, brought together devoutness and influence as a director of the Royal United Services Institute, fostering charitable causes to support destitute sailors abandoned by the nation they had once protected or served.

CHAPTER 14

A WANING OF GIFTS
January–November 1830

Seafarers bore witness to the timeless testimony of their incomparable chronicler Joseph Conrad, to 'the sea's senseless and capricious fury, its surface for ever changing, and yet always enticing, its depths for ever the same, cold and cruel, and full of the wisdom of destroyed life'. Those still cruising in *Black Joke* early in 1830 would have known exactly what he meant, even if they had not the words. They were familiar with the sudden tempests of the Gulf of Guinea. They had seen suffering and death come in forms as terrible as they were unpredictable.

In the months since being ravaged by fever, *Black Joke* had been replenished with some new hands. African sailors were increasingly visible in the squadron as – in response to the fever's toll, and in addition to Kru – young recaptives were being recruited; the brig *Clinker*, for instance, had just taken on 'six African boys from the Liberated African Department as apprentices'.[1] While details of *Black Joke*'s own company are hazy at this point, Kru hands still made up a significant portion – the Admiralty's prohibition on their assignment to tenders now being entirely ignored. She also had a new commander. Following the promotion of Lieutenant Parrey, a senior mate named William Coyde was at the helm.

The damage of recent months was not confined to her crew. In March, she had to put in at Freetown for further repairs. Although these were mainly to sails and rigging, her timbers had also taken a buffeting from tornados so the hull needed recaulking: while she still flew along with sleek assurance in a calm sea, *Black Joke* would be vulnerable when it rose in capricious fury.

It happened that conditions were easy on 1 April when, just two days out and some 200 miles south of Freetown, a suspicious sail was sighted. Together they raced west in a chase for twelve hours – sufficient for *Black Joke* to come up on a Spanish brigantine, the *Manzanares*.

Boarders were always prepared for trouble, with Spaniards especially. Cuba had become, in the words of one voyager, 'a *refugium peccatorum* for every ruffian', its trade in humans further bloodied by pirates noted for their brutality.[2] But despite the *Manzanares*'s superiority in fire-power and crew numbers, the master surrendered and the boarding party were in sufficient control to open the hatches for the captives.

No first-hand account of subsequent events survives. One despatch stated that, 'after the capture, and before the confusion attendant thereon had subsided, the slaves rose upon the captors'.[3] In fact, the chaotic circumstances point to a spontaneous reaction rather than a considered uprising. Those incarcerated below had no concept of being rescued. Opening the hatches triggered an eruption led by terror and instinct – another human surge so sudden 'it was impossible to imagine where they could all have come from'.

Violence was clearly unexpected as the first man to go down was an unarmed surgeon named Lane who had come on to inspect the captives' state. Caught up in a shrieking melee, he was badly beaten as men of the boarding party started to wield their swords. Gradually, naked Africans were driven back and below by flailing blades, leaving blood and limbs across the deck.[4]

But for their location, the taking of the *Manzanares* could well have evolved into disaster. As it was, just 200 miles from Freetown, they came to anchor four days later and a rare haste was brought to bear. A relatively low number of six deaths had occurred, probably from wounds, before an inspection by a surgeon the next day.

> [He] reported that among the slaves were a great many [with] sabre wounds and three amputated stumps arising from their having mutinied . . . He recommended that they be landed as soon as possible.[5]

So they were. And four weeks later, the 349 survivors – including 'several very severely wounded [but] now in a favourable state of recovery' – were declared emancipated. While there is no evidence to support any suppositions, it may be that some of these young freed men went on, like others, to serve the squadron.

Collier was not present to cast a fond farewell eye to the vessel whose voyage from enslaver to rescuer he had launched. Three years in the Navy's most desperate, unforgiving command had confounded this dutiful officer. He had fostered a cohort of dedicated young followers, marshalling his hopeless resources to decent effect, all the while battling apathy at home, helpless colonial officials and deadly natural forces. Memories of glory with Nelson were consigned to another world, over-shadowed by frustration in a war still far from victory.

The final blow was delivered by a new fever outbreak. Early in January, *Sybille* had captured two slavers in a week, her first in eight months. Carrying 659 men, women and children between them, the *Umbellina* and *Primeira Rosália* were sent on their way to Freetown with prize crews. Within days, men on *Sybille* were exhibiting baleful symptoms, and the ritual disposal of bodies overboard resumed.

From 25 January, *Sybille*'s logbook reads like a roll call of the doomed. Men were dying daily, from able hands to midshipmen, boys to marines, plus a lieutenant, the purser and the armourer. Jack Funnell was a rare death among the Kru. Worst of all for morale was the death of Tom Collins, the frigate's master, revered as 'the friend of every man on board'. According to one enduring yarn, old Tom went over the side just as a storm broke and a bolt of lightning caused the casket with his body to burst back up from the water as if bearing a ghost.[6]

Dread, along with exhaustion, had by now infected the lower deck with more than discontent. The spirit was mutinous. For three years, hands on *Sybille* and *Black Joke* had been immersed in human suffering of a kind known only to the witnesses, had cruised relentlessly without shore leave and with no end in sight. Men had had enough, they wanted to go home and throwing items overboard became a form of protest. A hand named Tom Wilkinson was given twelve lashes for casting stores into the sea. Others received between twelve and forty-eight for fighting and drunkenness. Usually the cat was in the bosun's hands, but he too – William Whitten – had turned rebellious, 'having thrown a sickbed overboard'. Flogging the bosun went beyond the pale, so Whitten had the bed's cost deducted from his pay.[7]

So pervasive was fear and mistrust that the surgeon, Dr McKinnel, staged a stunt to convince a superstitious company that yellow jack could not be spread by mouth: collecting black vomit from a dying man, he had it poured into a glass, raised it in a toast on the quarterdeck and drank it off; two hours later the man was dead while McKinnel continued to walk the deck as a demonstration of immunity.[8]

Such dedication, Collier reported, 'surpassed anything I ever experienced'.[9] But he also pointed out to the Admiralty that the flagship had reached breaking point. *Sybille* herself needed a 'major overhaul ... to clean her bottom', but the real concern was her company. Unless they were allowed to quit Africa he feared: 'We should lose half her remaining crew, not so much from sickness as the low despondency state they are in.'[10] Fortunately, even their lordships accepted the point.[11] On Collier's announcement from the quarterdeck that they were going home, unrest ceased directly. *Sybille* sailed from the Bights for the last time on 27 February, but by the time they reached Ascension, thirty-six of her company had died in this second fever wave.[12]

While mourning 'the sad wreck of my crew', Collier took 'proud satisfaction' in their record. In *Sybille*'s 32 months off Africa, she and *Black Joke* had rescued 6,575 captives, with another 11,914 credited to other vessels of the squadron under his command.[13] In a naval force that never numbered more than 958 men in that time, some 332 had died of disease, in accidents or in action.[14]

The spire of Portsmouth church was sighted from the maintop on a high summer's day in June. Of the 213 seamen on *Sybille* when she sailed from these waters three years and two months earlier, just eighty-eight were mustered on deck again that day and cast an eye to the Hampshire shore as she came to, firing a salute of fifteen guns.[15] An hour later, the log records: 'At 2 pm departed this life George Field, carpenter. Sent body of deceased to hospital.'[16] George Field's death in sight of home was mourned by his shipmates, but landfall also unleashed an explosion of frenzied celebration. Anchoring off Portsmouth Point brought an arrival of boats bearing troupes of gamey, resourceful women known as Portsmouth Polls. A week later, while gambols and carousing continued on the lower deck, the Admiralty paymaster and his assistants came up the side bearing sacks heavy with coin.

Among those coming forward that day were two Englishmen, a Scotsman and an Irishman, the sole survivors of the first twenty hands to come on board *Sybille* in 1827. William Wicks, William Crouch, Isaac Woodford and John Keily were due £88 1s 10d each for their three years' service, although in most cases this was reduced after deductions. Wicks, for example, would return to Norfolk with £63 8s 1d.[17]

Francis Collier came home to a knighthood and a pay-off of £2,133 7s 1d, a large portion of which was prize money.[18] The glaring social inequalities these figures reflect do not diminish the service of the Preventative Squadron's most successful commodore yet. At St Helena he had passed temporary command to Captain Alexander Gordon of *Atholl*, pending the appointment of a new commodore. Now back in England, Collier met his successor and pressed on him the reforms he saw as crucial to further progress in their campaign.

Logbooks can shine a deep light into a ship's life. What they could have related about events on captured slavers is a matter of conjecture as those records that were kept have not survived. It is safe to say, however, that what befell *Sybille*'s last prize, the *Umbellina*, after Collier despatched her for Sierra Leone, took forms of hell which no words could describe.

Once again, details are lacking as, although in this case a record was kept by the prize master, it was lost or destroyed.[19] Insofar as the horrors can be related, it is through statistics: *Umbellina*'s voyage from the Bight of Benin to Freetown, against what appear to have been winds and currents even more contrary than usual along the Gulf of Guinea, took a deadly fifty-seven days. As a result, 194 men, women and children died – a rate of between three and four every day; the surgeon who then came on board found cases of dysentery and smallpox, along with ophthalmia, a potential cause of blindness, and though he urged that the survivors be landed immediately, another twenty captives died. Of 377 humans loaded at Lagos, just 163 survived to be declared emancipated, rendering *Umbellina* among the most catastrophic captures made by the squadron. The horrors witnessed by, for example, two girls of 6 and 7, Arwonee (defining marks 'cuts all over') and Emgoloo ('cuts above navel'), were known only to those survivors.[20]

The scale of the tragedy led to an inquiry by the Mixed Commission at which the prize master, George Bamber, was required to appear. Because of the 'unusually great and lamentable number of deaths', the colonial surgeon James Boyle was asked about the likely cause. He hesitated to be specific but did say:

> I am confidently of opinion that the evil chiefly depends on want of knowledge on the part of the prize officers as to the management of such people, as well as of the treatment of diseases that ordinarily prevail among them.[21]

The clear implication was that Bamber had failed those in his charge, although how seamen with no medical knowledge were supposed to treat smallpox while navigating a death trap went unsaid. From the

BLACK JOKE

naval perspective, more damning was the duration of *Umbellina*'s passage of fifty-seven days, when twenty-three days was considered good and anything over thirty-five days disturbing. These figures bear comparing with the thirty-two days usually recorded for an entire trans-atlantic crossing to Bahia.[22] In *Henriqueta*'s case, it may be recalled, this had been reduced to twenty-eight days.

The management of captives had also been raised and here too there were concerns. Long-serving members of the squadron had been not only demoralised but hardened, even brutalised. Order was suffering, due to the barrels of aguardente found by prize crews on Brazilian slavers. In one recent case, a hand named John Ford sent on the *Não Lendia* had been given forty-eight lashes 'for getting drunk on board the Prize and ill-using the slaves', which may have been a recorded instance of a navy seaman raping female captives.[23] Three men from *Clinker* were flogged for 'drunkenness and insolence when on board slave vessels'.[24] These were not offences of a kind found in ships' records prior to the epidemic.

Disorder had spread ashore too. If Freetown's administration had been in a state of crisis before, it had since virtually collapsed. The departures of Ricketts as governor and Jackson as judge of the Mixed Commission introduced one of those phases of colonial feuding that would have resembled a comic opera had the consequences not been so grave.

A relatively junior army officer, Captain Alexander Fraser, had declared himself governor, a role for which he had neither credentials nor competence. Militaristic and boorish, he came into conflict with William Smith, the senior survivor in the Mixed Commission, and as their roles were interdependent – and as Smith had been the rock holding adjudications together – hearings and condemnation of slavers were delayed; and when the commission's Brazilian judge resigned in protest at Fraser's bullying, they were suspended altogether.[25] Smith, it appears, also harboured suspicions about William Cole, a wealthy merchant and one of Fraser's insiders at the commission, confiding to an ally at the Foreign Office that he was 'heartily tired of and disgusted with the connexion in my public duties that I have with these men'.[26] Smith's despatches did bring about Fraser's downfall – his actions were declared illegal and prompted a plea to Aberdeen: 'I throw myself on Your Lordship's kind indulgence.'[27] But by then no fewer than ten slavers had lain at anchor for up to two months awaiting condemnation, including *Umbellina*.

It could have been yet worse. To their credit, Smith and other officials had turned a blind eye to the rule that captives be held on their floating prisons until adjudication, so thousands had been landed to the overstretched care of the Liberated African Department 'and so distributed into different villages'.[28] The number freed was 2,235. But 428 had still died in transit on the ten captured vessels or after landing, more than half of them on *Umbellina*. Twelve ran away or simply disappeared.[29]

The arrival of a new governor, Colonel Alexander Findlay, opened the way to a resumption of condemnations, among which the *Umbellina* hearing shines another bizarre light on the nature of these cases.

Attending the hearing was her owner and master at the time of capture, none other than João Cardozo dos Santos. Formerly master of the *Henriqueta* and now one of Bahia's most experienced slavers, Dos Santos had profited sufficiently in his years as a protégé of José de Cerqueira Lima to buy his own schooner. Being captured for a second time – and by the same lumbering English frigate – had doubtless caused chagrin. But on appearing before Smith, he had no qualms about admitting to 'the illicit trade in slaves'. Although *Umbellina* was bound to be condemned, she would then be listed for auction, and there would be nothing to prevent him buying her back, quite legally.

Sure enough, a week after Smith ruled *Umbellina* an illegal slaver, she came under the hammer to one 'Joao Cardozo'.[30] Vigorous bidding had, it seems, been intended to thwart him, as £660 was an exceptional price for a schooner.[31] Just how the bill was paid is unknown, but Dos Santos had riches to draw on, having by now outstripped the fortune of his elder brother Manoel.[32] The *Umbellina* returned to Bahia and a year later embarked on her next slaving voyage.[33]

Laxity had too long left the door open to rampant abuse. The indefatigable Smith had no authority to deal with corrupt go-betweens, but he did have knowledge and insight, and, with the ear of the new governor, at least one bad egg was rooted out. Thomas Parker, an official recently dismissed under suspicion, paid £180 for a vessel at auction on behalf of a Spanish slaver. He was arrested and charged as 'an agent in an unlawful act'.[34] Released on bail, he was heard of no more.

Other known British criminals – vide William Savage – or suspects – William Cole – escaped justice. So too did Edward Jousiffe, the servant of former governor Charles Turner, who had set up a slaving enterprise at the Rio Pongos and, just as a force advanced to seize him, fled to Cuba, where he set up a profitable coffee business.[35]

The *Umbellina* calamity did raise some concern at the Admiralty about the mortality rates on passages to Freetown, eliciting an order that officers capturing vessels 'with a large number of slaves' must 'send with them a medical man when practicable'. That qualification relieved the Admiralty, as ever, of duty to provide the requisite resources. Collier's successor pointed out boldly in reply: 'The number of medical men here being hardly sufficient for the ordinary purposes of the squadron, it will be extremely difficult, if possible, to act upon these instructions.'[36]

Amid so much darkness, one voice emerging from the squadron at this time strikes a startlingly bright tone. Edwin Hinde was just 13, had been at sea for only six months and, finding himself in what his trembling mother declared 'a situation so perilous', wanted to reassure her. Sailing to Africa on HMS *Atholl*, the lad wrote home: 'The more I see of the sea life, the more I like it.'[37] His shipmates were kinder than she could imagine, the provisions quite excellent.

Edwin came from privilege, having been taken on the frigate *Atholl* by Captain Alexander Gordon, a family friend given interim command of the squadron. In times gone by, Edwin's position as a 'boy first class' might have heralded a rapid rise, to midshipman and on – to gold braid, battle and honours; and as *Atholl* made her way to Ascension for the handover from *Sybille*, his letters reflect some of that world, with youthful high jinks, swinging about on ropes and learning the use of a chronometer.

The boy's sangfroid was tested soon enough. Collier had passed on the command and *Atholl* was approaching Sierra Leone when a schooner was sighted and intercepted. Despite Edwin's age and innocence, he was with the boarding party sent by Gordon on *La Laure* and who then sailed her on to Freetown with 372 captives.[38] He seemed quite blithe about it all, writing to his mother:

> We lost 12 slaves who died in the passage, however the slaves are not so miserable as you would suspect. In general they are merry and come on deck. They used to sing and dance.[39]

Edwin was thrilled to hear that they were inheriting *Sybille*'s 'tender', the famous slaver-catcher. 'We have got the *Black Joke*, the fastest sailing vessel on the station. I expect we shall take plenty of prizes.'[40] A realisation had dawned, however, that *Black Joke*'s advancing frailty had left her too defective to cruise on her own until a major refit had been carried out.[41]

In June, they anchored off Princes Island to find the *Black Joke* 'hauled on shore and blocked, her cutwater being decayed and copper off her bows much damaged by the worms'.[42] While carpenters went across from *Atholl*, *Primrose* and *Clinker* to start repairs, Edwin wrote to his father:

> We are in a great state of anxiety for the *Black Joke*. [She] has been hauled up on the beach of this island to be refitted and we are very much afraid that she can not be got off without straining her a great deal which would spoil her sailing entirely.[43]

During the weeks of her refit, Edwin and others revelled in the beauty of an island escape from monotony and suffering:

Mountains with tops covered all over with magnificent trees, always green, inhabited only by birds of the most beautiful plumage, parrots, humming birds, kingfishers and eagles . . . not only the plumage but their song is beautiful. In fact, you could fancy yourself in one of the enchanted places of the Arabian nights.[44]

He enjoyed reading too – Goldsmith's histories of Greece and Rome in four volumes, loaned to him by a lieutenant from *Clinker* – and took to the water. 'I have almost learned to swim,' he informed his father proudly. 'This is the only place on the coast where you can bathe on account of the enormous quantity of sharks.'

His real desire, though, was for a berth on the restored *Black Joke*. Initially, he was disappointed. 'I am not going in her as I expected as the captain thinks I am not yet old enough,' he wrote.[45] But he had a powerful ally: William Ramsay was *Atholl*'s senior lieutenant, scion of a Highland baron distantly related to Edwin's own family.[46] Ramsay was to take command of *Black Joke* once she was ready for sea again and prevailed on Gordon for the lad to accompany him.

On 5 July, ropes were secured to her hull, the blocks removed, and under a light spread of canvas on *Primrose* and *Clinker*, and a chorus of 'Way, haul away' from the assembled companies, *Black Joke* was drawn slowly back into the water. 'Our tender is off and ready for sea,' Edwin reported. 'We have been very busy in boats getting her ballast and provisions on board.'[47]

No sooner had she made sail than another glitch appeared. The logbook, silent for more than a year, opened with the entry for 16 July: 'Set courses. Found the foremast much sprung.' After shortening sail to a passing squall, Ramsay had no option but to make for Fernando Po where 'carpenters were sent ashore to make a mast'. Reshaped timber was duly brought alongside and, with the help of hands from *Atholl*, a new foremast raised. Finally, on 27 July, they sailed again.[48]

Fundamentally, however, *Black Joke* was no longer reparable. Her essence, the timber that shaped her and defined her speed, could not be simply patched up repeatedly like torn rigging, or replaced like a sprung mast. She was not long for the sea. The question now was how to get the best out of what she had left to give.

The new commander's strategy was to emulate his predecessor by concentrating resources around the Bights, but whereas Collier had taken an active role in pursuit and capture, Gordon adopted a more cautious approach. It seems that *Sybille*'s high death rate had raised a psychological barrier. From this point, flagships kept slavers at a distance, rarely participating in physical contact with captives.

When the *Atholl* did make a capture while cruising off Bonny on 3 August, the prize crew came from *Black Joke* and, as she needed replacements, a berth was found for Edwin Hinde; the 'boy first class', his sights on a rise to midshipman, was brought on board by Lieutenant Ramsay. The very next day the log relates:

> Near entrance to River Bonny. At 11 obs'd a strange sail on lee bow. All sail in chase. 11.30 made out to be brig under French colours. 11.40 hove to and boarded *Paris* with 420 slaves.[49]

Edwin picked up the story in a letter home:

> Mr Ramsay and I went on board and when we told [the master] that we would take him he got into a rage and made us prisoners. However on seeing the *Black Joke*'s guns and all the men at their quarters he got quite civil and let us go on board again very quietly. However, as he was a Frenchman we could not take him.[50]

It did not end there. Between 5 October and 3 November, *Black Joke* intercepted another five French slavers with 1,642 captives – the highest number yet in so short a time. On one vessel were

> living men chained to dead bodies, the latter in a putrid state . . . The scalding perspiration was running from one to the other, covered also with their own filth.[51]

In total, these six vessels had been carrying 2,062 men, women and children to Martinique and Guadeloupe.[52] Yet they had to be allowed to proceed as all were sailing under the French flag – 'the banner of liberty, the vindicator of the rights of men!' as one member of the squadron remarked drily.[53] France and the United States saw the Navy's anti-slavery patrols as a form of economic warfare, a threat to be resisted, and had refused to submit to treaties; French slavers' exemption from capture – under the highly questionable undertaking that they would be dealt with by France's own anti-slavery operations – was a cause of rising frustration.

Young Edwin was nonetheless delighted with his new vessel. 'We live more comfortably here than on the ship,' he reported. 'Beside keeping a better mess we have the comfort of a large and airy cabin.' He had, moreover, been taken under the wing of an able commander, and Ramsay – having joined the Navy as a boy of 13 himself – knew how to foster a protégé. Edwin was kept on his toes, serving eight-hour watches and going 'to the masthead every four hours to look around', all the while learning to use a chronometer and other skills. 'Mr Ramsay takes great pains to teach me navigation which I find very easy and very amusing.'[54]

Action was never far away, however, and *Black Joke*'s next encounter had far-reaching consequences.

She advanced in November to the very corner of Equatorial Africa, where the Calabar and Cameroon rivers ran into the sea. Intelligence gleaned at Fernando Po indicated the presence of a slaver some 10 miles upriver from the mouth of the Cameroon where King Bell's Town, seat of the Douala monarchy, provided a steady supply of humans, if significantly fewer than the Bights to the west.

The slaver, believed to be Spanish, had been at King Bell's Town for months and Ramsay's decision to reconnoitre the river posed challenges. To seamen still familiarising themselves with this coast, Africa's swampy inland waterways were the dark unknown, and while mosquitoes were a discomfort – 'we are almost ate up', Edwin reported – there was a risk of real danger at the hands of a ruthless foe. As he explained to his family:

Instead of wearing our uniforms we all wear duck frocks . . . in case of going into action, the officers cannot be distinguished from the men, and the Spaniards receive a very great reward for every officer they kill, and as they are very good small arm men, it would be difficult to escape.[55]

On the evening of 8 November, a boat started upriver under the cover of darkness. No word came back, but early the next morning a vessel under sail was seen advancing down the river. At the sight of *Black Joke*, she turned about and started back up. Ramsay was evidently taken by surprise as men had to race aloft to set up the fore-rigging and three hours passed before they were able to make sail. In the meantime he ordered a gig 'manned and armed' to go in pursuit.

It was a mark of the sleek manoeuvrability of *Dos Amigos* – for that was the Spanish schooner's name – that she came to off King Bell's Town while the gig was still about two miles off. On the approach and with darkness falling, Robert Jenkins, the mate in charge of the gig, saw hundreds of naked black figures being borne ashore in canoes. There they were 'driven up into the bush by King Bell's people'.[56]

Jenkins fired pistol shots in warning before going on *Dos Amigos*. Below he found 'a slave platform much covered with human excrement' along with three tubs filled with between seven and twelve gallons more of shit, and slaving irons – but no captives.

The following morning, as *Black Joke* was seen coming up the river, King Bell's son came down and asked Jenkins her purpose. 'Very probably to fire on your town if King Bell does not send off the slaves,' he replied. In response, the king offered twenty-five captives 'which were all he had belonging to [*Dos Amigos*]'.[57] Ramsay declined. The number of captives initially loaded was never established. Jenkins said he had seen 'about two hundred' taken ashore, but the slaver's master told one hand there had been 563.

On one point Ramsay was certain. The *Dos Amigos* possessed the sailing magic that had once been his ailing brig's gift. In her decline, *Black Joke* may just have opened up a lifeline. There was even a hint of partnership in the capture – the *Dos Amigos* symbolising two friends.

Transition was by no means straightforward. The Freetown hearing lasted weeks and accumulated 'a mass of papers' presenting contradictory evidence from, on the one hand, master Juan Ramon de Muxica swearing on oath that *Dos Amigos*, being on a legitimate trade voyage, had no business in slaving, and on the other from Jenkins and his fellows, who presented different estimates of timing, of the numbers of canoes and captives emerging from *Dos Amigos*, and of the amount of excrement found on her decks, but as a result of which the adjudicators were able to agree:

> Persons in a state of excitement occasioned by being in action with an enemy have no accurate knowledge of the length of time passing under such excitement. The court therefore allows for the discrepancies.[58]

The evidence of De Muxica being found 'insincere and fictitious', the commission ruled *Dos Amigos* had been legally captured and she was condemned.

It was not a complete victory. An inventory of her contents at the time of capture found that a few items had been taken into *Black Joke*, including 'a set of sails, complete' along with casks of salt provisions and rice, and although the court agreed the purpose was 'for the public service', it could not be left there. *Black Joke* still being tender to *Atholl*, Gordon was held responsible for the loss and had £4 14s deducted from his pay.[59]

Out of this mountain of legalistic pedantry emerged one bright light. No captives may have been freed, but the *Dos Amigos* would prove among the most valuable of *Black Joke*'s prizes. A baton was being passed, from one reformed slaver to another. In the years ahead, she was to emerge under the White Ensign as the *Fair Rosamond*.

CHAPTER 15

'IS THIS UNPARALLELED CRUELTY TO LAST FOR EVER?'
November 1830–July 1831

The squadron's new commodore brought his flagship in at Freetown in November. With a long and fabled past at sea, John 'Magnificent' Hayes had seen much of the world but probably nothing quite like the scenes at a banquet held ashore by a local merchant to welcome HMS *Dryad*. The peculiarity, one of her company noted, was not the quantity of drink, although it left 'a few of the party *floored*', nor even a 'mania for speechifying during which the King's good English [was] murdered most cruelly', but rather a form of revelry bizarre to those unused to seeing men in gold braid dining with a mix of Africans and scoundrels.

> The Commodore was much amused at finding that he sat at a table opposite the black pilot who brought his ship into port – the Chief Justice sat cheek by jowl with a person he had tried for slave dealing just a week before – and the Governor had to nod acquaintance with at least half a dozen of the black rag-tag and bobtail of the colony![1]

The oddity, as *Dryad*'s surgeon saw it, was heightened by the fact that the governor in question was Colonel Findlay, an overbearing, blimpish figure who liked to sport plumes, epaulettes and spurs on grand occasions, while the chief justice, William Smith, was an assimilated white African with a black wife. Findlay and Smith were already at daggers drawn.

Commodore Hayes, for his part, came well briefed by his predecessor Collier and, unlike some of his officers, had little truck with prejudices of race or class. Scarcely had *Dryad* anchored than he took up the cause of prize money for the Kru, who, he informed the Admiralty, 'suspect the government is not acting fairly by them' and 'have never yet been paid what they had a right to look forward to'. Black hands, he added,

> have been used for many years to do the <u>deadly</u> work of the squadron and there can be no doubt of their labours having saved many European lives; and if they were to be withdrawn from the service the ships would soon be in a deplorable state.[2]

'Magnificent' Hayes came from a family of shipwrights, so had no ancestry to thank for his sobriquet, no grand bearing nor heroic feats in battle. His fame was born from the seamanship he showed in saving the 74-gun *Magnificent* from what appeared certain doom on a lee shore in 1812. To some it seemed remarkable that he had accepted the Africa command at all, particularly considering his 62 years. But another of his gifts, passed on by an uncle, was for ship design, notably of smaller vessels. As well as bringing reform to the squadron, Hayes was interested in how the new generation of Baltimore clippers was redefining fast sailing. His fascination with *Black Joke* soon became evident.

He sighted her for the first time coming to anchor on 19 January 1831 and she was in a sorry state. After taking *Dos Amigos*, Ramsay had diverted to Ascension – in hope of another refit. No help was forthcoming and some seven weeks were spent carrying out running repairs at sea, from a sprung main trysail tree to a lost fore topmast boom.[3]

Amid squalls casting forth thunder and lightning on Christmas Eve, *Black Joke* had to be handled cautiously back to Freetown.

At their first meeting over dinner in *Dryad*'s great cabin, Ramsay set out to Hayes the essentials to keep her operational – recoppering the hull and wedging the foremast.[4] Next he moved on to intelligence about the rising use of French colours; Ramsay's account of recently boarding no fewer than six Frenchmen with more than 2,000 captives, only to have to wave them on, confirmed a disturbing trend.

There was one question to which talk was bound to have evolved: how could the squadron's performance be improved?

The West Africa campaign had now been running for twenty years. Exactly what it had achieved was difficult to assess. Collier could claim to have saved more than 18,000 men, women and children from enslavement. Charles Bullen, his predecessor, might have pointed to rescuing more than 8,000 souls. How many had been brought to Freetown from slavers in the preceding decade or so is not accurately recorded – a number perhaps somewhere above 16,000.[5]

Yet just as captures had increased, so too had the numbers being transported across the Atlantic – and not just risen but in some respects surged. Vessels from Brazil, long the leading slaver nation, had landed an estimated 65,000 Africans in 1829, the highest number in its history.* On 3 May 1830, the emperor Dom Pedro announced publicly that, under the treaty with Britain, 'the slave trade has ceased'. Although this led to a sharp reduction the following year, it also set off a political crisis and, with it, Dom Pedro's downfall.[6] From 1834, the Brazilian trade would be resurgent.

In one respect there were signs of progress as the abolition movement in France gathered momentum and a reformist monarch, King Louis-Philippe, came to the throne. But all the while, Spanish vessels had been descending on West Africa in record numbers, taking to Cuba

* A significant but indeterminate number of these people had been shipped from Angola to Rio de Janeiro and were therefore outside the area policed by the Preventative Squadron.

more than 12,900 captives in 1828, rising to 14,900 in 1829 and a similar number in 1830; Spain had become, for the time being, the Preventative Squadron's principal foe.

William Smith, still doggedly adjudicating on a constant stream of atrocities, had written to the Foreign Office with obvious exasperation that year: 'So long as Great Britain continues to be the only power zealously endeavouring to effect suppression, it will never accomplish that much desired object.'

> The Natives of Africa will not believe that the slave trade can ever be repressed, and eagerly seek the opportunity to sell their fellow men ... They easily obtain their luxuries, and comforts, consequently will not exert themselves in cultivating the natural products of their country.[7]

One of Hayes's predecessors had pithily evoked the evils to which they all bore witness. 'It is necessary,' Robert Mends wrote, 'to visit a slave ship to know what the trade is.'[8] So it always was. A few weeks in Africa sufficed for Hayes to pen another impassioned despatch, a plea for more resources and diplomatic pressure:

> I say nothing of the Murders, horrible crimes worse than murder, perpetrated on these wretched creatures but beg of their Lordships to consider the offensive heat of the climate and to reflect on what must be the sufferings of upwards of five hundred of these miserable people chained together and crammed between the decks of a vessel only half the tonnage of a ten-gun brig.[9]

'Gracious God!' he concluded. 'Is this unparalleled cruelty to last for ever?' While that question was left hanging, Hayes weighed how he might rise to the challenge.

Among changes he had in mind was discipline. Despite a service record that dated from 1797, Hayes was part of a reformist group of officers who believed the Navy's old methods had seen their day, especially in a war against man's inhumanity to his fellow man. He intended to eschew flogging whenever possible. 'The Cat often irritates and makes the culprit worse,' he informed the Admiralty. 'Other methods of keeping the ship in good discipline' would be used instead.[10]

Old strains between sea and shore reignited almost immediately. With *Black Joke* still undergoing repairs, Hayes had two frigates, *Dryad* and *Atholl*, two brigs and two sloops to police more than 2,000 nautical miles of coast, when he was notified by the Admiralty of a request by Findlay 'for a vessel of war to be placed under his orders'.

The governor believed Collier had been mistaken in concentrating his efforts on the Bights – despite evidence that this was where most captives were embarked. Findlay also passed over the fact that most slavers detected in the vicinity of Freetown were under French colours and untouchable anyway. As an army man, he took relish in advising London about the squadron's 'inefficiency', claiming that commodores were interested only in prize money and 'increasing the expense of the British nation by bringing many thousands of slaves to this colony'.[11] Findlay was good at making enemies and not just among navy officers.

Hayes met his demand for a vessel with a brisk note: 'I find it a question too absurd for their Lordships to entertain for a moment.'[12] There it ended.

A more serious bone of contention arose from the thorny old issue of tenders. After lengthy consideration, the advocate general in London had ruled that *Black Joke* and her kind were *not* authorised 'to make captures of slave ships when acting separately and at a considerable distance from the ship to which she has been attached'.[13] Smith was obliged to reply on behalf of the Mixed Commission that, in future, 'we shall feel it our duty to restore such slave vessels on the ground of the irregularity of the capture'.[14] At a stroke of the pen, the fundamental gift of a tender to cruise independently of her clumsy companions had been lost.

In preparing for their first foray, Hayes was relying on what *Black Joke* could still offer, but already he had an eye to an heir. *Dos Amigos* was the ideal contender, and not just for the partnership with her captor implicit in her name. There was one obstacle. Their lordships were now likely to order that no more tenders be purchased. Hayes sent off another despatch, repeating the now-familiar wisdom – that 'the slave schooners here sail in a very superior way' and unless encountered close by at daylight 'there can be no chance of taking them' – before warning of the looming demise of the squadron's icon. The *Black Joke*, he reported, 'is worn out and in that state of <u>decay</u> not to be trusted to make a voyage to England'.[15] It made no difference. The Admiralty had indeed resolved to ban buying captured slavers. But Hayes had been left with one last opening. On 14 February, nine days after being condemned, the *Dos Amigos* was presented for auction at Freetown and a navy officer came forward with an order for £609 in payment.[16]

The officer concerned was William Turner. As *Black Joke*'s first commander, instigator of her rise to fame, he had returned to Africa and, although he may have looked on her lovingly (while perhaps eyeing *Dos Amigos* with a certain yearning too), that was not the Navy's way; Turner was second captain on *Dryad*, in effect number two to the commodore. The flagship had brought a string of other ambitious hopefuls who would be learning from Turner. One grateful junior later described him as 'a man of whom everyone spoke well, and of bitter material must have been that being who could bear other testimony of him'.[17]

Black Joke, patched up and ready to sail, was placed in the hands of William Castle, a lieutenant with almost twenty years of prominent service behind him. He replaced Ramsay, who had by no means been set aside but for the time being came on *Dryad* with his youthful protégé Edwin Hinde.

Dos Amigos was reborn as *Fair Rosamond*, named by Hayes after a legendary seductress and mistress of King Henry II. Her first commander was Henry Huntley, another senior lieutenant of long standing but with a strong aversion to the reformist political agenda emerging at home and, hence, his situation here: not only was the deployment of a squadron to suppress the slave trade 'a monotonous and idle absurdity', the whole endeavour 'to extend Christianity and civilization to Africa', he believed, 'has only resulted in an enormous loss of life, talent and treasure'.[18] Unlike most of his fellows, Huntley held to the bigotry characteristic of High Tory traditionalists.

Mortality, it may be noted, had remained high that year. A death rate of 11 per cent was a significant reduction on the calamity of 1829, but 72 men had still been lost in a force of 667.[19] *Dryad* came with a healthy new company who would replenish *Black Joke* and *Fair Rosamond*. They were volunteers, most rated Able, and – for better or worse – had just three smugglers among more than 200 hands.[20]

Black Joke's new company of thirteen Kru included the Prince of Wales, Tom Longlife and Jack Poorfellow. More freed blacks were also being taken on to train for the sea. The flagship's muster lists five 'Liberated African lads' as receiving a two-thirds pay allowance, while *Atholl*'s log shows '25 native Africans' as having recently entered.[21] Seafaring skills offered mobility, as the history of the Kru shows, and one officer believed the trend to be part of 'a wise and philanthropic design [that] must be of incalculable benefit to these poor beings'.[22] Enlistment by the Navy had begun late, however, and the number of freed Africans trained as seamen over the next thirty years is estimated at just 306. This compares with the 5,169 sent to the Army between 1808 and 1863.[23]

One unwelcome aspect of service for both officers and men came in the form of news that prize money – for those lucky enough to actually receive it – had just been halved. From an initial amount of £20 for men, £15 for women and £5 for children, the bounty paid for each freed captive had been reduced in 1824 to a standard £10. The Treasury had resolved that this was no longer sustainable, and from 5 October the rate would be cut to £5.[24] The last capture under the old system, the *Santiago* with 153 surviving captives, generated a payment of £1,530 to be distributed on a descending scale from captains to seamen, around a force numbering 677 men in all. Thereafter, it would have been cut to £765.

She may have remained fragile but she was fit enough to sail again and Hayes – having the same propensity for turning a blind eye to orders as his most illustrious contemporary – let her off the leash. *Black Joke* set forth alone on 10 February, independently of the flagship, in a test of her seaworthiness. For the time being, however, she was not to range far distant from Freetown and would lurk around the Gallinas estuary some 150 miles to the south-east.

The stranger was sighted at dawn, having pursued the usual slavers' strategy of loading in the evening and sailing after nightfall to stay under the cover of darkness – but without ruling herself quite beyond reach. At a distance of 11 miles, the schooner posed nonetheless a severe test for an eroded, ageing brig.

Once sails were raised and trimmed, men went again to the sweeps, and again they hauled under a tropical sun through the morning and on into the afternoon while temperatures rose to 90°F. Sufficient advance had been made late in the day for Castle to fire blank warning shots but the schooner's master ignored them, confident that nightfall would enable their escape. As dark came on, he blundered, bearing up in the belief that the pursuer would hold her course and race blindly on. But Castle had the blessing of a night-glass, a short telescope set for use at night.[25]

At around 10pm the slaver saw *Black Joke* looming out of the dark. He broke away, bearing south. It was too late. The brig's guns thundered again and this time not with blanks but balls that smashed into his starboard timbers. Resigned, fearful, he came to.

Most of the *Black Joke*'s party were boarding a loaded slaver for the first time to sail her to Freetown. As an induction, that was test enough: but the *Primera* was an example of the extreme overloading now common by Spaniards. To cram 311 people aboard, the schooner's lower deck had been allowed a depth of just 26 inches under the beams, possibly because almost half the captives were children.[26] Two of them and one of the crew had been killed by *Black Joke*'s fire. That left ninety-one boys aged 12 or under, and fifty-five girls, the youngest of whom was 8.

When the prize came in at Freetown eleven days later, two more captives had died. Of the four feeding mothers, one had just given birth and was observed, 'sickly and emaciated, suckling [the baby] on deck, with hardly a rag to cover herself or her offspring'.[27]

A doctor sent on board found women and children separated from the males, who were 'bound together in twos by irons rivetted round the ancles'.

> These chains were removed and they appeared much gratified. The countenances seemed lighted up at the prospect of being put on shore, towards which they often turned to gaze with an expression of wonder and impatience.[28]

Black Joke's latest capture had in fact been made in contravention of the latest legal instructions from London – she having been 'at a considerable distance from the ship to which she has been attached' – but, as a hardened observer, William Smith was not inclined to linger over that particular protocol. The commission 'unhesitatingly' pronounced *Primera* to have been legally taken and her 310 survivors emancipated.[29]

As commodore, however, Hayes could not afford to be insouciant about the legal implications. *Black Joke* – back in Lieutenant Ramsay's hands as a result of Castle's promotion and with an eager young Edwin Hinde at his side – returned down the coast. *Dryad* sailed with *Fair Rosamond* to join her at their rendezvous where, for the time being, they would cruise in concert, the flagship with her tenders at hand.

They left behind a colony that had fallen into a renewed state of civil war.

One newcomer to Sierra Leone that year was much taken on first sighting the place, its 'extensive lagoon bounded by a verdant and gentle acclivity . . . forming a sort of amphitheatre decorated with lofty trees and richly foliated shrubs'. It all presented to Peter Leonard 'a picture of the most agreeable character to the delighted eye'. He was impressed too by the resilience of once-enslaved Africans – a market 'crowded with liberated females, squatted on the ground or on mats, with their baskets of fruit, nuts or chilli peppers displayed around them and their naked, wooly-haired sable cherubs playing all around them, puckering their little, smooth, chubby visages into every form and degree of satisfaction'.[30]

Leonard, surgeon on *Dryad*, never doubted the worth and humanity of what Britain was trying to accomplish, and his own dedication to saving lives is evident. But nor did he pass over the toxic air poisoning Freetown's administration.

> The colony is agitated by perpetual broils and the most violent party spirit, caused, it is said, by the treacherous calumnies and malignant insinuations of some restless, hot-headed and evil-disposed individuals.[31]

Briefly, the mood had taken a more buoyant turn. Reform was sweeping through Westminster where a campaign to abandon Sierra Leone – to hand it over to the inhabitants and move British interests to Fernando Po – came before a select committee and was defeated. Years of uncertainty were ended. Property prices in Freetown revived and investment started to flow.[32] The anti-slavery movement in general gained further ground when a Whig government came to power under Earl Grey in November, giving fresh voice to Thomas Fowell Buxton and others seeking the emancipation of those still enslaved in British colonies. But at Freetown, familiar divisions soon reopened.

At the root lay an incompatibility between civilian and military authority that recurs throughout the imperial saga. The latest governor, Colonel Alexander Findlay, had little experience in administration and, although entirely without legal knowledge, was sitting on the Mixed

Commission. As such, he depended on William Smith who had long been holding the judicial process together and was unimpressed by his superior. 'Like all who preceded him,' Smith wrote to his confidant at Whitehall, 'he knows nothing at all about his duties and to tell you the truth he has nothing bright about him.'[33] Smith had fallen out with the previous governor over legal proceedings and was already exasperated.

Findlay's reliance on Smith and another member of the Mixed Commission opened a rift when he made demands that would have required contravention of a Foreign Office edict.[34] More serious strains emerged when Findlay suspended a young black clerk in Smith's office for organising a petition by eleven women, 'persons of colour', accusing a white militia member of 'cowardice'. Findlay was outraged by the claim, coming from 'illiterate females'. The clerk, David Wilson, the sole support of a widowed mother and grandmother, turned to Smith for backing.[35]

The mounds of despatches that started to land at the Foreign Office early in 1831 spell out a feud in progress thousands of miles away where communication had turned to letters-across-the-street mode. And because these despatches took months to reach London, events had already been overtaken by the time a bemused foreign secretary, Lord Palmerston, sat down to puzzle over the contents.

Findlay, seemingly in a state of paranoia, had already exceeded his mandate when in February he tried to seize the post of chief justice.[36] Smith pointed out that governors had no power over the Mixed Commission. Yet six months passed before a letter from Palmerston confirmed that Findlay had 'misconceived the extent of his authority'. A relieved Smith reported that his clerk Wilson had been duly reinstated 'and is most grateful for his Lordship's clemency'.[37] Smith himself was promoted to chief justice.[38] No longer in an acting capacity, he now sat in full control of the court.

Whitehall believed military types, fond of command, were suited for colonial rule. The trouble was that they were not familiar with debate. On taking office, the previous prime minister, the Duke of Wellington, found his first cabinet meeting an astonishing business. 'I gave them their orders,' he related, 'and they wanted to stay and discuss them.' Findlay was cut from the same red cloth.

Hostilities ashore may be compared with a relative harmony now prevailing at sea. That is not to say naval order was essentially less authoritarian – quite the contrary – but it had evolved out of a necessity for human cooperation in a confined space. And Hayes's method of maintaining order while eschewing the cat had gone down well on the lower deck. Seven months after sailing from Spithead, not one man had been flogged on *Dryad*, a singular statistic for a 36-gun frigate. The first recorded punishment came on 1 April, when John Walker, captain of the forecastle, was disrated for theft.[39] In most instances that would have earned him up to forty-eight lashes.

As newcomers, *Dryad's* company were introduced to the pleasures of Princes Island, where fresh meat and fruit were taken on and men might go ashore to be welcomed by women in a tropical idyll – 'a land so beautiful and romantic, covered with one continued impenetrable forest, from which issue miniature mountains, perpendicular rocks and undulating hills of singular and fantastic shape'.[40] For the officer class, hospitality awaited in the ample form of Madame Ferreira. 'The Queen of Princes' laid on evenings of 'artless and imperfect operas', but in this world of infinite paradox, surgeon Leonard noted wryly,

> banished as we are from the civilized world, the kindness of this good lady and the inelegant games and rustic entertainments performed by her half savage attendants afford us no small degree of gratification.[41]

Respite was brief. A passing British vessel reported that a number of slavers were awaiting captives at Duke's Town about 150 miles to the north. Ramsay's experience and zeal made *Black Joke* a clear choice over the untried *Fair Rosamond* – despite a new risk. According to reports reaching Hayes, such was the hatred among traders for the famous slaver-catcher that a vessel 'now on the coast' had been prepared with eight 32-pounders 'and is so armed for the express purpose of destroying the *Black Joke*'.[42]

When she sailed on 20 April it was at least with her firepower significantly enhanced by a third gun, an 18-pounder. At Fernando Po, Ramsay paused to take on a live bullock and fruit, along with further intelligence from a passing British palm-oil merchant: a large, fast and heavily armed Spanish brig was preparing to sail from Duke's Town; the merchant skipper had spoken to her master, a bullish fellow who declared his *Marinerito* could outrun or outgun any challenger.

Black Joke advanced to 4° 14′ N, 8° 15′ E, 50 miles from the river mouth and, at 11am on 25 April, sighted a sail in the north.[43] 'I had little doubt it was [*Marinerito*] and prepared accordingly for a severe contest,' Ramsay reported. 'A spirit was voiced in the whole of the officers and men, leaving me in no doubt of the result.'[44]

Whatever the appetite for an action that was always bound to be among *Black Joke*'s last, Ramsay's breezy confidence may strike an odd note: the Spanish brig had five guns, 25-pounders, against his three, and she was indeed – it had already become clear – a silky sailer with almost twice as many men, while *Black Joke* no longer had her old easy manoeuvrability to escape a tight corner. The truth was that in order to advance, naval officers of Ramsay's generation needed to show bravado. So did their acolytes, even 14-year-olds like Edwin Hinde.

The chase had gone into the night when guns from their quarry started to blaze redly in the dark. She still stood a mile ahead but, in another tense race conducted with the sweeps, *Black Joke* was closing. At midnight, regular fire roared out from both decks. As resistance was likely to be vigorous, Ramsay announced his plan for boarding.

On *Marinerito*, the master was given a chance to escape when his pursuer was taken aback – her sails driven against masts and stern – while he had the wind before him. But Francisco Cabieces detested

British interference, and he thought he had the advantage – may even have anticipated a reward in Havana were he to destroy the hated *Black Joke*. Rather than flight, he wore about to fight.[45]

As the Spaniard crossed *Black Joke*'s bow, 25-pounders roared from a starboard broadside. Isaac Foil, the quartermaster, failed to fall to the deck in time, was hit in the groin by grapeshot and died with his son William beside him, blood pouring from the femoral artery.[46] A return of incisive fire from *Black Joke*'s bow-chaser brought their antagonist up. Coming alongside, Ramsay lined up his boarders who included Edwin Hinde and they started to scramble across her side. Only fifteen men had reached the Spanish deck when a shift in the wind, or the current, or an element of collision between the hulls, caused the two vessels to drift apart.[47]

At this point, isolated and facing a company of desperate renegados four times their number, the Black Jokes demonstrated a spirit that went well beyond mere bravado. Ramsay led on, firing a pistol and sweeping his cutlass, followed by similarly armed men, blasting away as they came. A mate named Charles Bosanquet went down from a sabre blow, but the boarders' blood was up and they were driving the slavers back. Some Spaniards were thrown over the side and drowned.[48] One of the boarders, a midshipman named Pierce, also went overboard but managed to catch hold of a shredded sail as he fell and clambered back up.[49]

Two critical points followed within moments: *Black Joke* was brought back alongside by men hauling on sweeps and lashed to *Marinerito*; and Ramsay suffered a cutlass blow to his right arm. But any loss of his leadership was offset by a second surge of boarders; and from Edwin Hinde's account, the first wave had already secured the prize.

'I was determined to be able to say I killed a pirate in action,' Edwin reported to his brother at home. 'We all jumped on board, I with pistol in hand, going to let fly at the first Spaniard I saw . . . However I found the fun was over.'

Unfortunately they had all run below. I ran forward to rouse the fellows up on deck and received a bite in the finger from a parrot which I instantly hove overboard, so that all my bravery ended in the death of a parrot. However he gave me a good nip, so I can say I was wounded in the action on the 25th.[50]

Thirteen Spaniards had been killed and fifteen wounded. For all the insouciance of Hinde's account, there was plainly no regret at the toll, particularly in light of what was discovered in the aftermath.

Marinerito's master Francisco Cabieces had 600 captives ready for loading when it was found that many were suffering from dysentery. He shipped 475 anyway, although a large number also showed symptoms and were severely dehydrated. On the hatches being opened, faces looked up, as if from the medieval dungeon of an oubliette, pleading and shouting for water. The first group brought to a large tub on deck, Ramsay reported, 'pushed at it with such violence as to upset the whole and so great was their distress from thirst that they fell on their faces and licked it up from the deck'. When another tub was presented, another melee ensued.[51]

Within two days about thirty men, women and children had died.[52] In an atmosphere rank with panic and bowel effluent, Ramsay set *Black Joke* and her prize on a course for Fernando Po where, a few days later, a full medical examination found 107 men 'so afflicted by disease that to preserve their lives it is absolutely necessary that they be sent to the hospital'. An affidavit to this effect was sworn and signed by surgeons to head off any objection by nit-picking bureaucrats elsewhere.[53]

Danger did not pass with the evacuation and when *Dryad* came in two days later Hayes decided the best way to preserve lives was to divide the remaining captives between *Marinerito* and *Plumper*, another brig, for passages to Freetown.

An African propensity for song, whether at liberty or in chains, had long been noted and on *Marinerito* it came as a reassurance to the prize crew:

All slaves appeared to be fully sensible of their deliverance and upon being released from their irons expressed their gratitude in the most forcible and pleasing manner . . . The poor creatures took every opportunity of singing a song, testifying their thankfulness to the English and by their willingness to obey and assist rendered the passage to Sierra Leone easy to the officers and men.[54]

Peter Leonard witnessed similar scenes, accompanied by 'laughing and clapping of hands'; but he noted too the disenchantment among captives that followed on being brought ashore. 'When the gratification of setting foot on land once more had passed away [they] looked sullen and dejected.'

It struck me that on landing they expected to be allowed to go wherever they pleased and were disappointed and angry when they found themselves still under control.[55]

While *Marinerito*'s capture stands alongside *El Almirante*'s as the most lauded of *Black Joke*'s feats, traces of mystery and darkness were also left trailing in her wake.

A note from Ramsay stated that two Englishmen had been found among her company.[56] Only one British name can be associated with the slaver and he, Joseph Barrett, was actually an Irishman.[57] (Englishness tended to be used as a blanket identity for old naval hands.) He was nevertheless liable for trial and execution.

The particular brutality on *Marinerito* had roused in Hayes a desire for reprisal. The master Cabieces and two senior men would be taken with Barrett to Freetown. The rest, surgeon Leonard noted dispassionately, 'were sent in *Atholl* to the island of Anabona, where they were landed and turned adrift'.[58] He did not use the term, but they had been cast away.

It did not end there. Some weeks later *Black Joke* came across a makeshift canoe off Bonny with three men – bleached, parched and starving survivors of the castaways.[59] As they related, nine men had left Anabona in three canoes hoping to reach São Tomé when a tornado descended, sweeping their companions to oblivion. After ten days adrift they were reduced to the state of those they had once enslaved and two had 'little hope of recovery'. Leonard concluded: 'One would willingly discover a fearful retribution in all this.'[60]

Though *Marinerito*'s sailing qualities carried her to Freetown in just over three weeks, twenty-five more captives died. The cumbersome *Plumper*, meanwhile, took a month and, of the eighty Africans in her care, twenty-two were lost. 'Some in their mental agony and bodily distress [had] jumped overboard and were drowned.'[61] Of the 475 people initially loaded, only 373 survived to be settled at Sierra Leone.[62]

Barrett the Irishman was duly arraigned before a hearing with Cabieces and two others, charged with firing on *Black Joke* and killing Isaac Foil. Barrett, it was said, had been driven overboard and hauled up on a rope by his captors, so his claim to have been sick below and taken no part did not bear scrutiny. More plausible was his testimony that he had only shipped at Havana 'because he could not get anything else to do'.[63] Like many Irish hands, Barrett may well have served in the Navy until the mass post-war discharge.

The four were committed for trial on 1 July. They remained at Freetown gaol for five months, after which a hearing found insufficient evidence to prove any direct involvement in firing *Marinerito*'s guns, and they were freed.[64] What became of Joseph Barrett cannot be said. In previous times it is not inconceivable that he might have returned to naval service on a station always in need of able hands; but Hayes's detestation of anything connected with slaving ruled that out.

The *Marinerito* drama gave rise to some whimsy notable even by the standards of seamen's yarns. This was in large part down to Ramsay, whose broad Scotch speech and animation in relating a story while 'swinging his arms about' was noted by fellow officers.[65] With his own future assured, Ramsay saw advancing worthy aspirants as his bounden duty, especially in the case of a family friend.

Edwin Hinde, by his own droll account, had been late to the action and suffered to the extent of a parrot's peck on the finger. Yet in Ramsay's telling, the 14-year-old boy had saved the day after the vessels became separated: 'He at once took charge, ordered all hands to the starboard sweeps to get the *Black Joke* alongside.' Ramsay would repeat the story, which found its way into subsequent histories, and Hinde was also recorded among *Black Joke*'s six wounded.[66] Such elaborations were now crucial to advancement in a much pared-down Navy, and the lad, not short of spirit or dash, had won other plaudits, being 'unusually beloved on board', according to Captain Gordon.[67]

For a sharper contemporary account we turn to *Dryad*'s surgeon. Leonard had come to Africa an instinctive abolitionist – yet, his diary shows, with attitudes common at the time. Day by day, entries show his views evolving. On its publication two years later, *Records of a Voyage to the Western Coast of Africa* emerged as a campaigning tract – a diatribe against slaving states (Leonard advocated a simple strategy of boarding their vessels in port and setting them alight) and an exhortation that Britain press harder diplomatically for global abolition while investing more in Sierra Leone.

> Liberated Africans are seen labouring in the fields in every direction and appear as usual remarkably contented and happy . . . I am inclined to form a very favourable opinion of these poor people who are so cruelly traduced by a certain class of interested and heartless men . . . That the intellectual capacity and moral feeling of the liberated African black is in all respects equal to the civilised and educated individual with a skin of a different colour . . . I have with much gratification observed in numerous instances.[68]

He held other views that would have jarred with many, declaring a group of the freed African lads taken on *Medina* to train as seamen to be '*infinitely more* expert and active aloft than the white boys of the ship'. Those on *Dryad* instructed in skills including carpentry and rope-making showed a 'zeal, good humour and willingness to work' that earned 'the most unqualified praise'.[69]

Leonard's tribute to the real heroes of the *Marinerito*'s capture was likewise singular. Opinion had it that this 'was decidedly one of the most spirited' of the squadron's actions; Ramsay and Bosanquet were duly promoted while Hinde was made up to midshipman. But the surgeon's praise, both patronising and fond, went to *Black Joke*'s plain hands.

> It is gratifying to think that Jack is still the same – that he fights for the love of it just as he was wont to do – for it is not to be supposed that any notions concerning the inhumanity of slave-dealing or the boon of emancipation that he is about to confer on so many hundreds of his fellow creatures enter his thoughtless head when he begins the conflict. He is ordered – it is his duty: and, besides this, he likes it, being a pugnacious kind of animal, fond of a little excitement to vary the monotony of his life, hebetated [*sic*] by seclusion from the rest of the world, and to add another tale to the string of yarns he has to spin.[70]

Jack would long persevere in the same cause. Not so the brig Leonard termed the 'scourge of Africa's oppressors'. *Black Joke* was nearing her end. But a torch had been passed. *Fair Rosamond* was about to commence her rise.

CHAPTER 16

PASSING THE TORCH
June 1831–February 1832

The twin vessels seen ghosting along the African coast on an evening in the milder season of 1831 might have been likened to sea creatures. They had a predatory beauty, forms sculpted low in the water, raked masts and canvas like fins, bowsprits and booms arrowing fore and aft. Their menace was as evident as their beauty, for each had embodied terror as well as hope. *Black Joke* and *Fair Rosamond* had borne evil and delivered mercy. As to the why and how, it always came back to the human factor – the question of who was at the helm.

Officers of the Preventative Squadron, it bears repeating, embarked on a course in line with naval tradition. They had been sent out on orders, were glad to have posts, and did their duty in a demanding service with an eye to prize money. But amid constant suffering, many found themselves affected, driven by humanity. That *Black Joke* had become the most famous warrior in this campaign was due to a number of such men, from the dedicated William Turner to his devout successor Henry Downes and on to the aspiring young William Ramsay – all of their collaborations inspired by the brig's gifts.

There were also those who became sufferers themselves. As well as disease, mention has been made of men known to have been afflicted by mental disorders – the young hand William Wells, a gunner's mate

Edward Wood, unnamed others, all in an age when ignorance or stoicism tended to draw a veil over such matters. Another of *Black Joke*'s old company was Edward Butterfield, a promising young mate under Downes who, over fifteen years, became the longest-serving naval officer on the African coast before leaving his final command off Angola. At the age of 42, after what was described as a spell of 'melancholy . . . caused by his long residence in Africa', he committed suicide while staying at a family home in Bloomsbury. A jury, hearing from the servant who found him dead in bed at Torrington Square with his throat cut, attributed it to 'temporary insanity'.[1]

Ramsay's fellow commander on their cruise in the Bights was a more hard-nosed type. As the senior lieutenant to come out on *Dryad*, Henry Huntley was naturally delighted to be given charge of the *Fair Rosamond* but he had no intention of staying any longer than necessary. His aim was to 'fight [myself] into promotion' and find 'a station where nothing is so likely to happen as death from fever'.[2] He had little consideration for Africans: 'The negro's nature can be no more changed than the colour of his skin.'[3] But he did love his new vessel:

> Spreading every sail to a light land breeze, she glided out of the cove in so silent, stealthy and motionless a manner that she almost seemed sensible of her errand.[4]

As the *Dos Amigos*, she had a similar heritage to *Henriqueta* – made in America around 1830 to the Baltimore clipper model with a broad beam and shallow draught that enabled safe entry to estuaries. A later authority on sailing ships, Basil Lubbock, likened their design to the modern racing yacht in their bow and stern lines. But they were not identical twins. A schooner, *Fair Rosamond* ran to a length of just 75 feet with a displacement of 172 tons, compared with *Black Joke*'s upper deck of almost 91 feet and 256 tons. When it came to performance, Huntley believed that his schooner, 'though not equal to the sailing of the *Black Joke* by the wind, was her superior when going well "free"'.[5]

He had not known the brig in her heyday, however, and Ramsay thought her unique. *Black Joke*, he wrote, 'could forge ahead in a calm'.[6]

The bonds that hardened men formed with a structure of timber, rope and canvas is part of seafaring lore. Ships acquired an identity – as measures of success or failure, as theatres of sensation and as habitats, with all the associations of a home, for good or for bad. Among a superstitious fraternity of men, ships could be likened to living creatures imbued with human characteristics.

Occasionally, though, they entered a wider public consciousness. This was usually due to naval triumphs – the *Victory* and the *Temeraire* – or dramas of another sort – the *Bounty* and the *Beagle*. No such degree of fame attached to the *Black Joke*, but she had won a following among campaigners and readers of the popular prints and a renown with seafarers. 'Her success as a slave catcher,' wrote one authority on the age of sail, 'was not only the talk of the service itself but of shipping people generally.'[7] So it was only to be expected that, as she neared the end, her fate became the subject of intense debate.

The reforms introduced by Hayes wrought benefits across the squadron that year, from health to good temper. After the catastrophic toll of 1829, when 202 officers and men died – more than a quarter of the force – the number was reduced to twenty-two and would continue to fall over the next two years.[8] Flogging had been virtually abolished while discipline evolved in new forms. In one case, a mate named John Carpenter was brought before the commodore for striking a Kruman. This might have been passed over for, although Kru could only be beaten by their headmen, Carpenter was no common hand but an aspirant officer. In a display of regret and to make amends, Hayes had him confined.[9]

The commodore was also emboldened to push harder against Whitehall's constraints. In one instance, *Dryad* had to be taken to Ascension for stores and had Hayes obeyed the edict that tenders could not sail 'at a considerable distance' from the flagship, they would have

Discipline for hands eased under the command of John Hayes.

had to be removed from operations. Instead, he sent *Black Joke* and *Fair Rosamond* on prolonged independent cruises.

They had taken up positions in July – *Black Joke* roaming the Bight of Biafra, *Fair Rosamond* the Bight of Benin – with occasional encounters at the rendezvous of West Bay. Here Huntley recalled being presented with a basket of pineapples and oranges along with an invitation to join Madame Ferreira whom he found seated on her verandah in a state of déshabillé surrounded by black maids. After savouring a feast of fish, fruit, pastry and coffee, he happily accepted the offer of a bed.[10]

Ramsay had meanwhile resumed a spell of cruising off Bonny when on 11 July they intercepted a Spanish brig. Inspection showed she had no human cargo but Ramsay had no doubt of her purpose; *Rapido* was 'bound to Bonny for slaves'.[11]

Days later, alarming tidings came from below. For some time *Black Joke* had been shipping water. This was not in itself serious as caulked hulls started to leak sooner or later, and pumps were at hand. However, a measurement on 14 July showed a sudden and dramatic increase in the well. Energetic pumping reduced it to less than 13 inches before it started to rise again.

For the next two weeks *Black Joke* cruised by day until pumping resumed in the evening. But the leak was worsening, she was taking on more water – up from 13 inches to 20 inches then 25 inches – and hours more were spent at the pumps, a task for which the Kru proved themselves yet again indispensable. At the beginning of August they put in at West Bay for some patchwork caulking. That held the tide for little more than a week. On 15 August, she was found to be leaking badly again – now through the stem frame, the foremost curved timber of her bow. Water in the well was up to 27 inches.[12]

A further peril of their situation was spelled out a week later thanks to an encounter with a Liverpool palm-oil vessel whose master came aboard with intelligence from Bonny. While ashore he had met the masters of *Rapido* and a second Spanish slaver, the *Regulo*, who were awaiting captives but knew of *Black Joke*'s presence and pronounced that on sailing they would go on the attack. The scourge of slavers was to be destroyed. They certainly had the firepower: *Regulo* mounted fourteen 12-pounders, *Rapido* five 18-pounders.

To Ramsay's credit there was no wavering, no deviation from a daily resolve. *Black Joke* held to her course south of the river mouth while having to sustain pumping to stay afloat. Even so, the level rose at times to 28 inches.

That it would all have ended in blood and destruction seems probable, had it not been for a distant encounter two weeks later. *Fair*

Rosamond was refitting at Fernando Po when another English palm-oil trader came in and passed on the same word: *Regulo* and *Rapido*, he reported, had just loaded captives and were to sail with the full moon. Huntley, reasoning that there was just enough time, said he would head for Bonny to join *Black Joke* – to which the master replied: 'They'll sink you both so sure as you fall in with them.'[13]

On sighting mastheads on the morning of 6 September, Ramsay's first thought was of the Spaniards. As duty demanded, however, *Black Joke* 'bore up and made sail in chase'. It may be reasonably assumed a shout of delight went up when the advancing vessel proved to be *Fair Rosamond*.

Ramsay went on board for a dinner that had the air of a succession rite. Strictly speaking, Huntley, as he himself acknowledged, was 'poaching on another officer's station' but *Fair Rosamond* would have to play the leading role in any action.[14] Ramsay, his own promotion assured, was happy to extend opportunity to a rival. 'My dear fellow,' he is reported to have said, 'if there is to be any fighting, I hope you will have the whole of it.'[15]

The odds, if there was indeed to be any fighting, looked forbidding. With what were believed to be nineteen guns between them, the two brigs standing upriver mounted four times the firepower of *Black Joke* and *Fair Rosamond* combined.

Ramsay and Huntley had enjoyed a breakfast with marmalade and smoked salmon when a Kru lookout named Tom Peter shouted down 'Sail ho!'[16] As *Regulo* and *Rapido* emerged from the estuary jungle it appeared the challenge was at hand. Yet as their masters sighted two navy vessels awaiting them, instead of a solitary *Black Joke*, they anchored inside the outer bar. There they held for more than an hour before advancing as if to engage – when, Huntley wrote,

> on a sudden the *Rapido* bore up, set all her steering sails, and made a run for the river, hoping to be able to disembark her slaves before she could be seen doing so, and thus escape capture; under this

desertion on the part of her comrade, the *Regulo* had nothing left to do but the same.[17]

Fair Rosamond took the lead in pursuit, threading a risk-fraught path through shoals and channels to round the sandbar and there cross into the Bonny river mouth. Carried on by a long, rolling swell, she raced at the bar where waves were breaking in a steady line, and breaths were held until she passed around it unhindered. *Black Joke* followed, lagging at first before raising a full press of sail and closing to two cables' length, about 400 yards, as if to show she still had a turn of pace. Three miles ahead ran the *Rapido* with *Regulo* a mile astern of her.

Some five miles up the Bonny and still two miles from the slaving anchorage, several English palm-oil merchants stood dispersing their cargoes as the slavers raced past and, according to Huntley, at the sight of two vessels under the White Ensign a cheer went up and a boat came alongside bearing eight men with muskets. 'I have brought some volunteers, sir,' said the captain, 'for we thought you looked weakly manned.'[18]

As they approached the hindmost slaver, *Regulo*, it was seen that she had gone aground. Already canoes were racing out to take captives ashore. Huntley fired a warning shot, which brought the Spanish colours down. He left her for *Black Joke* to take possession of and *Fair Rosamond* raced on.

In her last river chase she had been the *Dos Amigos* in flight from *Black Joke*. On that occasion she had regained the bank and offloaded captives. This time events took a more diabolical turn.

A lookout shouted down: 'The leading brig is throwing her slaves overboard.' As they drew closer, events on *Rapido* became visible from the deck. Captives 'shackled together by the legs' were being 'pushed overboard and drowned'. Now *Fair Rosamond* was passing over water 'ruffled by the death struggles of slaves'.[19] A boat put out and a seaman wielding his boat-hook hauled up two men bound by shackles. Of the 450 captives estimated to have been loaded on *Rapido*, Okoorie and Olubarloo were the only ones to be rescued and taken to Sierra Leone.[20]

The *Fair Rosamond* drew up at point blank range and sent a ball from her pivot gun across the length of *Rapido*'s deck, followed by a volley of musket fire. Crossing to her deck wielding swords, boarders met the solitary figure of her master Santiago Alonzo. His men had fled below or ashore.[21]

The *Black Joke* had meanwhile come up and boarded the stranded *Regulo*, also without resistance. The slaver's guns, it turned out, numbered eight rather than fourteen 12-pounders. That still constituted a formidable arsenal, but not one had been fired. More than half her captives had been ferried ashore, doubtless to be enslaved and sold once more. The number found below was 207.

If any further evidence were needed, the captures of *Regulo* and *Rapido* confirmed a pattern: slavers bearing superior firepower and crew numbers, and with their entire venture at stake, usually chose to flee rather than resist; and, when chased down, quickly surrendered. Weapons represented a show of force they failed to deliver. Britain's naval prowess, honed by war, may have been intimidating; but thankfully, for the sake of all involved, most of these foes were as cowardly as they were heartless.

The toll at Bonny was nonetheless ghastly. The river's ebbing tide left all four vessels stranded and in the course of a week's desperate labour to get them off with the help of men from the English palm-oil traders, scores of shackled captives' bodies emerged from the mud.[22] How many had been cast into the water was not established; but after questioning Ramsay later, *Dryad*'s surgeon Peter Leonard put the figure at well over 100.

Leonard also used the disaster to rage against restrictions on the squadron. Had Ramsay (or Huntley), he wrote, been permitted to use all means at his disposal,

he could, and would, have gone up the river and destroyed [the slavers] with the greatest ease and thereby prevented the merciless cruelty that took place. But no! He dared not; because he was liable [to] heavy penalties had he even detained a Spaniard without having slaves actually on board.[23]

That no human captives had been found on *Rapido* posed a problem when her case came before the Mixed Commission. Santiago Alonzo, the master, swore on oath that his presence at Bonny had nothing to do with slaving. But the court had a resource awaiting – testimony from two of the men he had been in the business of enslaving. Okoorie and Olubarloo, speaking through an interpreter, said that of the 'great number of Blacks put on board' *Rapido*, they were the only survivors – thanks to being 'picked up in a boat manned by Englishmen'.[24] Okoorie was recorded as saying: 'Many other slaves were also forced either into the water or into canoes.'[25] *Rapido*, along with *Regulo*, was duly condemned.

The outcome still had other disturbing aspects, mainly in the losses among those 207 captives found on *Regulo*. On a surgeon's advice, Ramsay had landed five men with smallpox 'to prevent spreading that infectious disease'.[26] By the time she reached Freetown, thirty-nine had died and four more followed within days of landing. That did not deter the commission from declaring Ramsay's decision 'an unprecedented and in our opinion improper course to adopt'.[27]

The commission also went on to note 'the deficiency of an anchor' from *Regulo*, which, Ramsay explained, had been taken on *Black Joke* along with a cable in the salvage operations at Bonny. The return of these items was still demanded – so they could be auctioned for 'the military chest'. In the event, being in an 'unserviceable state', they fetched just £4 3s 4d.[28] William Smith continued to preside as chief justice but the governor's signature on these papers tends to indicate that Colonel Findlay persisted in his grudge against the oldest service.

She had taken her last slaver, made her final rescue – or so it must have seemed when Ramsay brought her to at Fernando Po in October. With hours of daily pumping needed to keep her buoyant, leaving men blistered in hand and grumbling at her vanishing graces, *Black Joke* could no longer sustain a cruise. Her future looked bleak when Hayes arrived in *Dryad* from Ascension two days later.

His first task was to conduct a survey 'to ascertain if she was seaworthy'.[29] What it showed was that for real benefit, repairs had to be extensive and – involving hauling her up on the beach – would take weeks, possibly months. Even then she would be vulnerable. Yet for Hayes this was not just about her capacity for capture, but her role as a symbol: *Black Joke* had become a talisman – raising morale, spreading fear among slavers. Neglect her and the campaign must suffer.

By 9 October she had been raised on to a slip, an improvised dock, and a team including eight men from *Dryad* were at work, replacing worn timbers with the island's plentiful supply of wood. After a month of steady progress a fever outbreak laid low the frigate's chief carpenter and four others, so the labour was taken over by craftsmen from *Atholl*. The completion of caulking on 1 December was marked by the installation of a new bowsprit and raising the lower masts – along with the distribution of double rations of rum.[30]

Also raising a glass was Ramsay. He was with Hayes on *Dryad* three days later when *Fair Rosamond* arrived with despatches from Freetown confirming his promotion and departure from *Black Joke* to what was deemed a more appropriate navy ship.[31] He took his leave with a note in the log on 5 December that simply reads, 'Mustered by Divisions. People employed variously. Sunset', followed by the signature 'Wm Ramsay'.

Young Edwin Hinde was more demonstrative, writing home that leaving *Black Joke* had been like

> parting from an old and faithful servant . . . Everybody that has been in her for long feels a pang at parting from her.[32]

Command was passed to Huntley. He may, with some justification, have felt aggrieved that *Regulo*'s capture had been credited to Ramsay, along with the prize money, when he and *Fair Rosamond* had taken the lead. It is noteworthy, however, that although she had proved herself a worthy successor, it was *Black Joke* whose command he now sought from Hayes. While her reputation was clearly a factor, Huntley's request suggests she was back in fair health, a significant indicator in light of her subsequent fate.[33]

No logbook of Huntley's command survives, so at this point a silence descends on life aboard *Black Joke*. It is known that in the weeks ahead she continued to prowl the Bights, as evidenced by sightings recorded on *Dryad* and others. Huntley would have kept his own log but it was either lost or, more probably, retained by him as a memento.

Details of her last capture are therefore scant. It was in any event achieved without resistance: she was back patrolling some 50 miles off Bonny when on 15 February 1832 she ran down a Spanish schooner, the *Frasquita*, bearing 290 captives.

It might have been treated as a significant moment. No slavers had been taken since the *Rapido* and *Regulo* five months earlier in a year that had shown a poor return for the squadron's efforts – just six vessels in 1831 compared with twenty-three in 1830. Starting the new year with a *Black Joke* prize proved there was life in her yet. But a decision as to her future had already been taken elsewhere.

A pause in captives' delivery at Freetown had at least given time for the authorities to tackle abuses. Over the past two years evidence had been accumulating that the earlier influx had had one malign consequence – a surge in 'liberated Africans selling their liberated brethren into slavery' – and if governor Findlay was suited to anything it was exercising authority.[34] His feud with William Smith had sufficiently cooled for them to cooperate on these infinitely more important matters.

Figures for what amounted to a local form of slave trading remain elusive. A return from the Mixed Commission in 1830 stated the number of captives emancipated and registered in the colony to be 23,310.[35] Another register that year showed 30,000 Africans had been liberated since 1808 – on the basis of which, according to one wildly flawed estimate at the time (it anticipated seven births for every death), Sierra Leone's population ought to have reached 50,000.[36]

Some recaptives, it is known, had chosen to make their way back to an Africa they comprehended. This developed into a trend in later years: William Johnson, a man of Yoruba origin who had profited by astute trading in goods and property at Freetown, bought a condemned slaver in 1841 and prospered further by selling groundnuts down the coast along with transporting other inhabitants wanting to return to their homelands.[37]

But many hundreds of recaptives had been sold by inhabitants to traders beyond the colony's borders. Records of the Liberated African Department show efforts to retrieve them, as in a note that year to the chief of the neighbouring Sherbro region accompanied by a reward of rum, bread and cloth, 'for the interest you have shown in rescuing a boy, a British subject'. It went on to request that in future any of his people found to have others 'in their possession' be sent to Freetown so it could be established how they had been obtained.[38]

A year of reckoning saw dozens of arrests by the colonial authorities. Peter Leonard, who had become a passionate abolitionist while serving on *Dryad*, noted that twenty-eight men were then in gaol awaiting trial, 'accused of decoying recently liberated Africans from home and selling them'.[39] Ten were convicted, including Thomas Cowan, a recaptive teacher at Bathurst, who was gaoled for five years for trading one of his pupils.[40]

The following year, 1831, measures hardened further with the hanging of three men. One, from the resettled Nova Scotian community, had seized a neighbour's child and sold him to the Bulom tribe. These public executions, it has been concluded, curbed kidnapping but did not stop it.[41]

Mistreatment of apprentices was also being subjected to closer scrutiny. With children as well as young men and women still to be acquired for 10 shillings and turned to domestic servitude without any form of policing, abuses had gone unpunished. A keen observer of Freetown society, Harrison Rankin, thought 'active cruelty' to be no part of Africans' disposition, but believed that the suffering endured by those once enslaved made them more apathetic to it.[42]

A new chief justice arriving from England, John Jeffcott, was taken aback by the cases awaiting him, concluding that 'for a considerable time past a very great and wanton cruelty had been exercised towards the great majority of Liberated African apprentices by their masters and mistresses', and cited a woman named Kisseah Bacchus, 'tried for the murder of her apprentice, a girl ten years of age, by beating her severely, rubbing pepper into her eyes and otherwise ill-using her'. What sentence Bacchus received was not stated but Jeffcott introduced a system of fining abusers £100 as well as cancelling the apprenticeship.[43]

Africans were not the only perpetrators. Jeffcott was appalled by the case of an Englishman named John Miller, an acting surgeon with the Mixed Commission brought to book for the 'disgusting and cruel treatment of his servant, a Liberated African boy'. William, as the lad was named, testified that after being deprived of food for two days he took food from a pantry, whereupon Miller 'flogged him on the back [and] rubbed the part lacerated with salt'. In other 'sickening details', Miller was recorded as having dipped William's head in a chamber pot and stuffed a pus-filled sock into his mouth. Miller was fined £50 and dismissed.[44]

Early in 1832, the Liberated African Department set in train measures to bring oversight across the expanding colony. A letter was sent to all village managers – who by now included some early black settlers – ordering them to record the name of every householder and apprentice, and to examine 'the manner in which they are treated by their masters or mistresses'. Any transgressions were to be reported.[45]

For all its flaws, bumbling and sometimes cruelties, the colony continued to inspire crusading spirits. Among them was Hannah Kilham. The teacher, who once despaired over children's education here, had persuaded her Quaker friends at home to support her in founding a new school. She returned to Freeetown in 1831.

On her previous visit, Hannah had contrasted the schools for children of the settlers from Nova Scotia and Jamaica with those for recaptive children. The first were taught in English by missionaries and 'native assistants' with results she found astonishing, especially among the boys. 'Never did I see a company of children in any school whose countenances struck me as more expressive of a lively disposition to imbibe instruction, and a quick capacity for receiving it.'[46] Village schools, on the other hand, had to tutor freed children from a range of linguistic backgrounds for whom English textbooks were incomprehensible and their difficulties were obvious.

Back in England and drawing on what she had learned in Yoruba, Hausa and other tongues, Hannah published a volume entitled *Specimens of African Languages Spoken in the Colony of Sierra Leone*. Her intention, she declared to the Friends, was to use this knowledge, 'to prepare an outline for elementary instruction in each language [to] introduce the pupils in the Liberated African Schools to a better knowledge of English than they possess'.[47] That mattered because, as the tongue of colonial authority, English was evolving into Sierra Leone's lingua franca.

When she sailed for Africa again, it was with a blend of faith and fear. As well as having narrowly survived a bout of fever at Freetown, she had a dread of the sea which, a close relative noted, 'almost overcame her'.[48] These doubts Hannah confided to a diary which became a form of prayer and a confessional of weakness.

On landing at Freetown, she was received by governor Findlay, who said he would be happy enough to hand rescued children into her care, 'provided no additional expense should be brought upon government'.[49] She set herself up in Charlotte, a village in a beautiful mountain setting overlooking Freetown, where she found 'the evening breeze around sunset delightful' and, provided with 'two ample rooms and a piazza', started classes for girls in Yoruba while introducing them to English using pictures as teaching aids.

Further tests lay at hand. On the landing of children from *Black Joke*'s last major capture, the *Marinerito*, she reflected, 'I cannot think it right we should pass them by', and wrote accordingly to Findlay.[50] Another twenty girls were duly sent, taking pupil numbers to forty-seven.[51] Some showed lingering signs of trauma. 'While they sleep their restless enemy pursues them and again all is distress and commotion,' she observed. 'One of the girls has an anxious countenance . . . perhaps her indisposition is occasioned by secret sorrow preying on her mind.'

> Sometimes, when she has done her little washing, she will sit down pensive by the brook, and fixing her eyes on the other side of the mountain on one particular spot, will silently weep and seem to wish not to be questioned as to the cause.[52]

Hannah often felt the absence of friends and the lack of any support besides one African teacher. She was frail herself, well into her fifties and suffered frequent bouts of ill health as well as doubt: 'I have been so much indisposed within the last few days that my faith was almost ready to faint, and my mind was tried with the apprehension that I have not physical strength for the work in prospect.'[53]

Yet months of perseverance brought uplifting reflection on what had been achieved by the girls from the *Marinerito*. 'I have certainly cause to be pleased and comforted with my dear children. It is scarcely eight months since [they] were taken from the slave-ship. Many can read the picture-lessons and also some of the Scripture-lessons as well as write from dictation the same lessons on their slates. They can answer questions from surrounding objects, are improving in reading and learn to repeat hymns.'[54]

The little school's resources were severely strained even before the Church Missionary Society closed its school at Bathurst, and Hannah, unable 'to reject attempting to do good to these dear children', agreed to take in another fifty-seven girls.[55] All the while, funding from Quakers at home was in the balance and, at the start of 1832, it ran out. 'Oh, that there might be a school for Africans in England!' she pleaded.[56]

Instead, seeking inspiration and finance, she looked to Liberia, the nearby colony recently established for freed black Americans and sustained by missionary zeal. With a free passage provided by the merchant John

McCormack, she prepared to sail while battling her fears and declining health right up to the eve of departure, stiffening herself with reason: 'How often have I found that a time of depression and apparent difficulty has been succeeded by a brighter day.'[57]

Shortly before sailing, Hannah noted the appearance off Freetown in January of four ships and wondered idly whether they had come from England. The date shows she was not mistaken. Not only were they from England, they were ships of the Royal Navy, and they had come bearing an admiral to pass judgment on the *Black Joke*.

CHAPTER 17

THEIR LORDSHIPS' JUDGMENT
January–May 1832

The commodore sensed trouble the moment he came in at Freetown to find a 58-gun flagship flying an admiral's pendant. Visits by admirals to the slave coast were unheard of and the impressive bulk of HMS *Isis* standing at anchor on 28 January hinted at change that was unlikely to be welcome. Sure enough, when Hayes went on board, Rear-Admiral Frederic Warren was waiting in the great cabin to deliver not just one thunderbolt but two.

The first was a letter from the Admiralty stating that Warren had been appointed commander-in-chief at the Cape of Good Hope. In itself, that was of no concern, but the order went on to add that the Cape station had been extended to take in West Africa, granting Warren jurisdiction over the Preventative Squadron. Hayes had been given no warning of what was coming, which meant being subjected to the command of a man who would be 3,500 miles distant from the theatre of operations, and for whom he had no great respect; Warren was a political appointee and, despite his rank, had a rather less distinguished service record than the man who would be his junior.

Next, Warren said he had orders for the *Black Joke* to be destroyed. There is no document from the Admiralty spelling out this unexplained decision, only letters showing that Hayes was told she had to be 'broken up'.[1]

He was mortified. Their lordships had long evinced hostility for tenders and, as Warren informed him, wanted to reduce the cost of sustaining operations off West Africa.[2] But he feared their verdict might have arisen from his reports of *Black Joke*'s decline – made at a time when he still hoped to add other captured slavers to the squadron. Now that had been ruled out, her preservation was essential. Hayes protested (as carefully as he could) that the recent repairs had been carried out 'at trifling expense . . . in a very ingenious and remarkable manner . . . so that the vessel is now as strong as when built'.[3]

At this point *Black Joke* was still cruising the Bights, so there was no question of her death sentence being carried out immediately, and Hayes's appeal did at least give rise to second thoughts. Hearing what was in the wind, governor Findlay renewed his request for a vessel of his own, writing to Warren: 'As the *Black Joke* is now put in such good repair, I think it would be a pity to cut up such a fine vessel when [the] government of this colony stands so much in need of one of her description.'[4]

For the time being, that question was left hanging while Warren prepared to make an obligatory, if perfunctory, tour of the waters now under his command and inspect *Black Joke* himself.

On the question of Hayes's status, the admiral said he was at liberty to stay with the squadron, but his rank would be reduced to captain. Or he could sail home under his commodore's pendant. There was no hesitation. 'I have to state that I prefer the latter alternative,' Hayes replied, adding with palpable vexation: 'I have also to state that not having had the slightest intimation of their Lordships' intentions, I am taken completely by surprise.'[5]

Hayes still retained hopes for *Black Joke*. Aside from his command duties, he was driven by a passion for ship design. Some years earlier he had written a pamphlet on naval architecture founded on the wild notion of a single-pattern structure for a range of ships. The idea had the potential to revolutionise shipbuilding, and a sloop, a corvette and a frigate based on his plan were contracted by the Admiralty. His theories may have been flawed: the *Seaflower*, a cutter of his design, had accompanied *Dryad* to Africa but utterly failed to test any Baltimore-built slaver. While innovation was taking a new direction – the *Pluto* had just become the squadron's first paddle-steamer – Hayes was still trying to absorb what British shipbuilders could learn from American designs.

He had one final voyage to make across his old domain. While the admiral and *Isis* ventured down the Gulf of Guinea, Hayes would take *Dryad* to Fernando Po to collect their stores before proceeding to Ascension and thence home. The two ships were to converge at a point where *Black Joke*'s fate would be resolved.

Few records survive to explain quite what passed after Warren's flagship encountered *Black Joke* off Bonny on 25 February, so events over the next few days are indistinct, like some other key episodes in her life. The rendezvous took place, however, just ten days after *Black Joke*'s capture of the Spanish schooner *Frasquita* off Bonny which, Huntley was doubtless pleased to point out, was the squadron's first prize in five months. This news failed to make much impression on the admiral.

Warren, interested in seeing how *Black Joke* performed against the latest British-built vessels, ordered Huntley to test her pace – her 'rate of sailing' – against his two brigantines – *Brisk* and *Charybdis*, which had been modified specifically to hunt down slavers.[6] There is no first-hand account of what followed, but according to the tale that went round the squadron and entered seafaring lore: 'The famous ex-slaver walked round and round them in a cable's length.'[7]

The admiral did not report the result to his superiors.[8] Instead, it was noted, being 'not too pleased with the exhibitions made of his best brigantines', he ordered an inspection of *Black Joke*.[9] It was made by Thomas Ogle, *Isis*'s commander, her master and two carpenter's mates. They returned, stating that her stem was 'decayed, several timbers in each side quite rotten', the deck 'very bad', and the outside timbers 'in a decayed state, particularly in the wake of the chains and near the head'. All in all, they added, 'She is not in our opinion a vessel calculated for HM Service.'

Perhaps the most revealing element of the report, however, is its conclusion:

> And we further declare that we have taken this survey with such care and equity that we are ready if required to make oath to the impartiality of our proceedings.[10]

That the admiral felt it necessary to have the inspection's 'impartiality' validated under oath points to the hostility it was going to meet, not just from Hayes but also public opinion at home. It was dated 29 February, along with a despatch to the Admiralty in which Warren stated that having previously 'suspended their Lordships' instructions' for *Black Joke* to be broken up, her condition had been found 'so much at variance with the statement of Commodore Hayes' that he had been directed 'to repair to Sierra Leone to attend to the breaking up of the *Black Joke*'.[11]

Also enclosed with the despatch were six small paper wrappers with what were described as 'Tastings' – fragments of wood taken from *Black Joke*'s starboard and larboard sides, the stem and the ceiling of the main hold. These were intended to show the state of her timbers. They remain part of the documentary records, attached to Warren's letter in their original wrappers. As each scrap is about a half-inch in length it is hard to imagine what they actually proved about her condition.[12]

Hayes was not party to Warren's report. Still proceeding under the illusion that he had secured *Black Joke*'s survival, he put in at Fernando Po on 29 February to find another letter from Warren, dated four days earlier, ordering her destruction.[13]

The admiral had just departed, but *Black Joke* remained at anchor with Huntley, who was able to explain in *Dryad*'s great cabin what had passed. Hayes was naturally – as he subsequently made clear – furious about the decision and the harm it would do to the campaign. But as a dedicated seaman and enquiring shipwright, he was also distraught that this object of beauty and mystery should be demolished. To a scholar of ship design, destroying so innovative a vessel, and one with her history, was an act of sacrilege.

Huntley had his own reasons to be bitter: *Black Joke*'s death would terminate his first command and – convinced that his diehard Tory values would exclude him from advancement under the current Whig government – he had little hope for the future. Huntley was the likely source for claims that *Black Joke* had run rings round *Brisk* and *Charybdis*.

The basic question remained. Why had Warren seen fit to have this icon of the war against slavery destroyed, the vessel that had achieved most in that endeavour? This was, after all, now his squadron. The answer is probably that, having only recently been advanced to flag rank and knowing his superiors' aversion to tenders, he saw this as no time to rock the boat.

But what followed took on another aspect. *Black Joke*'s final fate had about it the reek of vindictiveness.

News that *Dryad* was to sail home came to her company as 'a piece of intelligence not a little gratifying to us', as surgeon Leonard put it.[14] Even so, relief at being delivered from West Africa's deadly clime was followed by outrage at what it betokened. In a diary extract, Leonard wrote:

> We have been ordered to return [to Sierra Leone] in order to perpetrate the final destruction of this favourite vessel – the terror of slave dealers, the scourge of the oppressors of Africa – which has done more towards putting an end to the vile traffic in slaves than all the ships of the station put together . . . Her demolition will therefore be hailed as the happiest piece of intelligence that has been received at the Havannah, and wherever else the slave trade is carried on, for many years.[15]

Anger, according to Leonard, was not confined to officers and men. 'The Africans themselves are sensible of the boon she has conferred on so many of their countrymen,' he added. This may be thought somewhat fanciful. The surgeon, as has been seen, had become a zealous abolitionist and his account was later published as a campaigning tract. But his diary links the freed Africans at Fernando Po that day to the capture just months earlier of *Marinerito* and how her arrival then had set off rejoicing as 'friends and relations' were found among those on board. Now, hearing their deliverer was to be broken up,

> they, particularly the women, petitioned the commodore in the most earnest manner, not to destroy her. When they heard he had received orders for so doing, as he was taking final leave of the place, they crowded round him, and hugged and embraced him, and entreated him not to injure 'poor *Black Joke*'.[16]

Leonard went on to rail at 'the mistaken hope' that *Brisk* and *Charybdis* were any more suited to catching slavers than their predecessors. In sailing qualities, he wrote, they simply did not bear comparison with *Black Joke* – 'or slave vessels generally'.[17] The surgeon felt free, as no officer could, to spell out the consternation and sorrow arising from the wanton harm being done to the cause of rescuing the enslaved.

They sailed together for the last time, *Dryad* and *Black Joke*, on 2 March – the flagship to rendezvous with the admiral at Ascension, her tender for Freetown, there to await Hayes. He would return to supervise her dismantling and arrange for auctioning her remaining assets, such as sails and anchor.

A pervasive darkness had settled. Five days later a tornado descended as they neared Princes Island and blew both *Black Joke*'s topmasts over the side. *Dryad* sent a boat across to help her limp in to West Bay for two more days of repairs. On 12 March they sailed again, parting for their separate destinations.[18]

Two weeks later, *Dryad* anchored at Ascension Island where Admiral Warren was waiting. What passed at his meeting with Hayes is unrecorded. It may, perhaps, have given rise to a bitter exchange, but that seems unlikely as downright insubordination could have led to a court martial. However, Hayes made no secret of his feelings.

The next day Warren wrote to him:

> I have to desire that instead of [*Black Joke*] being broken up, which will take more time than is requisite to bestow upon her in a place where timber is of little value, and exposure on shore is dangerous, she shall be destroyed by hauling her up in a convenient place in Sierra Leone and burning her.[19]

To further assure the Admiralty that the matter was being handled in the most economical way, Warren wrote to their lordships that prior to being set ablaze, her 'copper, stores and furniture' would be removed for auctioning.[20]

The decision mystified even those who had no connection to *Black Joke*. Newspapers at home picked up on the subject. The *United Service Journal* ran a tribute to her later, a complete record of her captures, noting that the Admiralty had 'directed the destruction of the severest scourge to the slave trade ever known'. The daily press was more overtly critical, while the seafarer and historian Basil Lubbock later reflected on another aspect of this blockheaded vandalism: 'That her model was not considered worth preserving reflects on the admiral commanding the station and the Lords of the Admiralty themselves.'[21]

Hayes could only fulminate in private but he allowed himself one statement of candid dissent to the Admiralty, drawing on what he thought might have given rise to second thoughts among their lordships – the economics of waste: 'Such was the estimation in which this vessel was held,' he wrote with pointed emphasis, 'I would have obtained for her the sum of <u>twelve hundred pounds</u>.'[22]

Yet the bleak absurdity of the order for her destruction is best captured in a final note Warren sent to the Admiralty just before he sailed for his new station at the Cape of Good Hope. Headed 'A report of Slave Vessels detained by the Squadron under my command between

December 1831 and March 1832', it contains a solitary entry: '*Frasquita*', along with her captor, '*Black Joke*'.[23]

The arrival of *Black Joke*'s final prize at Freetown in March set off alarm bells. The *Frasquita*, it was noted by the Liberated African Department, was rife 'with the smallpox and other diseases'. Fifty of the 290 captives had died on her passage and special measures were ordered to take dozens of ailing survivors to Kissy hospital.[24]

Four still died before they could be landed and another eight at Kissy.[25] In a subsequent inquiry it was found that yams laid in *Frasquita*'s hold by the master to feed captives had been 'in a forward state of germination'. Along with smallpox and dysentery, diseases found among them were craw-craw and gonorrhoea.[26]

In all, 131 men, 19 women, 62 boys and 16 girls were the last Africans to be declared emancipated by the *Black Joke*. Of the men, roughly half were resettled in Gambia, for which they were required to give their assent.[27] Nine were taken on by the Navy. Some of the women also went to Gambia. The great majority of boys were apprenticed, but the youngest were sent with the girls to be schooled.[28] They included some of the youngest children rescued by the brig, two 7-year-old girls, Odomoo and Imboray, and a boy aged 6 named Orroh.[29]

Waiting to receive them was the school at Charlotte village started by Hannah Kilham. On sailing for Liberia a few weeks earlier Hannah had left her school in the hands of a matron with a range of instructions, particularly concerning any vulnerable arrivals. 'New girls received from [a] slaveship who are thin and weak should not do any heavy work,' she wrote. Cleaning and the washing of clothes were among her concerns. 'The stronger girls who have been here longer should do the work.'[30] Her lessons for teaching children freed from the *Marinerito* would also benefit those from the *Frasquita*.

But Hannah would not be there to supervise their education. She had completed her visit to study missionary schools at Monrovia before embarking on the return voyage to Freetown. A few days out, on

25 March, she made a final entry in the journal to which she had long confided her ailments, doubts and faith: 'We are becalmed and have been for some days . . . but I have cause to be thankful for hope. I have been weak and not well.'[31]

The next day a storm descended, the vessel was struck by lightning and started back for Liberia but was still at sea when Hannah died on 31 March. She was 57. Her body was consigned to the deep.

Appreciative citizens of Freetown joined in composing a letter of consolation to her relatives:

The name of Hannah Kilham is dear to many in this part of the world; we may say she was beloved and respected by all who knew her. Her loss is felt acutely by the poor people at Charlotte, particularly by her dear charge, the school children; they feel they have lost their dearest friend . . .

Her zeal in the great cause seemed to know no bounds; full proof of it is left behind, though her own life is laid down in her last efforts to benefit her fellow creatures.[32]

Hannah's journal survived, to be returned to her step-daughter and published in 1837, with a foreword that amounted to her final testament:

Africa will, I believe, be ever dear to my heart, and I would pray that no shrinking from danger should ever interfere with what is called for from me in this injured people's cause.

Four weeks after Hannah Kilham was buried at sea, and just days before tidings of her death reached Freetown, HMS *Dryad* came in with Hayes for the last time to oversee another passing. The *Black Joke* was already there at anchor and the next day a party of hands were sent across to start clearing her of stores and provisions.

She lay there, on the morning of 29 April, as she had at anchorages from Bahia to Bonny and Freetown to Lagos. Yet an enduring mystery rested within. While little more than eight years had passed since her launching into the waters off Baltimore, the thousands of lives that had been shaped and evolved – and, in many cases, ended – on her decks had moved on, in large part to unknown ends. While their experiences and worlds can be no more defined than they can be described, we may pause to reflect how that space – less than 91 feet in length and 27 feet in breadth – had held within it the fates of so many human beings, from a 6-year-old Yoruba boy like Orroh to the old-school bigot Henry Huntley, who went on to a knighthood and the governorship of Gambia.

There was no ignoring the evil side of her life. How can it be possible to comprehend the terror, the torment, the lamenting, that had passed in the darkness of the lower deck among those 3,040 souls estimated to have been delivered to the hands of José de Cerqueira Lima? How many had died there, ignored and alone, to be cast into seas where sharks cruised? And all while her master João Cardozo dos Santos kept his eye to the horizon, and his own mounting fortune.

What of those other, equally voiceless, humans – the common men who had handled her transition, turning her into the Royal Navy's most effective weapon against slavery? Men who, in reversing the Preventative Squadron's tide of failure, had helped to take 3,692 captive Africans from thirteen vessels bound for Brazil and the Caribbean? Seamen were no strangers to affliction. Many retained memories of war and impressment, of fellows torn from family or liberty ashore by cudgel-wielding press gangs. Although serving in Africa from need or duress rather than brute force, they might still feel the cat on their backs and most would return home to austerity if not downright destitution. Few, if any, would have seen themselves as saviours. But they understood suffering, they knew subjugation.

The identities of those who had manned *Black Joke* at the last are unknown, so they are nameless as well as voiceless.[33] They joined in the labours that took place over three days to prepare for the end, so that on 2 May she lay there still, but as spare and barren as a hulk. Her lower and upper decks had been cleared, masts taken down. That night Hayes wrote: 'Preparing to burn the *Black Joke*.'

He came up to the quarterdeck at dawn to a cloudy sky and a light breeze in the air. Bosuns' pipes mustered all hands on deck. Looking across at her now, they saw in that sleek brig a relic awaiting obliteration. Then, for the last time, they went over, set ropes in place, and began leveraging her from the sea.

Hayes's description was nothing if not succinct: 'Hauled *Black Joke* on shore and set her on fire.'[34]

Rising flames were to be seen from land and sea. On *Dryad* and *Fair Rosamond*, the men who had sailed with her watched, each with his own recollection. The people of Freetown too had gathered, among them some of those she had delivered; and high on the hill above, at Mrs Kilham's school for rescued girls in Charlotte village, rising smoke could be observed.

In her transformation from the *Henriqueta* to the *Black Joke* she had distilled redemption. The final act, of death by burning, had about it an element of sacrifice.

Timbers were blazing and crackling when a downpour began in the afternoon, sending sparks exploding into the sky.[35] Still the blaze ate into the hull, which began to blister and crumble. And still the rain poured down so, as night came on, the sparks flew up like fragments of lightning. But nothing expunged the flames except, at the end, the obliteration of wood once hewn from the forests of Massachusetts, gradually reduced to smouldering golden fragments, then ashes.

Hayes was among those who watched to the last. He then went ashore to inspect the remains. He returned to his cabin about midnight and wrote: '*Black Joke* entirely destroyed.'[36]

EPILOGUE

Commodore Hayes took *Fair Rosamond* home with him in order to preserve her from any further act of vandalism. In time – although not as soon as should have been requisite – *Fair Rosamond* would resume anti-slavery voyages off Africa with a success that marked her as a worthy heir to *Black Joke*.

Destroying the Preventative Squadron's most prolific predator and excluding her kind from operations did incalculable harm to the campaign. The Admiralty never relented on its decision against employing tenders, so even *Fair Rosamond*'s return was permitted only once she had been commissioned as a navy man-of-war.[1] The blind and flawed obstinacy that continued to insist on the superiority of British design served no one other than slavers and British shipyards; over the second half of 1832 just two slaving vessels, both Spanish, were captured off West Africa.

Hayes's arrival in England unleashed a flurry of press coverage. Newspapers initially focused on *Black Joke*'s final capture, *Frasquita*, implying with it criticism of the tender's destruction. The more overt disapproval expressed by the *Morning Advertiser* suggests that men like Hayes and Leonard had made plain their outrage:

The orders [to burn her] were peremptory and the vessel, by her wonderful sailing qualities the most calculated for the service, is lost for ever. On the circumstance being known at the large slaving place called Gallinas, the Spaniards there had a feast.[2]

Papers across the country picked up on the story, running a narrative of her heyday under Turner, Downes and Ramsay entitled 'Life and Adventures of the Black Joke, lately deceased at Sierra Leone' drawn from the *United Service Journal*.

Apart from the tiny fragments of her timber kept in the Admiralty records, no trace of the brig or her design survives, and the seafarer and writer Basil Lubbock thought it 'a great pity that [Hayes] did not think of taking off [her] lines before she was burned'.[3] Given Hayes's lifelong passion for ship design, that seems unlikely. (He did, as the naval historian J.K. Laughton observed, publish pamphlets on design, 'which were favourably received at the time, though now forgotten'.) In all likelihood, Hayes had studied and noted what few others could, the mystery of *Black Joke*'s magic and, ignored by or despairing at what Lubbock called England's 'pig-headed naval shipwrights', carried the secrets to his grave.[4]

Two years later a clergyman visitor to Sierra Leone was wandering through Freetown when his eye was caught by the sight of a cannon standing 'above water in the bay at half-tide'. A devout young man, Harrison Rankin had read of *Black Joke*'s exploits before coming to Africa. Now, looking out at the remains in the sand of her old 18-pounder, once a bearer of freedom, he 'recalled the stories of her heroic doings' and lamented this 'melancholy sight'.[5]

Soon after his glimpse of *Black Joke*'s remains, Rankin was a witness to the return of *Fair Rosamond*.

No prize had been brought to Freetown for months and Rankin had never seen a loaded slaver himself when a signal gun heralded the arrival of *La Pantica*, recently taken by *Fair Rosamond* in the Bight of Biafra. Prompted by 'painful interest', Rankin went on board to the harrowing visions, the overwhelming stench and the sheer, disgusting reduction of human beings recorded by other observers cited in this narrative.[6] Forty-seven of the 317 captives on the Spanish schooner died. Over the next six years *Fair Rosamond* went on to take another eight loaded slavers and, under a treaty of 1835 allowing the capture of vessels 'fitted for the slave trade', a further six of that description.[7] As a record, it bears comparison with that of *Black Joke*, although accomplished over a rather longer period; and *Fair Rosamond* never obtained the same fame.

The Preventative Squadron's 'excellent band of energetic and meritorious officers and men' were honoured by Rankin and other observers. But recognition at home for what remained the most taxing and dangerous naval duty of the era was scant. Long afterwards, tributes and records continued to cite at length heroics during the wars with France while passing perfunctorily over service in West Africa.

A special case in point is Edward Butterfield, once one of *Black Joke*'s young hopefuls, who continued to serve off Africa – despite having the 'interest' of an admiral father who might have secured him easier berths – and returned in 1839, this time to the Cape of Good Hope, captaining a sloop, the *Fantome*. He proved a leading light in the long-overdue extension of the campaign that legitimised captures south of the Equator, with a squadron of brigs off Angola. The *Fantome* alone is estimated to have rescued 5,628 Africans.[8] Nine years after returning home, Butterfield, as has been seen, was found dead in bed, his self-inflicted cut throat attributed to 'melancholy . . . caused by his long residence in Africa'.

Black Joke's first commander, William Turner, had also proved staunchness as well as ability while serving more than four years off West Africa, lastly under Hayes in *Dryad*. On their return home he was paid off, leaving with little more acknowledgement than the sword of tribute he received from his first commodore, Francis Collier, 'for his zeal and gallantry while commanding the *Black Joke* tender'. Turner remained ashore almost a decade later when, in token recognition of his previous duty, he was promoted to captain.

Henry Downes left with his own trophy from Collier, the wine cooler carved from *El Almirante*'s timbers. He too remained ashore, never attaining the rank of captain but living in comfort while serving the interests of less fortunate seafarers.

William Ramsay was among that minority of his officer generation to embrace the great maritime evolution just under way, captaining a steam-paddle frigate, HMS *Terrible*, the largest and most powerful vessel of that description built for the Royal Navy. He remained at sea for much of his life, never married and died a vice admiral and Knight of the Bath.

Henry Huntley returned to serve off West Africa and, despite his earlier view of the campaign as 'a monotonous and idle absurdity', evidently developed some affinity with the region. He went on to the governorship of Gambia and, after being knighted, to pen a lengthy protest against a policy that supported slave-grown sugar.

The boy Edwin Hinde returned to England with promotion to midshipman. After three years away, he wrote to his mother that he very much wanted to visit home, but it was important to stay on *Dryad* 'as it requires the greatest interest to be able to get a ship now' and if he took leave she might sail, leaving him high and dry.[9] He persevered and twelve years later was made lieutenant. Hinde remained forever grateful to his mentor Ramsay and to Turner, for his advice and kindness, but never became a captain.

For all their differences, most officers and men of the Preventative Squadron shared the opinion of one of their kin, who, years later – in pursuit of the same goal but off East Africa – could still rail against the

Englishmen who annihilate the slave-dealers and civilize Africa by their own comfortable firesides, little thinking of the hardships and privations their countrymen are undergoing to carry out their impossible theories.[10]

Once again, endeavours to suppress the trade could be found rubbing up against those for emancipation, and neither would be readily resolved.

A mood of reform had been simmering across Britain since the coming to power of Earl Grey's Whig government in 1830. Rising demands for working-class rights, accompanied by rioting, tended to overshadow the campaign for emancipation, but Thomas Fowell Buxton was now insisting that it must proceed on an 'immediatist' rather than a gradual agenda.[11] Nothing, needless to say, ever moved that fast in Parliament and it took a rebellion by the enslaved in Jamaica, the largest and bloodiest in British colonial history, to hasten freedom. Some 60,000 followers of a black deacon named Samuel Sharpe rose up at Christmas in 1831. As at Demerara eight years earlier, the military force at hand ensured they were crushed, with a toll that cannot be precisely assessed but numbered at least 200 and was followed by many random murders and the passing of 312 death sentences.[12]

Two years later Parliament passed the Slavery Abolition Act making slave ownership illegal, thus laying the way for Emancipation Day in 1834 and full freedom in West Indies colonies in 1838. Slave-owners received compensation of £20 million, the modern equivalent in purchasing power of £115 billion. For those previously deemed their property, there was no suggestion of reparation.

Slavers in Brazil were still reaping fortunes and insisting they would prevail against their oppressors. José de Cerqueira Lima's claim against the British state for £600,000 in damages was taken to London by his lawyer brother Manoel in 1834. Whitehall had long dismissed as 'grossly and systematically fraudulent' avowals by Cerqueira Lima that his captured vessels had been engaged in legitimate trade. The case was dismissed.

Brazil's government continued to regard treaties with Britain, in the words of consul William Pennell, 'as dictation of a superior authority from which it is lawful to escape, rather than as a compact which they are bound to enforce'.[13] Rebellions still spluttered, notably the Bahia uprising by Muslim slaves in 1835, the most significant and organised so far. Hundreds were executed.[14] Cerqueira Lima joined the local authorities in blaming the influence of *libertos*, the freed black population.

Bahia's most voracious slaver died in 1840, his age undetermined, his vast wealth – in the form of a private palace with its slaves, gold table service and jewels, along with several other houses and slaveships – bequeathed to his widow, Carlota, and numerous children.[15] It may be reasonably assumed that Cerqueira Lima went to his grave claiming to have overcome British tyranny.

His trading partner across the Atlantic continued to profit. Francisco 'Chacha' de Souza lived on until 1849, having turned gradually to a new export in palm oil, and helped to resettle hundreds of former slaves expelled from Bahia after the 1835 uprising. At the time of his death aged 94, he had still accumulated a fortune estimated at $120 million, making him one of the world's richest men.[16] Honoured in death by King Gezo, a statue of him was erected that still stands in Ouidah.

In the meantime, the number of Africans trafficked to Brazil had surged again, reaching in 1836 the highest estimate yet of 52,000, only to be surpassed by a figure of 54,000 a year later.[17] Most of the enslaved had come from Angola and other points south of the Equator but these were still dispiriting times for the West Africa squadron. The number of ships captured compared with the number that completed their voyages was minuscule and the figure for captives rescued in those two years was no more than 10,000.[18]

One aspect allowing for a little satisfaction was a new order that permitted the seizure and destruction of unloaded vessels obviously equipped for slaving. From 1836, most captured slavers fell into that category. Significantly more vessels were thus being removed year by year from trafficking. This, in itself, made all the more persuasive the case for converting them – like *Black Joke* and *Fair Rosamond* – into hunters. That remained beyond the pale for the Admiralty.

Yellow fever remained the curse of the squadron. No year again extracted so terrible a toll as 1829, when it carried off 202 officers and men – a quarter of the force – but disease returned in 1837 and the year after, killing 105 and 115 men, respectively. The total number of deaths over the squadron's lifetime is not known. The one study covering the twenty years between 1825 and 1845 put the figure at 1,328.[19] West Africa was clearly defined as far and away the most dangerous naval station in the world.

Why and how the slave trade continued for as long as it did is a study in itself. Diplomatic pressure was sustained and the number of cruisers assigned to the squadron increased – to thirteen, then to twenty. Yet the traders were now concentrating on sources south of the line. In 1846 the number of captives landed in Brazil rose again – to an estimated 62,600.[20]

The Navy blamed politicians for their diplomatic failure, and governments of both parties for severely cutting the naval budget as reform took priority in a time of peace. The Westminster establishment, naturally, pointed the finger straight back. The reflection of Lord Palmerston, foreign secretary of the day, later prime minister and always a dedicated servant of the abolitionist case, bears repeating:

No First Lord, and no Board of Admiralty, have ever felt any interest in the suppression of the slave trade, or taken of their own free will any steps towards its accomplishment, and whatever they have done in compliance with the wisdom of others they have done grudgingly and imperfectly.[21]

African leaders, it may be added, continued to feed the atrocity. In 1849, seventeen years after the *Black Joke* went up in flames, the explorer John Duncan returned to the kingdom of Dahomey. Duncan had been selected as a diplomatic go-between and came to the capital Abomey bearing a petition for King Gezo to stop plundering humans from neighbouring lands. As on his previous visit, Duncan arrived at Abomey to behold a slave-hunting expedition preparing for the Yoruba country and 'thousands of armed men and women rushing round their monarch, brandishing aloft their clubs and muskets, and yelling and shouting in the most fearful manner'. Gezo was the same 'frank, unassuming but intelligent man I had found him in 1845', Duncan reported, and listened attentively to his visitor's request. He then pointed out that, if the slave trade was indeed wrongful, it had taken Britain a long time to realise it.[22] The petition was rejected because, Gezo said, his people would not allow it. Duncan died in Africa a few months later, aged 44.

Ultimately, only new measures of force achieved victory. Navy ships, cruising off South America, started to attack and sink Brazilian vessels, exciting talk in Rio of war but in time bringing about a surrender. Brazil's slave trade ended in 1851.

An amphibious operation was launched that same year against Lagos, where the *oba* Kosoko ruled the last major slaving port in the Bights. A single vessel steamed upriver in December, went aground and Kosoko's musket-armed militia drove the intruders into a humiliating retreat. A second, far bloodier, incursion weeks later ended with Lagos in flames and Kosoko being driven into exile. A rival, Akitoye, took his place and signed a treaty to abolish the slave trade in his lands. When these tidings reached Gezo, he changed his mind and signed a similar declaration.

It was far from ending there. Palm oil started to replace human beings as the principal export from Lagos, but neither Akitoye nor Gezo was able to hold to his word, and traders in the Bights continued to smuggle captives to Cuba. Out of frustration, Palmerston, now prime minister, annexed Lagos in 1861.

There was never a moment of victory. Despatches from naval officers still cruising off Africa repeated as a mantra that slaver voyages had ceased, but they remained on station until 1867. Sixty years after its creation, having rescued an estimated 160,000 Africans, the Preventative Squadron was merged with the force at the Cape of Good Hope. The transatlantic slave trade was deemed to be at an end.

ACKNOWLEDGEMENTS

This book had its origins in the midst of pandemic confinements that made access to any original archival material impossible, so to find that some of these resources had been digitised and made available online by the National Archives at Kew turned what might have been months of frustrated meandering into a time of discovery. Most of the treasure at Kew is yet to be digitised, but that work goes on, and being able to access Foreign Office records relating to the slave trade was a lesson for me in the future that must benefit researchers everywhere with limited access or means.

Technology has preserved and made available other files that might have been beyond my reach. Projects sponsored by the British Library's Endangered Archives Programme have included digitising documents of the Sierra Leone Public Archives in Freetown which offer some insight into what became of the tens of thousands of rescued captives taken to the colony. For their work in this field I am grateful to Professors Suzanne Schwarz and Paul Lovejoy.

Once their doors were reopened, staff at the National Archives and the Caird Library in Greenwich were as efficient and helpful as ever in producing the naval records fundamental to any work of this sort.

Most of the historical documents in Brazil relating to that country's slave trade and its enslaved population were destroyed in 1891. Research at the State Archive of Bahia was conducted on my behalf by Naira Mota to clarify what remains.

Although I have spent some years studying maritime subjects, two books in particular formed an essential basis for further learning: Peter Grindal's *Opposing the Slavers* is a meticulous and extensive volume covering the Royal Navy's campaign to end the slave trade; it is much to be regretted that Grindal did not longer survive publication of this major work. Pierre Verger's *Fluxo e Refluxo* about the slave trade between the Bight of Benin and Bahia is another landmark study on which I came to depend for advancing my own research.

The team at Yale have provided that blend of encouragement, deliberation and probing that all authors of non-fiction need, along with fine timekeeping. This is the sixth book I have written with Julian Loose as editor, and as it is likely to be my last I wish to express a special gratitude for his contributions to the words that have emerged over more than twenty years of our work together. The production was managed by Rachael Lonsdale with precision, attention to detail and suggestions that improved the content as well as the presentation. My thanks go too to Frazer Martin for his part in this process, and creative help with images and maps, and to Lucy Buchan, who dealt with the proofreading and indexing. Robert Sargant's sharp eye as a copy-editor gave cause for relief as well as thanks.

Another long-term collaborator has been my agent, who, by extraordinary coincidence, has shared ancestral connections with more than one of my subjects. It's added to the fun. Caroline Dawnay, thank you once more.

Readers are what authors need above all, and it has been my blessing to have at hand during my writing life two wonderful readers ready to offer forthright and insightful criticism. Tom Fort is my dearest friend as well as a reader and writer himself. My wife Caroline is another voracious reader, a partner and, in her spirit and dedication, so much more. I could not have done any of it without her.

ENDNOTES

PROLOGUE

1. Grindal, p. 288.
2. Ibid., pp. 76–7 & 88.
3. These figures are cited by Grindal on p. 800.
4. Bethell, *The Abolition of the Brazilian Slave Trade*, p. 124.
5. Grindal, p. 290.
6. Gardiner, pp. 87–8.
7. Taylor, *Sons of the Waves*, p. 434.
8. ADM 51/3280, Log of the *Maidstone*, 23 Sept. 1825.
9. Ibid., 7 Oct. 1825.
10. FO 84/42/282–5, William Pennell to George Canning, 16 Nov. 1825.
11. Ibid.
12. Ibid.
13. Grindal, p. 303.

1 FROM BALTIMORE TO BAHIA: JANUARY–OCTOBER 1824

1. Taylor, *Sons of the Waves*, p. 8.
2. Chapelle, p. 130.
3. Ibid., p. 131.
4. Graham, p. 132.
5. Ibid., p. 138. Although the city is known today as Salvador, this text observes the contemporary appellation of Bahia. Maria Graham's observations come from her visit to the city late in 1821 as the wife of a navy captain and are therefore, broadly speaking, contemporary with this narrative.
6. Klein and Luna, pp. 152–3.
7. Robert Harvey's biography *Cochrane: The Life and Exploits of a Fighting Captain* (London, 2002) tells the story.

8. Klein and Luna, pp. 152–3. Although graphs show Rio surging above Bahia in captive arrivals from the 1820s, many of those landed in the capital had originally been transported to Bahia in vessels owned by traders there.
9. Wetherell, p. 20.
10. Berktay, pp. 36–7; see also Hicks, p. 121.
11. Graham, p. 148.
12. See database of slavevoyages.org.
13. Graham, p. 156.
14. Tinnie, p. 522. An official record states specifically that the one son of Cerqueira Lima who went on to attain prominence himself – and fell out with his father over the issue of slavery – was 'legitimate'. The palace became the official residence of the president of Bahia. It was demolished in 1927.
15. Grindal, p. 279.
16. Thomas, pp. 70–117.
17. Ibid., pp. 156–7.
18. Ibid., p. 203.
19. Ibid., pp. 244–6, 257, 264, 284.
20. Grindal, p. 185.
21. FO 315/65/60, the record of *Henriqueta*'s capture in 1827 gives his age as 23.
22. Verger, p. 365. The actual relationship between the two members of the Dos Santos family is, as the author says, unknown, but he concluded that they were brothers.
23. Ibid., p. 366.
24. Grindal, p. 248.
25. FO 84/31/182, Canning to Chamberlain, 6 Aug. 1824.
26. Grindal, p. 288. This, as we have seen, was the letter written by Bullen to the Admiralty soon after arrival on station.
27. In Britain, under the Dolben Act, or Slave Carrying Bill of 1788, the number of captives was limited to five for every 3 tons of carrying capacity and required all slavers to have a doctor on board.
28. FO 84/31/270, Chamberlain to José de Carvalho Mello, 10 Sept. 1824.
29. Ibid.
30. FO 84/40/31.
31. FO 84/40/15.
32. Dundas, pp. 42–3 testifies to Pennell's gout and his narrow survival from a stomach ailment.
33. Graham, p. 134.
34. *Dictionary of National Biography*, and *Gentlemen's Magazine*, March 1861.
35. See Harding for an account of the uprising.
36. Guenther.
37. Graham, p. 148.
38. Ibid., p. 144.
39. A place for their own worship was among the things denied to the enslaved of Demerara, but Mrs Graham may have erred on the side of blitheness. Months later, in June 1822, Pennell reported 'a rising among the Blacks in the isle of Itaparica . . . which was quelled by the militia, 20 Blacks were killed and about 20 wounded' (Verger, p. 292). Nothing else is known about this rebellion, however,

and as Itaparica was also used for disembarking newly arrived Africans it is possible that the violence arose from a spontaneous demonstration at the end of a voyage.

40. Ibid., p. 151.
41. Grindal, p. 247.
42. FO 84/12/147–54, Case of the *Emilia*.
43. Graham, p. 153.
44. Ibid., p. 133.
45. Hicks, p. 4.
46. Ibid.
47. Ibid., p. 17.
48. This was the composition of the *Henriqueta*'s company on her capture. See FO 315/65/60.
49. Hicks, p. ii.
50. FO 84/12/147, Case of the *Emilia*.
51. Verger, p. 397.

2 A HELL AFLOAT: OCTOBER 1824–JANUARY 1825

1. FO 315/65/60 contains notes from the logbook of *Henriqueta*'s voyage in 1827 prior to her capture.
2. These distances are based on the 1827 logbook.
3. As Howard Chapelle notes in *The History of American Sailing Ships*, no plans of the *Henriqueta* have survived, thanks to the nature of her end, so mystery surrounds the details of her design. She is presumed to have borne the rigging standard to American-made brigs. Chapelle, pp. 157–8.
4. Grindal, pp. 290 & 295.
5. LUB/39/21.
6. Based on the *Henriqueta*'s logbook in FO 315/65/60.
7. Ibid.
8. Grindal, p. 85.
9. Rediker, p. 77.
10. Law, *Ouidah*, p. 30. *Ouidah: The Social History of a West African Slaving 'Port'* is a closely researched study of this subject. See also pp. 12–16.
11. Ibid., pp. 31–46.
12. Verger, pp. 209 & 406. See also Law, *Ouidah*, and Araujo.
13. Law, *Ouidah*, pp. 167–8.
14. Ibid., pp. 183 & 74.
15. Ibid., p. 150.
16. Araujo, p. 91.
17. Thomas, pp. 696–7.
18. Huntley, p. 119 (also Rees, p. 167).
19. Thomas, p. 696.
20. Verger, p. 11.
21. Forbes, p. 109. This journal by a naval officer, Frederick Forbes, dates from a visit some twenty-five years after the *Henriqueta*'s first voyage, but conditions are held to have been largely consistent during this period of rule by the kings of Dahomey.
22. Ibid., p. 109. An analysis of religious life in Dahomean Ouidah is found in Law, *Ouidah*, pp. 88–98.

23. Huntley, p. 119.
24. Ibid., pp. 116–17.
25. See Law, *Ouidah*, pp. 74–5, 160.
26. Duncan, vol. 1, pp. 193 & 204.
27. Ibid., pp. 224–5 & 250.
28. Ibid., pp. 226–7.
29. Ibid., vol. 2, p. 305.
30. Ibid., vol. 1, pp. 259–60.
31. Ibid., vol. 2, pp. 265–6.
32. Ibid., vol. 1, p. 259.
33. Huntley, p. 114.
34. Duncan, vol. 2, p. 297.
35. Thomas, pp. 395–6.
36. Law, *Ouidah*, pp. 174–5.
37. Forbes, p. 122.
38. Park, p. 319.
39. Thomas, p. 395.
40. Law, *Ouidah*, pp. 138–44, contains a comprehensive account of the process up to embarkation.
41. FO 84/63/92.
42. Law, *Ouidah*, p. 142.
43. Ibid., p. 143.
44. Ibid., p. 151. Mahommah Baquaqua was enslaved and shipped to Pernambuco in Brazil in 1845, about twenty years after the events described here. He was subsequently taken to Rio de Janeiro and placed on a ship before escaping to New York. His memoir 'An Interesting Narrative Biography of Mahommah G. Baquaqua' was written 'from his own words' by author Samuel Moore.
45. Law, *Ouidah*, p. 141.
46. FO 315/31/398.
47. Rediker, pp. 37–8.
48. Law, *Ouidah*, p. 144.
49. Grindal, p. 53.
50. Hicks, pp. 152–3.
51. Grindal, p. 51, Tinnie, pp. 512–16. Tinnie concluded that each survivor of the *Henriqueta's* six voyages as a slaver had been confined in a space of 4.75 square feet. This was based on the average number of 507 Africans sharing an area of 2,415 square feet. However, this makes no allowance for the additional platforms.
52. Walsh, vol. 2, pp. 481–2.

3 'THE MOANS, THE WEEPING, THE CRIES': JANUARY–JULY 1825

1. Tinnie, p. 525.
2. ADM 55/11, folio 13. This document formed the basis of the published *Journal of a Second Expedition into the Interior of Africa*, but Clapperton's observations on Ouidah and De Souza were omitted.
3. Ibid.

4. This figure for the return voyage is calculated from the number of days between the failed pursuit of the *Henriqueta* by the *Maidstone* off Lagos on 7 October 1825, and her arrival back in Bahia on 3 November. Because Brazilian slavers' records were falsified after 1820 to show that they were sailing from south of the Equator, most of these logs cannot be treated as an accurate record.

5. The news was brought by another of Cerqueira Lima's vessels, the *Conceição Estrela*, which came into Bahia on 2 February. See Tinnie, p. 524.

6. Ibid., p. 525.

7. Ibid.

8. FO 84/42/250, Pennell to Canning, 17 Oct. 1825.

9. Ibid.

10. Records of voyages by vessels entering Bahia in 1825 are missing from the archives. Tinnie, p. 526.

11. Verger, p. 430.

12. Grindal, p. 47.

13. See Ribeiro. Voyages from Angola to Bahia were longer in distance but ran with a more favourable current.

14. Falconbridge, p. 20.

15. Grindal, p. 53.

16. Hicks, p. 157.

17. Ibid., p. 153.

18. Thomas, p. 426.

19. Falconbridge, p. 25.

20. Rediker, pp. 274–6.

21. Ibid., pp. 265 & 306.

22. Ribeiro, p. 13.

23. APEB, Livros do Banguê.

24. Graham, pp. 155–6.

25. Bethell, *The Abolition of the Brazilian Slave Trade*, p. 4.

26. FO 84/42/202, Return of slaves imported at Bahia.

27. Graham, pp. 135–6.

28. Ibid.

29. Walsh, vol. 2, p. 354.

30. Ibid., vol. 1, p. 366.

31. Koster, p. 441.

32. Ibid., p. 326. The author was describing an auction in 1828 at Rio, rather than Bahia.

33. Ibid., p. 325.

34. Berktay, pp. 78–9. Names adopted by the enslaved in Brazil were often derived from those claiming their ownership.

35. Ibid., pp. 36–7.

36. Tinnie, p. 527.

37. Walsh, vol. 2, p. 355.

38. Klein and Luna, p. 82.

39. Verger, p. 438.

40. Klein and Luna, p. 118.

41. Bethell, *The Abolition of the Brazilian Slave Trade*, p. 4.

42. FO 84/71/136, Pennell to Canning, 9 Jan. 1827. The word 'renewed' has been inserted as, although the sense is clear, the original is illegible.

43. FO 84/42/282, Pennell to Canning, 16 Nov. 1825. Values in sterling are calibrated here in terms of a guide provided by the National Archives. Brazil's currency was the milreis but against the dollar or pound sterling it fluctuated wildly in value. See Tinnie, p. 527.

44. Walsh, vol. 2, p. 354. Walsh's words were: 'The natural tendency to cruelty and oppression in the human heart is continually evolved by the impunity and uncontrolled licence in which they are exercised.'

45. Ibid., vol. 2, p. 291.

46. FO 84/42/266, Tristão Pio dos Santos to Pennell, 23 Oct. 1824

47. FO 84/42/264, Application of Joseph Cerqueira Lima, 23 Oct. 1824.

48. FO 84/42/244, Pennell to Canning, 10 Sept. 1825.

49. FO 84/71/232, Pennell to Viscount Dudley, 10 Aug. 1827.

50. FO 84/42/270, Pennell to Manuel da Costa, 6 Oct. 1825.

51. The position was 22° 55′ S and 34° 30′ W. Report of Robert Roddam, FO 84/42/302.

52. FO 84/42/336, Contract signed by Manoel dos Santos, 26 Jan. 1825.

53. Details of the case in full can be found in FO 84/42/83–92.

54. *The Interest* by Michael Taylor is a comprehensive exploration of the subject.

55. Ibid., pp. 54 & 64.

56. FO 84/42/237, Pennell to Canning, 1 Apr. 1825.

57. FO 84/42/242, Pennell to Canning, 15 Apr. 1825.

58. Graham, p. 149.

59. Taylor, *Sons of the Waves*, pp. 371–2.

60. FO84/42/225, Pennell to the Marquês de Queluz, 21 Nov. 1825. The *Carlota* is described as 'a Spanish schooner', but sailing under false colours was a common maritime ruse and as she was the same type as the vessel owned by Cerqueira Lima, there seems little doubt they were one and the same.

61. Grindal, pp. 132–3.

4 GIFTS FOR THE KING: AUGUST–OCTOBER 1825

1. FO 84/40/31, Statement of Manoel dos Santos, 2 Feb. 1824.

2. Ibid.

3. Grindal, p. 279.

4. It may be argued that servitude is a more apt word than slavery, but a survey of the practice from ancient times has observed that what defined those described as slaves were individuals – whether men, women or children – who were dependent on masters who disregarded the basic ties of family, kin and community common to even the lowest free persons. In West Africa, chiefs were known to use their servants for human sacrifice and other practices now deemed inhuman.

5. Lovejoy, 'Patterns in Regulation and Collaboration in the Slave Trade of West Africa'.

6. Mann, pp. 2–3 & 26. This work offers a cogent analysis of the early societies of Benin.

7. Ibid., p. 30.

8. Ibid., pp. 32–3. Rio de Janeiro's principal source of slaves remained Angola.

9. See Law, 'The Chronology of the Yoruba Wars of the Early Nineteenth Century: A Reconsideration'.
10. Mann, p. 64.
11. Ibid., p. 67.
12. Ibid., pp. 66 & 80.
13. Ibid., p. 62.
14. FO 84/42/282, Pennell to Canning, 16 Nov. 1825.
15. Mann, p. 52.
16. Memoir of Samuel Crowther in the *Church Missionary Record*, Oct. 1837.
17. Clapperton, p. 74.
18. Ibid., p. 39.
19. Ibid., p. 36.
20. Ibid., p. 20.
21. Ibid.
22. Ibid., p. 95.
23. Memoir of Samuel Crowther in the *Church Missionary Record*, Oct. 1837.
24. Grindal, p. 264.
25. The single greatest loss of the era in British ships was the wreck of the *St George* and the *Defence* off the coast of Denmark on Christmas Day in 1811. Sixteen men reached the shore alive while 1,380 died.
26. Grindal, p. 180.
27. Ibid., p. 800.
28. These figures are compiled from Grindal, pp. 769–71.
29. Ibid.
30. Memoir of Samuel Crowther in the *Church Missionary Record*, Oct. 1837.
31. Grindal, p. 295.
32. Verger, p. 403.
33. Ibid.
34. Grindal, p. 47.
35. Ibid., pp. 47 & 76.
36. ADM 51/3280, log of the *Maidstone*, 6 Oct. 1825, and FO 84/42/282.
37. FO 84/42/282, Pennell to Canning, 16 Nov. 1825.
38. ADM 51/3280, log of the *Maidstone*, 7 Oct. 1825.
39. The *Henriqueta*'s use of her sweeps to escape is mentioned in Pennell's report, FO 84/42/282.
40. ADM 51/3280, log of the *Maidstone*, 7 Oct. 1825.
41. Anderson, 'Uncovering Testimonies of Slavery and the Slave Trade in Missionary Sources'.

5 'THERE HAS BEEN CONCEALMENT': OCTOBER–NOVEMBER 1825

1. FO 84/31/217.
2. Klein and Luna, pp. 1–34.
3. FO 315/65/60, Papers of the brig *Henriqueta*. List of Crew. This relates to her voyage of 1827.
4. Ibid.

5. Hicks, p. 117.
6. Ibid., pp. ii, 122, 129.
7. Quoted in Candido.
8. Walsh, vol. 2, pp. 340–1.
9. Klein and Luna, p. 192.
10. Ibid., pp. 242–3.
11. Hicks, p. 115.
12. See Hawthorne.
13. Grindal, p. 192.
14. Hawthorne, p. 420.
15. FO 84/12/132.
16. FO 84/12/147, Henry Hayne to the Marquis of Londonderry, 21 Sept. 1821.
17. Hawthorne, p. 420.
18. Ibid.
19. In her study 'The Sea and the Shackle', p. 4, Mary Ellen Hicks defines men like Gorge as a category of black mariners, mobile and cosmopolitan, who 'leveraged their ability to operate in the disparate cultural milieus of West Africa and Bahia, limiting their own marginalization and facilitating great autonomy from their owners'.
20. FO 315/65/60.
21. Rediker, p. 220. Newton is remembered as the slaver master who repented, became an evangelical minister and wrote numerous hymns, notably 'Amazing Grace'.
22. FO 315/65/60.
23. Ibid. The conversion rate is based on figures in Tinnie, p. 527.
24. Ibid.
25. Hicks, pp. 250 & 251. It is pointed out that Cerqueira Lima's high evaluation of the *sangrador* Barilio was related to his claim for damages from Britain over the *Independência*.
26. Hicks, pp. 148–9.
27. Bethell, *The Abolition of the Brazilian Slave Trade*, pp. 49–51.
28. FO 84/42/357.
29. FO 84/42/370, Robert Hesketh to Henry Chamberlain, 19 Oct. 1824.
30. FO 84/42/163.
31. FO 84/42/268, William Pennell to George Canning, 18 Oct. 1825.
32. FO 84/42/206, Henry Chamberlain to George Canning, 19 Nov. 1825.
33. FO 84/42/282, William Pennell to George Canning, 17 Nov. 1825.
34. See Ribeiro.
35. FO 84/42/284, William Pennell to George Canning, 17 Nov. 1825.
36. FO 84/42/286, ibid.
37. FO 84/42/284, ibid.
38. The figure of £30 comes from Pennell's letter to Canning: FO 84/42/282.
39. FO 84/42/285, William Pennell to George Canning, 17 Nov. 1825.
40. FO 84/71/209, William Pennell to the Vice President of Bahia, 6 June 1827.

6 BONDED BY SUFFERING: NOVEMBER 1825–OCTOBER 1826

1. Thomas, p. 629.
2. Ibid., p. 160.
3. Verger, p. 11.
4. Huntley, vol. 1, p. 119.
5. Ibid., p. 120.
6. Duncan, vol. 2, p. 266. It may be noted that a persistent argument over the extent of 'African agency' in the slave trade has been addressed by academics, and will no doubt continue. That the transport of humans from their homelands to the equivalent of a separate planet was only made possible by Europeans and their technology is beyond dispute. Equally evident is the fact that the rulers who bartered their own kind also engaged in other practices that today appear utterly inhumane. In the case of Dahomey, these included ceremonial human sacrifices: humankind has a long history of ritual being used to demonstrate power over subject peoples, so while the accounts by nineteenth-century British travellers in Africa like Duncan may be treated with suspicion, they can also shine a light into the dark corners that exist in all societies.
7. Law, *Ouidah*, p. 171.
8. Law, 'Chronology of the Yoruba Wars'.
9. The original journal and related papers are held at the National Archives in ADM 55/11. After Clapperton's death it was edited by John Barrow and published in 1829 as the *Journal of a Second Expedition into the Interior of Africa, from the Bight of Benin to Soccatoo*. Another volume, of the original journal and other Clapperton papers, was edited by Jamie Bruce Lockhart and Paul E. Lovejoy and published in 2005 as *Hugh Clapperton into the Interior of Africa: Records of the Second Expedition, 1825–1827*. All three sources have been consulted here.
10. Lockhart, p. 152. These states covered territory running across the Bight of Benin from west to east.
11. Lovejoy, 'Islam, Slavery and Political Transformation in West Africa', p. 278.
12. Lockhart, pp. 150–1.
13. Clapperton, p. 13.
14. Ibid.
15. Ibid., pp. 71–4.
16. Ibid., p. 94.
17. ODNB.
18. Clapperton, p. 81.
19. Ibid., p. 102.
20. In 'Islam, Slavery and Political Transformation in West Africa', Paul Lovejoy writes: 'According to Clapperton, only "refractory slaves" were sold, all others being retained within the caliphate or sold north to other Islamic areas' (p. 279). Clapperton's published journal actually states: 'The slaves sold to the sea coast are generally taken in war, or refractory and intractable domestic slaves' (p. 95).
21. Clapperton, pp. 170–1.
22. Lockhart and Lovejoy, p. 57.
23. Clapperton, p. 197.
24. Ibid., p. 204.

25. See, for example, Barcia.
26. FO 84/57/318, William Pennell to George Canning, 7 Apr. 1826.
27. Ibid.
28. Thomas, p. 422.
29. Barcia, pp. 11–12.
30. Klein and Luna, pp. 194–202.
31. See Reis.
32. Walsh, vol. 2, p. 480.
33. Ibid., pp. 482–3.
34. Ibid., p. 331.
35. Ibid., p. 334.
36. Rediker, pp. 301–2.
37. FO 84/57/318, William Pennell to George Canning, 7 Apr. 1826.
38. FO 84/57/345.
39. Bethell, *The Abolition of the Brazilian Slave Trade*, pp. 55–6.
40. Ibid., pp. 57–60.
41. Smith, pp. 6–7.
42. Grindal, p. 311.
43. FO 84/71/206, William Pennell to George Canning, 8 June 1827.
44. FO 84/57/371, William Pennell to George Canning, 17 Nov. 1826.
45. FO 84/57/357.
46. FO 84/57/341.
47. FO 84/57/318.
48. Tinnie, p. 524.

7 'THE MOST SANGUINE AVARICE': OCTOBER 1826–SEPTEMBER 1827

1. Graham, pp. 137, 143, 146 & 147. The original unedited sentence has been slightly amended. It concludes '. . . show too plainly that they are intruders, ever to be in harmony with the scene'.
2. Ibid., p. 142.
3. Bethell, *The Abolition of the Brazilian Slave Trade*, p. 64.
4. FO 84/71/136–141, Pennell to Canning, 9 Jan. 1827.
5. In Cuba, too, slaves were able to obtain their freedom. The island's 200,000 population in 1817 included an estimated 24,000 free blacks. Thomas, p. 635.
6. See Berktay.
7. FO 84/71/144, Pennell to Canning, 7 Apr. 1827.
8. FO 84/71/142, Pennell to Canning, 20 Mar. 1827.
9. FO 84/71/154, Pennell to Canning, 18 Apr. 1827.
10. Ibid.
11. Verger, p. 271.
12. FO 84/71/159, Pennell to the President of Bahia, 21 Apr. 1827.
13. In some publications, including Tinnie, the departure date is incorrectly given as 13 April. Pennell recorded it was 13 May in his letter to Canning of 4 July 1827: FO 84/71.
14. Ibid.
15. FO 84/71/160, Pennell to the President of Bahia, 21 Apr. 1827.

16. FO 84/71/203, Pennell to Canning, 3 June 1827.
17. FO 84/71/191, Pennell to Canning, 1 June 1827.
18. FO 84/71/189, Pennell to the Vice President, 31 May 1827.
19. FO 84/71/191, Pennell to Canning, 1 June 1827.
20. FO 84/71/199, Vice President to Pennell, 30 May 1827.
21. FO 84/71/192, Pennell to Canning, 1 June 1827.
22. Ibid.
23. FO 84/71/206, Pennell to Canning, 8 June 1827.
24. FO 84/71/201, Pennell to Canning, 2 June 1827.
25. FO 84/71/195 & 206.
26. Taylor, *The Interest*, p. 144.
27. Ibid., p. 62.
28. ADM 37/7363, Muster of the *Beagle*.
29. FO 84/71/224, Pennell to Canning, 4 July 1827. Dos Santos's use of the US flag is in Verger, p. 372.
30. Ibid.
31. FO 84/71/227, Pennell to Dudley, 12 July 1827.
32. FO 84/66/66.
33. Ibid.
34. FO 84/71/229, Pennell to Dudley, 20 July 1827.
35. FO 84/71/237, Pennell to the Vice President, 30 July 1827.
36. FO 84/71/250 & 254.
37. FO 84/66/1.
38. Verger, pp. 322–4 & 366.
39. Ibid., p. 366.
40. FO 84/95/247, Earl of Aberdeen to Viscount d'Itabayana, 10 March 1829.
41. Verger, pp. 323–4.
42. FO 84/66/14, Report of the Mixed Commission, 18 June 1827.
43. FO 84/71/257, Pennell to Dudley, 1 Dec. 1827.
44. Walsh, vol. 2, p. 322.
45. Dundas, p. 41. See also Guenther, p. 13.
46. FO 84/71/259, Pennell to Dudley, 24 Dec. 1827.
47. Thomas, p. 631.
48. This can be inferred from the list of captives made after the *Henriqueta*'s capture.
49. FO 315/65/60, Papers of the *Henriqueta*.
50. Ibid.
51. Ibid.
52. FO 315/31/398.
53. Ibid.

INTERLUDE

1. Taylor, *The Interest*, pp. 1–14.
2. Ibid., p. 54.
3. Ibid., pp. 73 & 160.
4. Ibid., pp. 146–7.
5. Grindal, p. 136.

8 COMMODORE COLLIER'S PURCHASE:
SEPTEMBER–DECEMBER 1827

1. ADM 51/3466, Log of the *Sybille*.
2. Grindal, p. 322.
3. FO 84/66/203, Report of the capture of the *Henriqueta*.
4. ADM 51/3466, Log of the *Sybille*.
5. FO 84/79/50.
6. Rankin, vol. 2, p. 103.
7. Holman, vol. 1, pp. 107–8.
8. In one instance, the navy sloop *Kangaroo* took thirty-nine days in 1812 (Ward, p. 47).
9. FO 84/66/203, Report of the brig *Henriqueta*.
10. Ibid.
11. Fyfe, *A History of Sierra Leone*, p. 134.
12. FO 84/77/128, Jackson to the Earl of Aberdeen, 20 Sept. 1828.
13. FO 315/23/169.
14. This is a calculation based on a disparity in the figures in the above two documents.
15. FO 315/31/398.
16. Anderson, *Abolition in Sierra Leone*, p. 2.
17. Ryan, p. 42.
18. Rankin, vol. 1, pp. 16–17.
19. This figure is based on the number of captives recorded in Grindal, Appendix A, as having been released from the end of 1822.
20. The allowance is specified in EAP 443/1/18/2, folio 291.
21. Rankin, vol. 1, p. 204 & vol. 2, p. 116.
22. Ibid., vol. 1, pp. 223–4.
23. EAP 443/1/18/2, Denham to the Treasury, 14 Oct. 1827.
24. Anderson, *Abolition in Sierra Leone*, p. 119.
25. Ibid., p. 122.
26. Rees, pp. 131–2.
27. EAP 443/1/18/3/31 & 18/4/32. Maeve Ryan's *Humanitarian Governance* takes a more critical view of Cole's performance. See pp. 192–3.
28. EAP 443/1/12/12, folios 59–92, contain the assignations of *Henriqueta*'s recaptives.
29. EAP 443/1/18/3, folio 238, Cole to Thomas, 22 May 1828.
30. EAP 443/1/12/12, folios 59–92.
31. Ibid.
32. Curtin, p. 332.
33. In his study of Wright's narrative, Philip Curtin suggests that he was on board the Brazilian vessel *Velas* and that she was taken by HMS *Maidstone* in March 1827. However, although the *Maidstone* intercepted five vessels that month, none was named *Velas*, and none had captives aboard.
34. Curtin, p. 314.
35. Ibid., p. 315.
36. Grindal, p. 122.
37. Ibid., p. 313.

38. Ibid., p. 303.
39. These figures are compiled from the table in Grindal, Appendix A.
40. Ward, p. 128. Grindal, p. 318, argues that there was no suggestion of impropriety on Bullen's part.
41. FO 84/66/164, 24 July 1827.
42. FO 84/66/5, 4 Nov. 1827.
43. Fyfe, *A History of Sierra Leone*, pp. 195–6.
44. FO 84/79/13, Accounts for sale of the *Henriqueta*.
45. ADM 51/3466, Log of the *Sybille*, 14–21 Sept. 1827.
46. ADM 1/1682/5, Collier to Croker, 29 Oct. 1827.
47. ADM 51/3466, Log of the *Sybille*.
48. Ibid., Collier to Croker, 31 Dec. 1827.
49. Wikipedia.
50. Ryan, p. 33.
51. Lloyd, p. 16 & Rankin, vol. 1, p. 49.
52. EAP 443/1/12/12, folios 59–92.
53. Macaulay, pp. 104 & 106.
54. Values are based on the Bank of England's inflation calculator.

9 EXORCISING DEMONS: JANUARY–APRIL 1828

1. ADM 51/4090, Log of the *Black Joke*.
2. Knight, p. 629. Vice Admiral Sir George Collier died in 1795 when Francis was just 8. He is not to be confused with Sir George Ralph Collier, the commodore of the West Africa Squadron from 1818 to 1821. The two men were not related.
3. ADM 37/7734, Muster of the *Sybille*, lists the order as Edward Webb, Henry Downes, William Hargood and Turner. Webb had been promoted to commander in October 1827.
4. This description of a Baltimore clipper comes from Lloyd, p. 35.
5. There is no official muster for *Black Joke*'s company as hands were drawn from HMS *Sybille* and turned over regularly as circumstances dictated. The only list recorded was compiled by Henry Downes as a memento of the action with *Almirante* (Log/N/41).
6. ADM 37/7737, Muster of the *Sybille*.
7. Charles Dickens described this Southwark gaol, where his father was sent for debt, as 'a living grave'.
8. ADM 37/7737, Muster of the *Sybille* & ADM 35/4489, Paybook of the *Sybille*.
9. Log/N/41.
10. Grindal, pp. 326–7.
11. These figures come from the database of slavevoyages.org.
12. Burroughs and Huzzey, pp. 3–5.
13. ADM 1/1682/14, Collier to Croker, 29 Oct. 1827.
14. ADM 51/4090, Log of the *Black Joke*.
15. Grindal, p. 68 & Rees, pp. 38–9.
16. ADM 51/4090, Log of the *Black Joke*.
17. Ibid.
18. Huntley, p. 106.
19. Rooks, p. 58.

20. Leonard, p. 77.
21. ADM 51/4090, Log of the *Black Joke*.
22. Ibid. The martingale was a stay, or rope, securing part of the bowsprit known as the jib-boom against the upward drag of the fore-topgallant stays.
23. Lloyd, pp. 79–81 & Grindal, p. 203.
24. Log/N/41, from Downes's notebook.
25. FO 84/79/76.
26. ADM 1/1683/294, Collier to Croker, 14 Aug. 1828.
27. Mather's name is unmentioned in the Admiralty list of Officers' Service Records.
28. See ADM 1/1/52 & FO 84/101/104.
29. Burroughs and Huzzey, p. 83.
30. Rees, p. 6.
31. Brooks, p. 3.
32. See Gunn.
33. See Brooks.
34. Leonard, p. 55.
35. It was not only for service on the water that the Kru were sought. Hugh Clapperton hired a number to accompany his ill-fated second expedition to Sokoto.
36. Brooks, p. 7.
37. FO 84/87/114.
38. Gunn, p. 88.
39. Grindal, p. 337.
40. Rankin, vol. 1, p. 74.
41. Ibid., pp. 4–5.
42. Ibid., vol. 2, p. 127.
43. ADM 1/1682/22, Collier to Croker, 14 Dec. 1827.
44. ADM 51/4090, Log of the *Black Joke*.
45. Rankin, vol. 1, pp. 143–4.
46. ADM 37/7734, Muster of the *Sybille*.
47. Taylor, *Sons of the Waves*, p. 372.
48. ADM 37/7734, Muster of the *Sybille*.
49. Huntley, p. 49.
50. ADM 51/4090, Log of the *Black Joke*.
51. Ibid.
52. ADM 1/1683/217, Turner to Collier, 4 Apr. 1828.
53. Ibid.
54. Ibid.
55. ADM 1/1682/148, Collier to Croker, 13 May 1828.

10 'A COSTLY GRAVE FOR BRITISH SUBJECTS': APRIL–JULY 1828

1. Huntley, p. 125 & Leonard, pp. 118–19.
2. Rees, p. 171.
3. ADM 51/4090, Log of the *Black Joke*, 20–23 Apr. 1828.
4. Huntley, p. 100.
5. ADM 51/4090, Log of the *Black Joke*, 16 May 1828. All details of the case come from the log, the only account of the *Vengador*'s capture.

6. These figures are based on the comprehensive list of suspected slave-vessel deten-
tions between 1807 and 1839 in Grindal, Appendix A. Not all the captive
numbers on the 390 vessels were recorded.

7. Walsh, vol. 2, pp. 481–2.

8. ADM 35/4489, Paybook of the *Sybille*.

9. ADM 51/4090, Log of the *Black Joke*, 21 May 1828.

10. Ibid., 19 May 1828.

11. Ibid., 22 May 1828.

12. Ibid., 26 May 1828. Although the log previously referred to 'sick men' coming
from the prize, the unstated reason for Wells's and others' removal suggests trauma.

13. ADM 35/4489, Paybook of the *Sybille*.

14. Rankin, vol. 2, pp. 119–23, contains an account of captives' processing.

15. All details of *Vengador*'s captives come from FO 315/32.

16. Rankin, vol. 2, p. 125.

17. Anderson, *Abolition in Sierra Leone*, pp. 84–5.

18. Anderson, 'Uncovering Testimonies'.

19. Rankin, vol. 1, p. 327.

20. Ibid., vol. 2, p. 108.

21. Ibid., vol. 2, p. 110.

22. The digitised records of the Sierra Leone archives are accessible at the British
Library, ref. EAP 443.

23. Colley, p. 314.

24. Rankin, vol. 1, p. 22.

25. EAP 443/1/17/12, folio 129.

26. EAP 433/1/18/2, folios 297, 293 & 295.

27. FO/84/77/114, Smart to Aberdeen, 6 Aug. 1828.

28. Fyfe, *A History of Sierra Leone*, p. 173.

29. Ibid., p. 165.

30. Ibid., p. 175.

31. ADM 1/1684/54, Collier to Croker, 2 Dec. 1828.

32. Fyfe, *A History of Sierra Leone*, pp. 142 & 153. An example of Savage's legal
presentation is seen in FO 84/84/60 & 77.

33. Anderson, *Abolition in Sierra Leone*, pp. 245–6.

34. FO 84/79/227.

35. FO 84/79/233.

36. ADM 1/1684/54, Collier to Croker, 2 Dec. 1828.

37. Fyfe, *A History of Sierra Leone*, pp. 225 & 218, and research on ancestry.co.uk.

38. FO 84/89/36.

39. ADM 1/1684/54, Collier to Croker, 2 Dec. 1828. No first-hand account in Turner's
words can be traced and *Black Joke*'s log contains no entries from 1 to 27 June.

40. Rooks, pp. 99–100.

41. ADM 1/1684/54, Collier to Croker, 2 Dec. 1828.

42. Ibid.

43. Ibid.

44. ADM 1/1685/198, Collier to Croker, 20 Feb. 1829.

45. Log/N/41.

46. ADM 35/4489, Paybook of the *Sybille*.

47. Rankin, vol. 1, p. 149.

48. ADM 35/4489, Paybook of the *Sybille*.
49. ADM 1/1683/154, Collier to Croker, 15 Apr. 1828.
50. Grindal, p. 337.
51. ADM 1/1683/303, Collier to Croker, Sept. 1828.
52. Grindal, p. 339.
53. Bethell, *The Abolition of the Brazilian Slave Trade*, p. 124.

11 RISING TO RENOWN: AUGUST 1828–APRIL 1829

1. ADM 51/4090, Log of the *Black Joke*.
2. ADM 1/1683/290, Collier to Croker, 8 Sept. 1828.
3. Ibid., Turner to Collier, 28 Aug. 1828.
4. Britons' role in the Cisplatine War sustained a trend in South American naval affairs started by Thomas Cochrane. In addition to officers and sailors, both forces had British commanders – James Norton, a former navy officer, in the case of Brazil, and William Brown, an Irishman who settled in South America, of the embryonic Argentine navy. His success brought him acclaim as a national hero.
5. FO 6/29, Moreno to Aberdeen, 4 Mar. 1829.
6. FO 6/28/115, 31 July 1828.
7. Ibid. Prouting was evidently using the name Beasley as an alias at the time.
8. FO 6/25/122, 3 Jan. 1828 & FO 6/28/107, 6 Jan. 1829.
9. FO 6/28/115.
10. ADM 1/3715, Jones to Croker, 30 Jan. 1829.
11. Ibid., Transcript of Proceedings, folios 83–4.
12. ADM 1/1683/290, Collier to Croker, 8 Sept. 1828.
13. Ibid., Turner to Collier, n.d.
14. ADM 1/3715, Transcript of Proceedings, folio 53.
15. ADM 1/1683/290, Turner to Collier, n.d.
16. ADM 1/3715, Transcript of Proceedings, folios 55–6.
17. ADM 1/1683/290, Turner to Collier, n.d.
18. *The Times*, 14 Feb. 1829.
19. Log/N/41, 5 Sept. 1828.
20. ADM 37/7736, Muster of the *Sybille*.
21. ADM 1/3715, Transcript of Proceedings, folios 58–9.
22. Log/N/41, 5 Sept. 1828, states that there were thirty-nine British prisoners, but a letter from Collier dated 30 Nov. makes it clear that there were seventy-one in total. ADM 1/1684/41.
23. ADM 1/3715, Transcript of Proceedings, folios 69–70.
24. ADM 1/1683/290, Collier to Croker, 8 Sept. 1828.
25. ADM 1/3715, Admiralty Sessions, folio 112.
26. ADM 1/1684/26, Collier to Croker, 25 Nov. 1828.
27. ADM 51/4090, Log of the *Black Joke*.
28. Ibid., 5 Oct. 1828.
29. ADM 1/1683/152 & 1/1685/230.
30. ADM 51/4090, Log of the *Black Joke*.
31. Grindal, p. 340.
32. ADM 51/3466, Log of the *Sybille*, 26 Feb. & 22 Mar. 1828.
33. ADM 1/1683/167 & 168.

34. ADM 1/1683/290, Collier to Croker, 8 Sept. 1828 & ADM 1/1684/41, Collier to Croker, 30 Nov. 1828.
35. What became of the other thirty-one prisoners from *Presidente* is a mystery. Although it had been intended that they too should be shipped to England, some were not British subjects.
36. ADM 1/3715, Jones to Croker, 7 Feb. 1829.
37. ADM 1/3715, Admiralty Sessions, folio 11.
38. Ibid., folio 83.
39. Ibid., folio 96.
40. Ibid., folio 106.
41. Ibid., folio 112.
42. Ibid., folio 125.
43. Ibid., folios 125–35.
44. *The Times*, 9 Apr. 1829.

12 'SHE SEEMED TO EXULT IN WHAT SHE HAD DONE': NOVEMBER 1828–MAY 1829

1. Seniority was rated by the date when officers passed their examinations. The *Sybille*'s four lieutenants were listed as Edward Webb, first lieutenant, Henry Downes, second lieutenant, William Hargood, third, and William Turner, fourth. Webb had been promoted to commander in October 1827 (ADM 37/7734).
2. O'Byrne & ADM 1/1684.
3. PROB 11/2154/346 at the National Archives. Downes's will makes clear his strong Christian faith, citing 'my working Bible' as part of his legacy.
4. Log/N/41.
5. See Burg.
6. ADM 1/2427/439, Rodney to Croker, 7 Dec. 1815.
7. ADM 1/1259/161, Report of inquiry into discipline on *Africaine*.
8. ADM 1/2427/488.
9. ADM 1/1259/161.
10. Neither of *Africaine*'s two senior lieutenants, William Sturgess or William Meadows, served again.
11. ADM 51/3466, Log of the *Sybille*, 11 & 16 Dec. 1828.
12. Lubbock, p. 5.
13. Log/N/41.
14. ADM 51/3466, Log of the *Sybille*, 26 Dec. 1828.
15. Log/N/41.
16. Ibid. Downes's papers include records of *Black Joke*'s company and notes which show that he stayed in touch with a number of them. Eason went on to pen a verse in praise of the brig.
17. ADM 1/1685/174, Collier to Croker, 4 Mar. 1829 & Log/N/41.
18. Lubbock, p. 23.
19. Log/N/41. Caps were large blocks of wood holding the lower and upper sections of masts together.
20. ADM 1/1685/171, Collier to Croker, 7 Jan. 1829.
21. ADM 51/3466, Log of the *Sybille*, noted 24 Jan. 1829.
22. Ibid.

23. Log/N/41.
24. ADM 1/1684/130, Collier to Croker, 11 Feb. 1829.
25. Ibid.
26. Log/N/41.
27. Ibid.
28. Ibid.
29. ADM 1/1684/130, Collier to Croker, 11 Feb. 1829.
30. Log/N/41.
31. Ibid.
32. Ibid.
33. Ibid.
34. ADM 1/1684/107 & 109, Collier to Croker, 24 & 29 Jan. 1829.
35. ADM 1/1685/181, Collier to Croker, 20 Feb. 1829.
36. ADM 1/1684/130, Collier to Croker, 11 Feb. 1829.
37. Ibid.
38. ADM 1/1685/234, Collier to Croker, 1 June 1829.
39. ADM 1/1685/235, Collier to Croker, 2 June 1829.
40. ADM 51/3466, Log of the *Sybille*.
41. Ibid., 19 Feb. & 10 Apr. 1829.
42. AMD 51/3270, Log of the *Medina*, 18 Feb. 1829.
43. ADM 51/3466, Log of the *Sybille*, 16 Apr. 1829.
44. Log/N/41.
45. Ibid.
46. Rankin, vol. 1, p. 148.
47. ADM 37/7737, Muster of the *Sybille* shows that sixteen Kru entered *Black Joke* on 6 March, the day of *Carolina*'s capture.
48. ADM 1/1685/277, Collier to Croker, 7 July 1829.
49. The 'Song by Thomas Eason' is part of Log/N/41 and is noted as having been written at sea on 15 March, nine days after the capture of the *Carolina*.
50. Ibid. Although Downes is not identified as the author of the additional verses, the implication is clear.
51. Ibid.
52. The cooler is held at the National Maritime Museum in Greenwich, which attributes its source to timbers from *El Almirante*.
53. ADM 35/4489, Paybook of the *Sybille*.
54. The note is found at ADM 1/1684/130, Collier to Croker, 11 Feb. 1829.
55. Quoted in *The Times*, 18 Apr. 1829.
56. See britishnewspaperarchive.co.uk.
57. Wikipedia; rusi.org.
58. The painting and the cooler were noted in Downes's will as being bequeathed to his brother William. The artist is not identified but, although William Huggins is associated with a popular image of the action, Nicholas Condy painted the one known oil of the subject.

13 PLAGUE AT SEA: MARCH–DECEMBER 1829

1. Walsh, vol. 2, pp. 482–3.
2. Ibid.

3. ADM 51/3270, Log of the *Medina*.
4. FO 84/89/10, Jackson to Aberdeen, 23 Mar. 1829.
5. FO 84/87/50.
6. EAP 443/1/17/13, from folio 65.
7. FO 84/87/114, Jackson to Aberdeen, 5 Jan. 1829.
8. Ryan, p. 6.
9. Anderson, *Abolition in Sierra Leone*, pp. 232–3, also addresses what has been called the Cobolo War of 1832.
10. Fyfe, *A History of Sierra Leone*, p. 188.
11. EAP 443/1/18/3, folio 108.
12. EAP 443/1/17/13, folio 65 & 18/3, folios 135 & 118.
13. EAP 443/1/18/3, folio 108, Ricketts to Hay, 31 Jan. 1829.
14. Ibid., folio 154.
15. Ibid.
16. Kilham, *Report on a Recent Visit to Sierra Leone*, p. 17.
17. ODNB.
18. Kilham, *Report on a Recent Visit to Sierra Leone*, pp. 22–4.
19. Fyfe, *A History of Sierra Leone*, p. 137.
20. FO 84/77 contains correspondence prior to Jackson's appointment suggesting that he may have been in financial need.
21. FO 84/66/103 & FO 84/95/154.
22. FO 84/87/114, Jackson to Aberdeen, 5 Jan. 1829.
23. FO 84/77/202, Jackson to Aberdeen, 29 Nov. 1828.
24. FO 84/90/125.
25. FO 84/90/33.
26. FO 84/90/125, Jackson to Aberdeen, 15 Apr. 1829.
27. Quoted in ADM 1/1685/249, Collier to Croker, 6 May 1829.
28. Ibid.
29. Ibid.
30. FO 84/77/167, Jackson to Boyle, 9 Oct. 1828.
31. ADM 1/1685/229.
32. ADM 1/1685/249, Collier to Croker, 6 May 1829.
33. FO 84/87/246, Jackson to Aberdeen, 14 Apr. 1829.
34. The logs of both *Black Joke* and *Sybille* give this as the date of Downes's departure and Parrey's arrival.
35. Grindal, Appendix G.
36. ADM 1/1685/198, Collier to Croker, 10 May 1829.
37. ADM 1/1685/278, Collier to Croker, 13 July 1829.
38. ADM 1/1685/234, Collier to Croker, 1 June 1829.
39. Grindal, p. 358.
40. See Watt.
41. ADM 51/3466, Log of the *Sybille*.
42. ADM 37/7736, Muster of the *Sybille*.
43. ADM 51/3270, Log of the *Medina*.
44. Grindal, p. 355.
45. ADM 1/1685/313, Collier to Croker, 22 Aug. 1829.
46. ADM 37/7737, Muster of the *Sybille*.
47. Ibid.

48. Quoted in Rees, p. 142.
49. This account of the *Cristina* case is based on reports in FO 84/89/90 & 94.
50. ADM 37/7737, Muster of the *Sybille*.
51. ADM 1/1/52, Collier to Croker, 19 Nov. 1829.
52. FO 84/87/284, Smith to Ricketts, 6 June 1829.
53. Ibid.
54. Rankin, vol. 1, p. 19.
55. Scanlan, p. 128.
56. Rankin, vol. 1, p. 167.
57. William Smith Junior succeeded his father to duty with the Mixed Commission, acting as registrar, and married one of Kenneth Macaulay's daughters, with whom he formed another influential family.
58. FO 84/101/104, Lewis to Smith, 30 Jan. 1830.
59. FO 84/90/185, Ricketts to Aberdeen, 26 Sept. 1829.
60. Information from ancestry.co.uk.
61. Fyfe, *A History of Sierra Leone*, p. 196.
62. Grindal, p. 799.
63. Ibid., pp. 357–8 & Lloyd, p. 134.
64. ADM 37/7737, Muster of the *Sybille*.
65. ADM 35/4489, Paybook of the *Sybille*.
66. Ibid.
67. ADM 51/3466, Log of the *Sybille*.
68. Ibid.

14 A WANING OF GIFTS: JANUARY–NOVEMBER 1830

1. ADM 51/3130, Log of the *Clinker*, 14 Feb. 1830.
2. Walsh, vol. 2, pp. 472–3.
3. FO 84/104/54, Findlay to Aberdeen, 12 May 1830.
4. These scant details come from FO 84/104/23, 32, 54 & 56.
5. FO 84/104/56, Report of the *Manzanares*.
6. Lubbock, p. 160.
7. ADM 51/3466, Log of the *Sybille*.
8. Grindal, p. 368.
9. Ibid., p. 369.
10. ADM 1/1/128, Collier to Croker, 28 Mar. 1830.
11. Grindal, p. 369.
12. ADM 1/1/134, Collier to Croker, 25 May 1830.
13. ADM 1/1/475.
14. Figures from Grindal, Appendix G, and muster of the *Sybille*.
15. ADM 37/7737, Muster of the *Sybille*. In addition to deaths, a significant number had been discharged, mainly for health reasons.
16. ADM 51/3466, Log of the *Sybille*.
17. ADM 35/4489, Paybook of the *Sybille*.
18. Ibid.
19. FO 84/103/174, Report of the *Umbellina*.
20. FO 84/102/175.
21. FO 84/103/178.

22. Anderson, *Abolition in Sierra Leone*, pp. 79–80.
23. ADM 51/3270, Log of the *Medina*, 11 Dec. 1829. Taylor, *The Interest*, p. 45, cites cases of rape on slaveships.
24. ADM 51/3130, Log of the *Clinker*, 28 Oct. 1829.
25. FO 84/101/141, De Paiva to Fraser, 6 Feb. 1830.
26. FO 84/101/124, Smith to Bandinel, 6 Feb. 1830.
27. FO 84/102/88 & 36, Fraser to Aberdeen, 27 Mar. 1830.
28. FO 84/103/123, Smith to Aberdeen, 6 Apr. 1830.
29. FO 84/102/135.
30. FO 84/103/235, Sale of the *Umbellina*.
31. Ibid.
32. Dos Santos was not the only one of *Henriqueta*'s former company to have made a fortune. Miguel Vianna, the pilot at the time of her capture, had since bought his own schooner, the *Emilia*. She too was taken, by HMS *Atholl*, off Lagos with 187 captives, in December 1829 (FO 84/90/197).
33. Verger, p. 394.
34. FO 84/102/181, Findlay to Aberdeen, 13 July 1830.
35. FO 84/117/229, Findlay to Palmerston, 28 Dec. 1831.
36. ADM 1/1/457, Hayes to Elliot, 19 Feb. 1831.
37. HIN/1/2, Hinde to his father, 11 Sept. 1829.
38. ADM 51/3017, Log of the *Atholl*, 1 Oct. 1829.
39. HIN/1/3, Hinde to his mother, 23 Feb. 1830. The slaver in question, *La Laure*, was sailing under French colours with captives recovered from a wrecked Spanish schooner. Grindal, pp. 362–3.
40. HIN/1/6, Hinde to his mother, 6 June 1830.
41. Grindal, p. 369.
42. ADM 51/3017, Log of the *Atholl*, 14 June 1830. The cutwater was the forward edge of the prow.
43. HIN/1/7, Hinde to his father, 5 July 1830.
44. HIN/1/4, Hinde to his mother, 26 Apr. 1830.
45. HIN/1/7, Hinde to his father, 7 July 1830.
46. The connection between their families is stated in Hinde's letter to his grandmother in HIN/1/4.
47. HIN/1/7, Hinde to his father, 7 July 1830.
48. ADM 51/4090, Log of the *Black Joke*. As stated elsewhere, there are unexplained and significant gaps in her logbook but this concluded the longest of nineteen months, from 28 Nov. 1828.
49. Ibid.
50. HIN/1/8, Hinde to his father, 7 Sept. 1830.
51. ADM 1/1/256, Hayes to Elliot, 20 Jan. 1831.
52. These figures come from *Black Joke*'s log, ADM 51/4090.
53. Leonard, p. 151.
54. ADM 51/4090, Log of the *Black Joke*.
55. HIN/1/8, Hinde to his father, 7 Sept. 1830.
56. FO 84/117/48.
57. FO 84/117/49.
58. FO 84/117/59.
59. FO 84/127/7.

15 'IS THIS UNPARALLELED CRUELTY TO LAST FOR EVER?': NOVEMBER 1830–JULY 1831

1. Leonard, p. 100.
2. ADM 1/1/177, Hayes to Croker, 4 Dec. 1830.
3. ADM 51/4090, Log of the *Black Joke*.
4. Ibid.
5. These figures are based on Grindal, Appendix A.
6. Bethell, *The Abolition of the Brazilian Slave Trade*, pp. 67–8.
7. FO 84/102/108, Findlay and Smith to Aberdeen, 15 June 1830. Although Findlay was a signatory, all such correspondence was in Smith's hands.
8. Grindal, p. 282.
9. ADM 1/1/256, Hayes to Elliot, 20 Jan. 1831.
10. ADM 1/1/627, Hayes to Elliot, 29 July 1832, quoting an earlier letter of 17 Feb. 1831.
11. Grindal, p. 375.
12. ADM 1/1/227, Findlay to Elliot, 31 Jan. 1831.
13. FO 84/102/196, Findlay and Smith to Aberdeen, 16 Sept. 1830.
14. Ibid.
15. ADM 1/1/239, Hayes to Elliot, 21 Jan. 1831.
16. FO 84/117/94.
17. Lubbock, p. 202.
18. Lloyd, p. 73, Huntley, pp. 25–6.
19. Grindal, Appendix G.
20. ADM 37/8019 & Muster of the *Dryad*.
21. Ibid. & ADM 51/3017, Log of the *Atholl*, 5 Oct. 1829.
22. *The Journal of Lieutenant George Bedford, 1835–6*, The Naval Miscellany, vol. 153 (2008).
23. Anderson, *Abolition in Sierra Leone*, p. 98.
24. Grindal, p. 371.
25. Details from ADM 51/4090, Log of the *Black Joke*, and ADM 1/1/307, Hayes to Elliot, 4 Mar. 1831.
26. Leonard, p. 104.
27. Ibid.
28. Ibid., p. 105.
29. FO 84/117/97.
30. Leonard, pp. 38 & 49.
31. Ibid., p. 96.
32. Fyfe, *A History of Sierra Leone*, p. 178.
33. FO 84/102/93, Smith to Bandinel, 22 May 1830.
34. The despatches in FO 84/116 trace the feud to a letter from Lord Palmerston at the Foreign Office in December 1830 that Smith, having been appointed chief justice *pro tempore*, was not to give his opinion on the slave trade when attending meetings of the colonial council, of which he was also a member. Despite pressure from Findlay, Smith insisted that he had to stand down from the council.
35. FO 84/116/266. Smith stated specifically that Wilson was 'a young man of color' as if to illustrate the nature of the dispute.
36. FO 84/116/290, Findlay to Smith, 14 Feb. 1831.

37. FO 84/116/399, Smith to Palmerston, 1 Oct. 1831.
38. FO 84/116/239.
39. ADM 51/3141, Log of the *Dryad*.
40. Leonard, p. 117.
41. Ibid., p. 208.
42. ADM 1/1/418, Hayes to Elliot, 6 May 1831.
43. ADM 51/4090, Log of the *Black Joke*.
44. ADM 1/1/431, Ramsay to Hayes, 28 Apr. 1831.
45. FO 84/117/123, testimony of Charles Bosanquet.
46. ADM 1/1/435.
47. ADM 1/1/431, Ramsay to Hayes, 28 Apr. 1831.
48. FO 84/117/111, citing an undated report by Ramsay.
49. Grindal, p. 416.
50. HIN/1/12, Hinde to his brother, 28 May 1831.
51. ADM 1/1/418, Hayes to Elliot, 6 May 1831.
52. Leonard, p. 133.
53. FO 84/117/119.
54. Grindal, p. 417.
55. Leonard, p. 133.
56. FO 84/117/111.
57. FO 84/117/127.
58. Leonard, p. 136.
59. ADM 51/4090, Log of the *Black Joke*.
60. Leonard, pp. 212–13.
61. Ibid.
62. FO 84/117/118.
63. FO 84/117/123–7.
64. FO 84/117/225.
65. *Captain Boteler's Recollections*, Navy Records Society, 1942.
66. Ibid. & Lubbock, p. 214.
67. HIN/1/5, undated letter from Gordon.
68. Leonard, pp. 252–3.
69. Ibid., pp. 254–5.
70. Ibid., pp. 131–2.

16 PASSING THE TORCH: JUNE 1831–FEBRUARY 1832

1. *Dover Telegraph*, 12 Apr. 1851.
2. Huntley, p. 206.
3. Ibid., p. 32.
4. Ibid., p. 198.
5. Ibid., p. 145.
6. LUB/39/21.
7. Ibid.
8. Grindal, p. 799.
9. ADM 51/3141, Log of the *Dryad*, 24 Sept. 1831.
10. Huntley, p. 132.
11. ADM 51/4090, Log of the *Black Joke*.

12. All details from the Log of the *Black Joke*.
13. Huntley, p. 197.
14. Ibid., p. 205.
15. Ibid.
16. Ibid., p. 207.
17. Ibid., p. 209.
18. Ibid., p. 211.
19. Ibid., pp. 214–15.
20. FO 84/127/95.
21. Huntley, p. 216. In his memoir, Huntley called the master 'Don Felippe' and described him as 'a fine looking man' and 'a brave but despicable slave dealer', which may have been intended to add swagger to the account. FO 84/127/29 names him as Santiago Alonzo.
22. The Admiralty subsequently took the rare step of writing to the owners of the *Huskisson* of Liverpool and the *Rolla* of London acknowledging 'the meritorious conduct of the Masters'. Grindal, p. 424.
23. Leonard, p. 236.
24. FO 84/117/215.
25. FO 84/117/208.
26. FO 84/127/29.
27. FO 84/117/195.
28. FO 84/127/133.
29. ADM 51/3141, Log of the *Dryad*, 3 Oct. 1831.
30. Ibid.
31. Ibid.
32. HIN/1/9, Hinde to his mother, undated.
33. Grindal, p. 432.
34. FO 84/102/209.
35. FO 84/116/15.
36. Fyfe, *A History of Sierra Leone*, p. 183. This figure would have included the colony's other black inhabitants, the resettled former slaves from Nova Scotia and the Maroons from Jamaica.
37. Fyfe, 'Four Sierra Leone Recaptives'.
38. EAP 443/1/18/5, folio 32.
39. Leonard, p. 78.
40. Fyfe, *A History of Sierra Leone*, p. 183.
41. Ibid., p. 184.
42. Rankin, vol. 2, p. 109.
43. FO 84/116/185, Jeffcott to Findlay, 11 July 1831.
44. Ryan, pp. 173–4. FO 84/116/183, Findlay to Palmerston, 11 July 1831.
45. EAP 443/1/18/5, folio 53.
46. Kilham, *Report on a Recent Visit to Sierra Leone*, p. 5.
47. Ibid., p. 6.
48. Kilham, *Memoir of the Late Hannah Kilham*, p. 366.
49. Ibid., p. 371.
50. Ibid., p. 410. The *Marinerito* is not named in Kilham's memoir, but the vessel can be identified by the date of her diary entry.
51. Ibid., p. 410.

NOTES to pp. 276–288

52. Ibid., p. 425.
53. Ibid., p. 383.
54. Ibid., pp. 435–6.
55. Ibid., p. 443.
56. Ibid., p. 453.
57. Ibid., p. 465.

17 THEIR LORDSHIPS' JUDGMENT: JANUARY–MAY 1832

1. ADM 1/74/20, Hayes to Warren, 1 Feb. 1832.
2. Grindal, p. 431.
3. ADM 1/74/20, Hayes to Warren, 1 Feb. 1832.
4. Ibid., Findlay to Warren, 29 Jan. 1832.
5. ADM 1/74/25, Hayes to Warren, 30 Jan. 1832.
6. Grindal, p. 432.
7. Lubbock, p. 226. It may be added that Lubbock drew on Peter Leonard's account, and *Dryad*'s surgeon was not, strictly speaking, a witness, but heard the story a few days later.
8. Grindal, p. 432.
9. Lubbock, p. 226.
10. ADM 1/74/57, Warren to Elliott, 29 Feb. 1832.
11. Ibid.
12. Ibid. Also attached is a typewritten note dated April 1958 stating: 'A small quantity of the "tastings" of the timbers of HMS *Black Joke* have been sent to Lagos for exhibition in a museum there.'
13. ADM 51/3141, Log of the *Dryad*.
14. Leonard, p. 251.
15. Ibid., pp. 259–60.
16. Ibid., pp. 260–1.
17. Ibid., p. 261.
18. ADM 51/3141, Log of the *Dryad*.
19. ADM 1/1/608, Warren to Hayes, 27 Mar. 1832.
20. ADM 1/74/55, Warren to Elliott, 28 Mar. 1832.
21. Lubbock, p. 141.
22. ADM 1/1/604, Hayes to Elliott, 7 May 1832.
23. ADM 1/74/68, Warren to Elliott, 1 Apr. 1832.
24. EAP 443/1/18/5, folio 58.
25. FO 84/127/104.
26. FO 84/127/104 & 107.
27. EAP 443/1/17/14.
28. Ibid.
29. FO 84/127/163.
30. Kilham, *Memoir of the Late Hannah Kilham*, p. 416.
31. Ibid., p. 473.
32. Ibid., pp. 473–4.
33. Unlike the muster of HMS *Sybille*, which names those hands sent by Collier to man *Black Joke*, the *Dryad*'s muster (ADM 37/8545) gives no similar detail.
34. ADM 51/3141, Log of the *Dryad*.

35. Ibid.
36. Ibid.

EPILOGUE

1. Grindal, p. 450.
2. *Morning Advertiser*, 30 July 1832.
3. Lubbock, p. 227.
4. Ibid., pp. 212–13.
5. Rankin, vol. 2, pp. 136–7.
6. Ibid., p. 120.
7. These figures are compiled from Grindal, Appendix A.
8. These figures come from O'Byrne and from Sullivan.
9. HIN/1/17, Hinde to his mother, 31 July 1832.
10. Burroughs and Huzzey, p. 10.
11. Taylor, *The Interest*, p. 186.
12. Ibid., pp. 212–13.
13. FO 84/71/206.
14. Klein and Luna, pp. 209–10.
15. Tinnie, p. 527.
16. The only biography, *Francisco Félix de Souza, mercador de escravos*, by Alberto da Costa e Silva, is in Portuguese.
17. Grindal, p. 801.
18. Figures compiled from Grindal, Appendix A.
19. See Bryson.
20. Lloyd, p. 140.
21. Bethell, *The Abolition of the Brazilian Slave Trade*, p. 124.
22. Rees, pp. 272–3.

BIBLIOGRAPHY

COLLECTIONS

The National Archives of the United Kingdom

Admiralty

ADM 1/1 – Letters from Flag Officer West Africa
ADM 1/74 – Letters from Commander-in-Chief, Cape of Good Hope
ADM 1/1682, 1683, 1684, 1685, 1966 – Letters from Captains
ADM 1/3715 – Letters from Admiralty Solicitor
ADM 7/293–6 – Miscellanea journals
ADM 34 & 35 – Ships' paybooks
ADM 37 – Ships' musters
ADM 51 – Captains' logbooks
ADM 55/11 – Journal kept by Captain Clapperton, surveying West Coast of Africa
ADM 68/313 – Prize money distribution

Foreign Office

FO 6 – Foreign Office Correspondence with Buenos Aires
FO 84/12, 84/31, 84/40, 84/42, 84/57, 84/71, 84/84, 84/95, 84/108, 84/112 – Foreign Office Slave Trade Correspondence with Brazil commissioners, 1821–30 (available online in digitised format)
FO 84/63, 84/66, 84/77, 84/79, 84/87, 84/89, 84/90, 84/101, 84/102, 84/103, 84/104, 84/116, 84/117, 84/118, 84/127 – Foreign Office Slave Trade Correspondence with Sierra Leone commissioners, 1827–32 (available online in digitised format)
FO 315 – Archives of Sierra Leone Slave Trade Commission

Caird Library, National Maritime Museum

LOG/N/41 – Logbook of *Black Joke* and *Sybille* with crew list, letters, notes and verses
kept by Lt Henry Downes
HIN/1 – Letters from Edwin Hinde to his family from 1829 to 1832
LUB/39/21 – Notebook of Basil Lubbock on the histories of the *Black Joke* and *Fair Rosamond*

British Library

EAP 443 – nineteenth-century documents of the Sierra Leone Public Archive. These
records of the Liberated African Department between 1808 and 1894, digitised
under the Endangered Archives Programme, are among a far larger collection of
valuable documents thus preserved and made available online

Arquivo Público de Bahia, Salvador

APEB – records of Santa Casa de Misericórdia

BOOKS

Anderson, Richard Peter, *Abolition in Sierra Leone: Re-Building Lives and Identities in Nineteenth-Century West Africa*, Cambridge, 2020.
Bay, Edna, and Mann, Kristin, *Rethinking the African Diaspora: The Making of a Black Atlantic World in the Bight of Benin and Brazil*, London, 2001.
Bethell, Leslie, *The Abolition of the Brazilian Slave Trade*, Cambridge, 1970.
Bolster, Jeffrey, *Black Jacks: African American Seamen in the Age of Sail*, Cambridge, MA, 1997.
Bonner-Smith, David (ed.), *Captain Boteler's Recollections 1808–1830*, Navy Records Society, vol. 82, 1942.
Brooks, George: *The Kru Mariner in the Nineteenth Century: An Historical Compendium*, Newark, DE, 1972.
Bryson, Alexander, *Report on the Climate and Principal Diseases of the African Station*, London, 1847.
Burroughs, Robert, and Huzzey, Richard (eds), *The Suppression of the Atlantic Slave Trade: British Policies, Practices and Representations of Naval Coercion*, Manchester, 2018.
Chapelle, Howard, *The History of American Sailing Ships*, New York, 1935.
Clapperton, Hugh, *Journal of a Second Expedition into the Interior of Africa, from the Bight of Benin to Soccatoo*, London, 1829.
Colley, Linda, *Captives: Britain, Empire and the World, 1600–1850*, London, 2002.
Costello, Ray, *Black Salt: Seafarers of African Descent on British Ships*, Liverpool, 2012.
Curtin, Philip (ed.), *Africa Remembered: Narratives of West Africans from the Era of the Slave Trade*, Michigan, 1967.
Duncan, John, *Travels in Western Africa in 1845 and 1846*, London, 1847.
Dundas, Robert, *Sketches of Brazil, Including New Views on Tropical and European Fever*, London, 1852.

Falconbridge, Alexander, *An Account of the Slave Trade on the Coast of Africa*, London, 1788.

Forbes, Frederick, *Dahomey and the Dahomans, Being the Journals of Two Missions to the King of Dahomey in 1849 and 1850*, London, 1851.

Frost, Diane, *Work and Community among West African Migrant Workers*, Liverpool, 1999.

Fyfe, Christopher, *A History of Sierra Leone*, Oxford, 1962.

Gardiner, Robert, *Frigates of the Napoleonic Wars*, London, 2000.

Graham, Maria, *Journal of a Voyage to Brazil and Residence There during Part of the Years 1821, 1822, 1823*, London, 1824. (See also Hayward and Caballero for reprint.)

Grindal, Peter, *Opposing the Slavers: The Royal Navy's Campaign against the Atlantic Slave Trade*, London, 2016.

Harding, Thomas, *White Debt: The Demerara Uprising and Britain's Legacy of Slavery*, London, 2022.

Hayward, Jennifer, and Caballero, M. Soledad (eds), *Maria Graham's Journal of a Voyage to Brazil*, Anderson, SC, 2010.

Holman, James, *Travels in Madeira, Sierra Leone, etc. etc.*, London, 1840.

Huntley, Henry, *Seven Years Service of the Slave Coast of Western Africa*, London, 1850.

Kilham, Hannah, *Report on a Recent Visit to the Colony of Sierra Leone*, London, 1828.

————, *Memoir of the Late Hannah Kilham, edited by her Daughter-in-Law, Sarah Biller*, London, 1837.

Klein, Herbert, and Luna, Francisco Vidal, *Slavery in Brazil*, Cambridge, 2010.

Knight, Roger, *The Pursuit of Victory: The Life and Achievements of Horatio Nelson*, London, 2005.

Koster, Henry, *Travels in Brazil*, London, 1816.

Lambert, Andrew, *The Challenge: Britain against America in the Naval War of 1812*, London, 2012.

Law, Robin, *Ouidah: The Social History of a West African Slaving 'Port', 1727–1892*, Woodbridge, 2004.

Leonard, Peter, *Records of a Voyage to the Western Coast of Africa in His Majesty's Ship Dryad during the Years 1830, 1831 and 1832*, London, 1833.

Lloyd, Christopher, *The Navy and the Slave Trade*, London, 1968.

Lockhart, Jamie Bruce, *A Sailor in the Sahara: The Life and Travels in Africa of Hugh Clapperton, Commander, RN*, London, 2008.

Lockhart, Jamie Bruce, and Lovejoy, Paul E., *Hugh Clapperton into the Interior of Africa: Records of the Second Expedition, 1825–1827*, Leiden, 2005.

Lovejoy, Paul, and Schwarz, Suzanne (eds), *Slavery, Abolition and the Transition to Colonialism in Sierra Leone*, Trenton, NJ, 2015.

Lubbock, Basil, *Cruisers, Corsairs and Slavers: An Account of the Suppression of the Picaroon, Pirate and Slaver by the Royal Navy during the 19th Century*, Glasgow, 1993.

McCarthy, Matthew, *Privateering, Piracy and British Policy in Spanish America, 1810–1830*, Woodbridge, 2013.

Macaulay, Kenneth, *The Colony of Sierra Leone Vindicated from the Misrepresentations of Mr Macqueen*, London, 1968. (Reprint of 1827 edition.)

Mann, Kristin, *Slavery and the Birth of an African City: Lagos, 1760–1900*, Bloomington, IN, 2007.

Moore, Samuel, *Biography of Mahommah Baquaqua, a Native of Zogoo in the Interior of Africa*, Detroit, MI, 1854.

O'Byrne, William, *A Naval Biographical Dictionary*, London, 1849.

Olusoga, David, *Black and British: A Forgotten History*, London, 2016.

Park, Mungo, *Travels in the Interior Districts of Africa in the Years 1795, 1796 and 1797*, London, 1799.

Rankin, Harrison, *The White Man's Grave: A Visit to Sierra Leone in 1834*, London, 1836.

Rediker, Marcus, *The Slave Ship: A Human History*, London, 2007.

Rees, Sian, *Sweet Water and Bitter: The Ships that Stopped the Slave Trade*, London, 2009.

Rooks, A.E., *The Black Joke: The True Story of One Ship's Battle against the Slave Trade*, New York, 2022.

Ryan, Maeve, *Humanitarian Governance and the British Antislavery World System*, New Haven, CT and London, 2022.

Scanlan, Padraic, *Freedom's Debtors: British Antislavery in Sierra Leone in the Age of Revolution*, New Haven, CT and London, 2017.

Smith, George, *The Case of our West-African Cruisers and West-African Settlements Fairly Considered*, London, 1848.

Sullivan, Anthony, *Britain's War against the Slave Trade: The Operations of the Royal Navy's West Africa Squadron, 1807–1867*, Barnsley, 2020.

Taylor, Michael, *The Interest: How the British Establishment Resisted the Abolition of Slavery*, London, 2021.

Taylor, Stephen, *Sons of the Waves: The Common Seaman in the Heroic Age of Sail*, New Haven, CT and London, 2020.

Thomas, Hugh, *The Slave Trade: The History of the Atlantic Slave Trade 1440–1870*, London, 1997.

Thomas, Sarah, *Witnessing Slavery: Art and Travel in the Age of Abolition*, London, 2019.

Vale, Brian, *Independence or Death: British Sailors and Brazilian Independence, 1822–25*, London, 2022.

Verger, Pierre, *Trade Relations between the Bight of Benin and Bahia from the 17th to the 19th Centuries* (translated by Evelyn Crawford from *Fluxo e Refluxo*), Ibadan, 1976.

Walsh, Robert, *Notices of Brazil in 1828 and 1829*, London, 1830.

Walvin, James, *Black Ivory: A History of British Slavery*, London, 1993.

Ward, W.E.F., *The Royal Navy and the Slavers: The Suppression of the Atlantic Slave Trade*, London, 1969.

Wetherell, James, *Stray Notes from Bahia*, Liverpool, 1860.

Wills, Mary, *Envoys of Abolition: British Naval Officers and the Campaign against the Slave Trade in West Africa*, Liverpool, 2019.

Woodward, Llewellyn, *The Age of Reform 1815–1870*, Oxford, 1962.

ARTICLES AND THESES

Anderson, Richard, 'The Diaspora of Sierra Leone's Liberated Africans: Enlistment, Forced Migration and "Liberation" at Freetown, 1808–1863', *African Economic History*, vol. 41, 2013.

————, 'Uncovering Testimonies of Slavery and the Slave Trade in Missionary Sources: The SHADD Biographies Project and the CMS and NMS Archives for Sierra Leone, Nigeria and the Gambia', *Slavery & Abolition*, vol. 38, no. 3, 2017.

Araujo, Ana Lucia, 'Forgetting and Remembering the Atlantic Slave Trade: The Legacy of Brazilian Slave Merchant Francisco Felix de Souza', in *Crossing Memories: Slavery and African Diaspora*, ed. Ana Lucia Araujo, Mariana Candido and Paul Lovejoy, Trenton, NJ, 2011.

Barcia, Manuel, '"An Islamic Atlantic Revolution": Dan Fodio's *Jihād* and Slave Rebellion in Bahia and Cuba, 1804–1844', *Journal of African Diaspora Archaeology and Heritage*, vol. 2, no. 1, 2013.

Berktay, Asli, 'From Freedom in Africa to Enslavement and Once Again Freedom in Brazil: Constructing the Lives of African *Libertos* in Nineteenth-century Salvador da Bahia', PhD thesis, Tulane University, LA, 2015.

Bethell, Leslie, 'Britain and Brazil, 1808–1914', in *Brazil: Essays on History and Politics*, ed. Leslie Bethell, London, 2018.

Browne-Davies, Nigel, 'William Smith, Registrar of the Courts of Mixed Commission: A Photograph of an African Civil Servant in the Nineteenth Century', *Journal of Sierra Leone Studies*, vol. 3, no. 2, 2014.

Burg, B.R., 'The HMS *Africain* Revisited: The Royal Navy and the Homosexual Community', *Journal of Homosexuality*, vol. 56, no. 2, 2009.

Candido, Mariana, 'Different Slave Journeys: Enslaved African Seamen on Board of Portuguese Ships, *c.*1760–1820s', *Slavery and Abolition*, vol. 31, no. 3, 2010.

Everill, Bronwen, 'Bridgeheads of Empire? Liberated African Missionaries in West Africa', *Journal of Imperial and Commonwealth History*, vol. 40, no. 5, 2012.

Fyfe, Christopher, 'Four Sierra Leone Recaptives', *Journal of African History*, vol. 2, no. 1, 1961.

Guenther, Louise, 'The British Community of 19th Century Bahia: Public and Private Lives', University of Oxford Centre for Brazilian Studies, 2001–2.

Gunn, Jeffrey, 'Homeland, Diasporas and Labour Networks: The Case of Kru Workers, 1792–1900', PhD thesis, York University, Toronto, 2019.

Hawthorne, Walter, 'Gorge: An African Seaman and his Flights from "Freedom" back to "Slavery" in the Early Nineteenth Century', *Slavery and Abolition*, vol. 31, no. 3, 2010.

Hicks, Mary Ellen, 'The Sea and the Shackle: African and Creole Mariners and the Making of a Luso-African Atlantic Commercial Culture', PhD thesis, University of Virginia, 2015.

Law, Robin, 'The Chronology of the Yoruba Wars of the Early Nineteenth Century: A Reconsideration', *Journal of the Historical Society of Nigeria*, vol. 5, no. 2, 1970.

Lovejoy, Paul, 'Islam, Slavery and Political Transformation in West Africa: Constraints on the Transatlantic Slave Trade', *Revue Française d'Histoire*, 2002.

————, 'Patterns in Regulation and Collaboration in the Slave Trade of West Africa', *Leidschrift*, vol. 22, no. 1, 2007.

Northrup, David, 'Mortality in the Atlantic Slave Trade: The Case of the Bight of Biafra', *Journal of Interdisciplinary History*, vol. 9, no. 1, 1978.

Reis, João José, 'Slave Resistance in Brazil: Bahia, 1807–1835', *Luso-Brazilian Review*, vol. 25, no. 1, 1988.

Ribeiro, Alexandre, 'The Transatlantic Slave Trade to Bahia, 1582–1851', in *Extending the Frontiers: Essays on the New Transatlantic Slave Trade Database*, ed. David Eltis and David Richardson, New Haven, CT and London, 2008.

Schwarz, Suzanne, 'Reconstructing the Life Histories of Liberated Africans: Sierra Leone in the Early Nineteenth Century', *History in Africa*, vol. 39, 2012.

Tinnie, Dinizulu Gene, 'The Slaving Brig Henriqueta and her Evil Sisters: A Case Study in the 19th-Century Illegal Slave Trade to Brazil', *Journal of African American History*, vol. 93, no. 4, 2008.

Walls, Andrew, 'The Legacy of Samuel Ajayi Crowther', *International Bulletin of Missionary Research*, vol. 16, no. 1, 1992.

Watt, James, 'The Health of Seamen in Anti-Slavery Squadrons', *Mariner's Mirror*, vol. 88, no. 1, 2002.

INDEX